S. Eisenbach   C. Sadler

PASCAL
for Programmers

With 78 Figures

Springer-Verlag
Berlin Heidelberg New York 1981

Susan Eisenbach
Computer Unit
Westfield College (University of London)
Kidderpore Avenue
London NW3
Great Britain

Christopher Sadler
Computer Assisted Teaching Unit
Queen Mary College (University of London)
Mile End Road
London E1
Great Britain

ISBN-13: 978-3-540-10473-5   e-ISBN-13: 978-3-642-67911-7
DOI: 10.1007/978-3-642-67911-7

Library of Congress Cataloging in Publication Data
Eisenbach, S. 1951 - PASCAL for Programmers "The material for this book first
appeared in the magazine Personal computer world, as a series of articles
which ran from September 1979 to June 1980."
Bibliographie: p. Includes index. 1. PASCAL (Computer program language).
2. Electronic digital computers–Programming. I. Sadler, Christopher, 1948-
joint author. II. Title. QA76.73.P2E36. 001.64'24. 80-26856

Preface

The material for this book first appeared in the magazine Personal Computer World, as a series of articles which ran from September 1979 to June 1980. It was designed to appeal to a new (in 1979) sort of reader -- the microcomputer enthusiast, both amateur and professional -- about whom two assumptions were made. The first was that the reader was someone who had already learned to program (probably in BASIC) and who wanted to create programs in as systematic and proficient a fashion as possible. The second was that the reader would not be adverse to an occasional glimpse of how the underlying machine played its part in executing these programs. As a result of these, no attempt was made to teach the "problem-solving" aspects of programming (although the Top-Down philosophy for program design formed a key feature) and no apology was made for the repeated references to the way in which a Pascal compiler "viewed" some particular code fragment.

In preparing this material for publication as a single volume, there has been little deviation from this policy. Nevertheless, it should be remarked that the first five chapters contain all the material one would need to cover in an initial course in programming (up to the level of most BASIC's) while the second half of the book tackles some of the more sophisticated techniques available to the Pascal programmer. For illustrative purposes, it has been felt necessary to incorporate some fairly extensive working

VI

programs into the text. Pascal is a language for which
"readability" was a design goal, and this is exploited here
in the sense that very little explanatory material appears
outside of the program listing. Instead, the reader is
expected to read the program to ascertain its function and
the tactics behind its design, and only refer to the
accompanying text for particular features and additional
details.

Finally, acknowledgements are due to Dave Tebbutt,
editor of Personal Computer World, for his guiding hand; to
John Boreham, for helping to keep the text-editting
hardware alive; to Helen Eisenbach for the typing and to
Carol Nicholls for the illustrations.

Susan Eisenbach
Christopher Sadler
London
August, 1980

Table of Contents

VIII

Chapter 1. Introduction

Why Pascal?

How many people who program picked "their language" by consulting unbiased experts, reading books, and then making a rational choice before they began? Most of us learned our first language because it was the one available at the time. Implicit with learning a first language is learning to mechanize problem-solving, and hence to control a powerful, and captivating, machine -- the computer. There's little wonder that some programmers form an emotional loyalty to their language which makes the learning of a new one almost an infidelity.

Because there are a great variety of them available, and because a second language is much easier to learn than the first one, it seems short-sighted to stick passionately to one that was so accidentally selected. As designers have gained from past mistakes, so the structure of programming languages has evolved and, while one doesn't want to devote a great deal of time to digesting some fantastic syntactic edifice too big and complicated to run on a real machine, there are several modern languages which may amply repay the trouble taken to learn them. We hope the the potted history of programming languages that follows will persuade the reader that Pascal, in particular, is worth looking into.

The early machines had no formal languages; they were programmed in machine code. It soon became clear that this

procedure was unnecessarily tedious and that the speed and
accuracy of the computer itself could be employed to
overcome the problem of slow, error-prone transcription.
Assembly languages were designed therefore, to allow
programmers to use mnemonic codes rather than numbers, and
an <u>assembler</u> translated these programs into machine code
for execution. Using an assembly language, the programmer
still had the same control over the computer as with
machine code but avoided having to remember and key in long
and indistinguishable number codes. Unfortunately an
assembly language must be designed for a particular
processor so that a program written on one model will not,
in general, execute on another.

     The second generation of machines proved so much
faster than the first that it became no longer at all
necessary for the programmer to have complete control over
every processor cycle. General-purpose, high-level
languages came into being as a consequence. If all
processes within a program could be reduced or adapted to a
limited number of fixed sequences of machine code
instructions, then each such fixed sequence could be
represented by a single statement in the high-level
language. The problem of the high-level language designer
was, therefore, to specify the set of sequences which would
effectively cater for the range of problems he wished to
solve. The variety of languages developed at this time (as
typified by FORTRAN, COBOL and ALGOL 60) aptly demonstrates
the differing approaches adopted by their designers.
Learning to program came to involve learning the vocabulary
of a (human-oriented) language, of which each word
corresponded to a particular operation, or set of operations
performed by the computer. Programming became faster to
learn and easier to do (although not necessarily easier to
do well). In addition, a program written in a high-level
language should, in theory, execute on any machine

possessing the appropriate <u>compiler</u> (a program that
generates machine code sequences from high-level language
statements).

Of these early high-level languages, FORTRAN, still
the most popular "scientific" language, was closest in
style to the actual machine processes. This had two
results -- firstly, it was relatively straightforward to
produce an efficient, fast FORTRAN compiler for a wide
range of machines, and secondly, FORTRAN programmers were
compelled to structure their algorithms in machine-oriented
terms, so that the actual programs were also efficient, and
fast. It is these features, its machine-efficiency and
wide availability, that account for FORTRAN's continued
popularity.

The other two major languages of this period made
greater concessions to the human programmer at the expense
of a degree of machine efficiency. COBOL, the "business"
language, is written in English-like code, has a wide range
of data storage and handling facilities, but, compared to
FORTRAN is relatively limited in its (mathematical)
processing power. ALGOL 60, the "academic" language, was
designed, on the other hand, so that the mathematical
specification of the problem (the algorithm) could be coded
as naturally as possible by the programmer (mathematician)
-- this criterion has led to the class of "structured"
languages, about which more later. ALGOL 60, however, had
very limited data-manipulation facilities and neglected to
incorporate general Input/Output routines, thus making
ALGOL programs almost completely machine-dependent.

Taken together these languages contain features which
can be said to epitomize a well-designed, general purpose
high-level language. These are:

1. Algorithms should be expressible in a natural way.
2. A variety of means of storing and handling different types of data should be available.
3. The language should compile and execute efficiently on a variety of machines.
4. I/O instructions should be machine-independent and, as far as possible, straightforward to use.
5. The language should be self-consistent and coherent so that it is easy to learn and open to standardization and hence program-portability.

The mid-sixties brought the second generation of high-level languages. Although in some ways these languages represented an improvement over the originals, none of them adequately took account of all of the five points detailed above. PL/1, the "IBM language", attempted to incorporate all known facilities of all the languages into one monolithic creation. However the entire might of IBM could not persuade programmers to drop their FORTRAN or COBOL in favour of such a large, ungainly language.

BASIC, the "people's language", represented a different tack. It was designed as a teaching language for students who would normally have been taught FORTRAN. It took advantage of the interactive facilities which by then had become available (i.e. online terminals), eliminated the need to learn about compilers, loaders, linkers, and even editors, and allowed the students to concentrate purely on the programming. Although the BASIC syntax is closer to English than FORTRAN, and the Input/Output is much simpler, BASIC betrays its parentage in its data handling facilities and in the algorithmic style it imposes on its adherents. While no standardized BASIC exists , variations on the BASIC theme (from 2K Tiny BASIC to monstrous 32K Commercial BASIC compilers) abound throughout the micro-world. It is worth noting that very few programs will convert from one system to another without a degree of fiddling about between the different (and often idiosyncratic) dialects.

The mid-sixties also saw the convening of the working party of the International Federation for Information Processing (IFIP) who had previously produced ALGOL 60. This group felt that the algorithmic approach of ALGOL 60 was correct and that its limited impact had been due to its restricted data-handling facilities and non-existent general I/O statements. Their final report on ALGOL 68 appeared in early 1969. ALGOL 68 was designed to be as comprehensive as PL/I in that the failings of ALGOL 60 had been more than made up, but the compactness of the ALGOL 68 design formalism gave it a greater degree of coherence than PL/I. It is still a vast and complex language which is difficult to learn and even more difficult to implement on the huge machines it requires. Also, as a European language, it was slow to be implemented on hardware designed, manufactured and primarily marketed in the USA, and has not been at all enthusiastically received there.

Niklaus Wirth, a member of the IFIP working party, watched his colleagues painstakingly constructing their heavy-weight language with a certain measure of disquiet. He wanted a language which would not only incorporate the strengths of existing languages but which could also be implemented on an reasonably-sized computer (as with FORTRAN). He put his ideas into the language Pascal, an ALGOL-like language in machine-realizable form (i.e. easy to compile and not too big).

Actually, Pascal didn't catch on straight away either, even though it is implementable on a wide variety of machines and contains most of the major features of ALGOL

68. However, today, with the onslaught of micro-computers (requiring smallish, efficient compilers) and with the demand amongst professional programmers for "structured" programming languages, Pascal is coming into its own.

Of course there have been other languages designed on completely different lines (take, for instance, APL), but if the construction philosophy is to be based on the five points that have been established above, then Pascal must certainly be worth a closer look.

While this survey could in no way be described as being comprehensive, the major micro languages have been covered for comparison.

Pascal Nuts and Bolts

Any algorithm or computer program consists of two complementary elements -- a description of the "actions" which are to be performed, and a description of the data on which the actions are to be performed. Clearly, therefore, any programming language must supply one with the means of expressing these two descriptions and the better the language, the more elegant, efficient, understandable (readable) and error-free the programs of a given programmer are likely to be. The aim of Pascal is to provide a set of statements (action) and data types which are at the same time comprehensive (to cover all eventualities); and succinct (to convey the meaning without getting too complicated). Anyone familiar with another language will recognise that the action and data types described in Pascal can usually be accomplished in that language too, so that comparison is not so much about what they can do but more how elegantly and efficiently they do it.

Data Types

In machine code, the bit patterns in a location may be
interpreted in any way the programmer chooses, but in
high-level languages, the language designer must decide
what interpretations the programmer will be permitted to
employ. In BASIC, for instance, information is held as REAL
numbers (with or without a decimal point) or STRINGS of
characters. These are known as data types. Pascal has four
data types:
> BOOLEAN -- has values: TRUE or FALSE
>
> INTEGER -- has values: an implementable subset of
> the whole numbers
>
> REAL -- has values: an implementable subset of
> floating point real numbers (A REAL usually
> occupies twice as many storage locations as an
> INTEGER)
>
> CHAR -- has values: a single alphabetic, numeric
> or special character.

Pascal also offers the facility of defining a new data
type if the above four seem restrictive. For instance
> TYPE SUIT = (HEART, DIAMOND, CLUB, SPADE)

defines SUIT as a data type which can have any "value" as
specified in parenthesis. Likewise
> TYPE DAY = 1..31

allows only one of the defined values, and no other, to be
assigned of a variable of the DAY type. Similarly
> TYPE STRING = ARRAY [1..15] OF CHAR

defines a 15-element BASIC-like character string. While
> TYPE LONGSTRING = ARRAY [1..80] OF CHAR

would be suitable to describe (say) a punched-card format
record.

In addition to its data types, Pascal allows for the
creation of certain data structures, namely ARRAYs,

RECORDs, SETs and FILEs. An ARRAY is a data structure
containing two or more elements of the same type -- these
are particularly useful in certain mathematical algorithms.
The commercial counterpart is a RECORD consisting of two or
more "fields" which may be of any type. SETs are a special
case of ARRAYs while FILEs provide the means whereby data
in any form can be extracted from or introduced into the
program from (external) mass storage. In addition Pascal
enables the programmer to pack data to maximum density by
enabling the specification of variable ranges and limited
range data-types.

Control Structures

Most programmers agree that any computable problem can
eventually be subdivided and thence analysed (and so
programmed) in terms of three fundamental operations known
as structured constructs. These appear in Figure 1.1 with
comparative examples in BASIC and Pascal.

There are obviously other constructs which could be
employed, and, equally, any loop construct could be
replaced by an equivalent conditional. So why does Pascal
seem to have three different forms of loop? The answer
appears to lie in the balance between supplying the
programmer with enough techniques to do his work elegantly
and adequately while keeping the language simple enough to
operate it efficiently and effectively. Pascal is, at the
same time, comprehensive as a problem solver, and succinct
as a language.

```
        BASIC                              Pascal
        -----                              ------

1. The Sequence

    LET A=B+C                              SUM := NEXTONE + SUM
    A = B + C                              DEALCARDS
    GOSUB 4900                             DEALCARDS (FIRSTPLAYER)

2. The Loop

    FOR I = M TO N ... NEXT I              WHILE condition DO action
    FOR I = N TO M STEP -1 ... NEXT I      REPEAT action UNTIL condition
                                           FOR I := M TO N DO action
                                           FOR I := N DOWNTO M DO action

3. The Conditional

    IF condition THEN 4900                 IF condition THEN action ELSE action
    ON K GOTO 100, 200, 300                CASE N OF
                                              1 : FIRSTACTION
                                              2 : SECONDACTION
                                                    etc.
                                           END
```

Fig. 1.1. Comparison of BASIC and Pascal Language Constructs

Of course, this brief description doesn't illustrate
Pascal any more than a dictionary describes the English
language. What is needed are some examples used in actual
programs, and also some practice in formulating the
problems in the "Pascal way".

Niklaus Wirth, author of Pascal, was very firm on the
idea of standardization, and we shall use his book Pascal
User Manual and Report (Kathleen Jensen and Niklaus Wirth,
Springer-Verlag) as the ultimate reference work for this
series. However, the team at the Institute for Information
Systems at the University of California in San Diego, like
most other compiler writers, could not resist "improving"
the language slightly for their version, which is designed
for an interactive environment. Since this version is
currently the most widely available on microcomputers, the
occasional differences between "Wirth Pascal" and "UCSD
Pascal" will be pointed out as they arise.

Chapter 2. Fundamentals: Action and Data

Every language (computer or human) has grammatical rules. However, it is difficult to achieve fluency from a list of rules -- examples bring individual points to light. In this text, sample programs are used to illustrate new ideas and, more formally, rules are provided so that the new constructions can be more generally applied and checked for legality.

Format of a Program

A good programming language is one that can achieve an acceptable compromise between the following conflicting goals. First, it should provide the programmer with sufficient flexibility to allow programs to be written in a natural, logical way, and second, the programs should have a highly predictable structure so that the compiler (the program that translates the source program into a machine-code object program) can be fast and efficient.

In some languages, each statement must appear on its own line. This is equivalent to saying that the statement separator is CR LF (i.e. the result of pressing RETURN). This limits the maximum length of a statement to some fixed value (usually 80 characters); it also makes a program with lots of short statements very stilted and space-wasting. In Pascal the statement separator is a semi-colon which allows several short statements to be compressed onto one line, or

a single statment to overflow onto several lines. In
either case, the compiler can still rapidly sort out one
statement from another.

     It has become accepted that every language must
include some means of documenting a program within the code
itself. This provides the reader with additional
explanations beyond the bare lines of essential code. In
Pascal the primary method of documentation comes about
through the use of a very flexible naming convention.
Every name (or identifier), whether it is the name of the
program itself or that of one of the variables or other
elements within the program, can consist of an unlimited
number of characters. The only restrictions are:
     1. that the identifier should not be a reserved
     word i.e. one of the instructions of the
     language, like WRITE etc.
     2. that the first character should be a letter
     followed by an unbroken string of alphanumeric
     characters.
     3. that only the first eight characters are
     recognized by most compilers. Any additional
     characters will be there for the benefit of the
     reader, to explain the functions of the object
     being named.

Thus line 1 of the program in Figure 2.1 has the form:
          PROGRAM   EVENINGALL   ;
          (reserved word) (identifier) (separator)
The identifier "EVENINGALL" gives some idea of what the
program is about. The same approach should be adopted when
naming variables, strings and all the other program
elements, although care should be exercised to ensure that
the first eight characters are unique, for the sake of the
compiler. For instance it would probably treat identifiers
ACCOUNTSPAYABLE and ACCOUNTSRECEIVABLE as being identical.

The second method of documentation is the comment. In
Pascal this consists of a string of explanatory text
enclosed by the character pairs (* and *) as shown on line
5 in Figure 2.1. (* You can use curly brackets if you can
find them on your keyboard *). When the compiler encounters
the left-hand <u>delimiter</u>, it ignores everything until the
right hand delimiter, so that the message contained therein
is for the human reader only.

Good programmers always use a lot of documentation in
their programs, whatever language they are writing in.
However, in Pascal they would probably concentrate their
documentary efforts on the various identifiers chosen and use
correspondingly fewer comments than they would include in
(say) BASIC or FORTRAN, which have more restricted naming
conventions.

```
1: PROGRAM EVENINGALL ;
2: BEGIN
3:    WRITE('HELLO') ;
4:    WRITE(' ','HELLO HELLO') ;
5:    WRITELN ; (*MOVES TO A NEW LINE*)
6:    WRITELN('AND WHAT DO WE HAVE HERE?') ;
7:    WRITELN('HELLO HELLO HELLO')
8: END.
```

Fig. 2.1. EVENINGALL

The program in Figure 2.1 illustrates the general
format of a Pascal program. The line numbers down the left
hand side are <u>not</u> a part of the syntax of Pascal but have
been edited in for ease of reference when the program is to
be "talked through".

EVENINGALL consists of a program title (line 1), an
action part (lines 2-8) and a terminator (the full stop on
line 8). All programs must close with a full stop as this
is a message to the compiler to say that the end of the
program has been reached. The actual executable part of
the program stretches from line 3 to 7.

The instruction WRITE causes whatever follows it in brackets to be output. WRITELN will have the same effect except that CR LF are appended to the end of the text and will cause the type-head to move to the beginning of the next line, after the text has been output. If there is no text after a WRITELN, the type head is simply moved to the beginning of the next line. Thus lines 3 to 5 in Figure 2.1 have the same effect as line 7. The brackets which enclose the output are "output delimiters", while the single quotes surrounding each item are "string delimiters". More than one item can appear in a single statement (see line 4) and these are separated by commas.

The output of EVENINGALL would appear on the terminal as:

```
HELLO HELLO HELLO
AND WHAT DO WE HAVE HERE?
HELLO HELLO HELLO.
```

This assumes that the program is being run on an interactive system so that input and output relate directly to the terminal keyboard and screen. Wirth's Pascal definition allows for a less flexible arrangement where input comes from a disc-file named INPUT and output is directed to another named OUTPUT. Since all microcomputer systems adopt the former approach, the details of the less interactive method will be left to a later chapter.

The structure of the program and various subsections are illustrated, by means of syntax diagrams, in Figure 2.2. These syntax diagrams show what a program looks like, from the point of view of the compiler, and as such are worth taking a bit of trouble over. A knowledge of how the compiler will view a program can be a useful tool in producing correct code, provided the ideas behind the program have been properly thought out beforehand.

PROGRAM

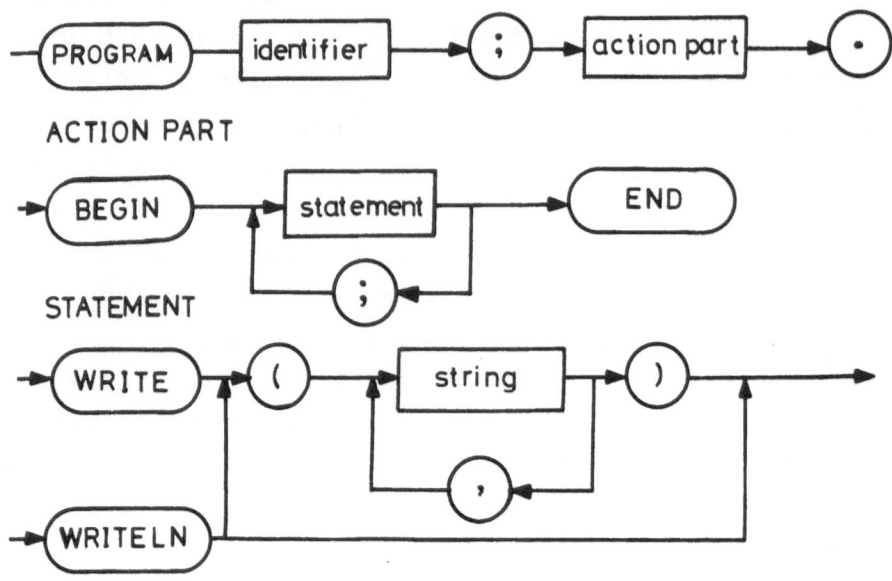

Fig. 2.2. Syntax Diagrams for PROGRAM, ACTION PART and STATEMENT

Looking at the first diagram in Figure 2.2, when the compiler encounters the word PROGRAM (a reserved word), it searches for a ";". Anything between these is the identifier or program name (provided it obeys the rules). Likewise, everything between the ";" and the "." is the action part which, looking at the second diagram, starts with the reserved word BEGIN and finishes with the reserved word END. Between these are statements, separated by ";"s and they are defined in the succeeding diagram. Each statement from 3 to 7 in Figure 2.1 can be checked against the definition of a statement in Figure 2.2 to ensure that each one is "legal" -- this is exactly what the compiler has to do.

In the course of this text, the elementary definitions will be expanded and enhanced to include all the Pascal facilities. In the meantime, below are some rules for interpreting a syntax diagram.

1. Symbols in <u>circles</u> are Pascal punctuation
marks -- i.e. separators, delimiters and
terminators etc.
2. <u>Sausages</u> contain either the reserved words (in
capitals) or one of "letter", "digit" or
character" -- which includes anything on a
keyboard.
3. <u>Rectangles</u> enclose names of elements which are
defined in other diagrams (e.g. "action part" in
the first diagram is defined in the second).
They can be considered therefore as symbols for
other complete diagrams.

In Figure 2.3, two diagrams are presented to complete the
set of definitions begun in Figure 2.2 and stated earlier
in the text.

Programs that Do Things

Almost every program functions by obtaining some data
(input), manipulating or processing this data and
presenting its results (output). In Pascal, this functional
aspect of the program (the "action part" of the previous
section) is separated from the more organisational task of
deciding how the information is to be stored and used at
each stage of the operation. These decisions must be made
and announced in a "declaration part" immediately before
the action part is begun.

In program PAY, Figure 2.4, lines 2 & 3 form the
declaration part while lines 4 (i.e. BEGIN) and onwards
constitute the action part. Looking first at the action
part, lines 5 & 6, together with the first line of output,
below, show how a dialogue can be constructed within a
program. WRITE outputs text but allows the response to be

typed on the same line. READLN requires a CR to terminate
the input. Finally, line 11 is a typical <u>assignment</u>
statement. The values of the variables HOURS, RATE and
OVERHOURS are arithmetically manipulated, together with the
value 1.5 (from OVER), to produce a numeric value which is
assigned to the variable WAGE. The <u>assignment</u> <u>operator</u> ":="
is used to emphasize that this activity occurs in the

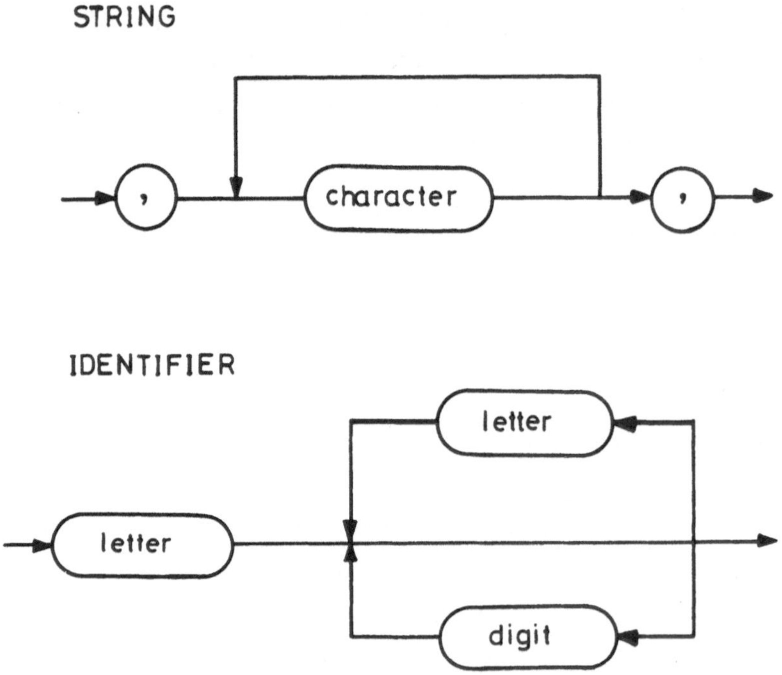

STRING

IDENTIFIER

Fig. 2.3. Syntax Diagrams for STRING and IDENTIFIER

```
 1: PROGRAM PAY ;
 2: CONST OVER=1.5 ;
 3: VAR HOURS, RATE, OVERHOURS, WAGE : REAL ;
 4: BEGIN
 5:    WRITE('NORMAL HOURS WORKED --') ;
 6:    READLN(HOURS) ;
 7:    WRITE('RATE OF PAY --') ;
 8:    READLN(RATE) ;
 9:    WRITE('OVERTIME HOURS - TYPE 0 IF NONE') ;
10:    READLN(OVERHOURS) ;
11:    WAGE := HOURS * RATE + OVER * RATE * OVERHOURS ;
12:    WRITE('WAGES = ', WAGE, ' POUNDS')
13: END.
```

Fig. 2.4. PAY

action part, and indicates that the contents of a memory location (referenced by WAGE) is to be altered. A typical run of PAY might look something like:

```
NORMAL HOURS WORKED--40
RATE OF PAY--2
OVERTIME HOURS -- TYPE 0 IF NONE--3
WAGES = 89 POUNDS
```

The final diagram in Figure 2.6 defines all the new statements introduced in program PAY.

Although the action part of this program must seem straightforward, the declaration part may look rather peculiar. At machine-code level, all data is represented by sequences of ones and zeroes at specific locations in memory. Higher level languages must provide a means of accessing and interpreting this data in a more readable form -- numbers and characters, arrays and words. Generally, memory locations are accessed by means of variable names (or identifiers) and some languages use restrictions in the naming conventions to help the compiler to interpret the data stored at the named location. FORTRAN distinguishes between names for REALS and those used for INTEGERS, while BASIC has REALS and STRINGS (of characters).

These restrictions are inefficient in two ways -- first, program readability is hindered and second, the programmer has to force his data into the rigid data types provided. Thus, in most versions of BASIC, a flag (taking values 1 or 0) which need only occupy one bit will, in fact, occupy 32 bits in the guise of a REAL variable. In Pascal, variable identifiers have no such restrictions so one function of the declaration part is to give the programmer the opportunity to name variables and state what type they are. So Figure 2.4, line 3 reads:

```
VAR              HOURS, RATE, OVERHOURS, WAGE   :   REAL
(reserved word)          (identifiers)              (type)
```

This enables the compiler to set up all the necessary memory locations at one go (before starting on the action part). Clearly this is more efficient than the alternative, where memory allocation must occur in conjunction with other compilation activities.

Moving from efficient compilation to efficient execution brings up another Pascal feature, the <u>declared constant</u>. When a computer executes an arithmetic assignment, all the relevant numbers have to be extracted (via the variable identifiers) from memory. Because this activity uses a significant fraction of the execution time required for the operation, the facility exists to incorporate actual values into an arithmetic statement. Hence Pascal allows for the declaration of constants (line 2, Figure 2.4). When the program is compiled, every occurence of the specified identifier (OVER) is replaced by the value indicated (1.5). No location in memory is associated with constant identifiers.

Constants can also be used in the more traditional way. For example line 11 in Figure 2.4 could have "1.5" instead of "OVER". But if union negotiations managed to push up overtime rates to doubletime, someone (imagine a larger program with tax and NI calculations, etc.) would have to look through the entire program to adjust it everywhere

```
 1: PROGRAM TEMPERATURECONVERSION ;
 2: CONST FREEZING = 32 ;
 3:       LINE = '   ---------------' ;
 4: VAR CENTDEGREE, IFAHRENHEIT : INTEGER ;
 5:     RFAHRENHEIT : REAL ;
 6: BEGIN
 7:    WRITE('PLEASE TYPE IN A TEMPERATURE IN DEGREES CENTIGRADE --) ') ;
 8:    READLN(CENTDEGREE) ;
 9:    RFAHRENHEIT := CENTDEGREE * 9/5 + FREEZING ;
10:    IFAHRENHEIT := CENTDEGREE * 9 DIV 5 + FREEZING ;
11:    WRITELN(LINE) ;
12:    WRITELN(CENTDEGREE,'C =', RFAHRENHEIT,' F OR APPROX',IFAHRENHEIT, ' F') ;
13:    WRITELN(LINE)
14: END.
```

Fig. 2.5. TEMPERATURECONVERSION

it occurred. On the other hand, when a constant is
declared, only one change need be made.

The role of the declaration part is therefore to
allocate memory locations and to assign constant values for
use by the action part. The first three diagrams in Figure
2.6 cover the descriptions of the last few paragraphs. The
third diagram in particular shows the exact format of
constant and variable declarations. In Figure 2.8 the words
"constant identifier" and "variable identifier" occur.
These refer to a legal identifier that has been previously
declared in a constant or variable declaration.

TEMPERATURECONVERSION in Figure 2.5 contains a wider
range of data types. On line 3 there is an example of a
string constant. This facility will be familiar to most
programmers. In line 4 CENTDEGREE and IFAHRENHEIT are
declared as INTEGERS. This means that they can only take
whole number values (and in machine terms take up less
storage space than REALS).

If the left hand side of an assignment statement is a
variable of type INTEGER, then all terms on the right hand
side must also be INTEGERS. When adding, subtracting and
multiplying two integers, the result will always be an
integer. However, when dividing two integers, the result
may be a real. Pascal provides two division operators. "/"
(as in line 9, Figure 2.5) is the division operator for
reals and it always produces a real result. It can be used
between integers but the result must be assigned to an
identifier that has been declared as REAL. The operator
DIV (as in line 10 in Figure 2.5) is used between two
integers when an integer result is required. Any
fractional part is chopped off (that is truncation rather
than rounding occurs). So 11/4 gives 2.75 while 11 DIV 4
gives 2.

DECLARATION PART

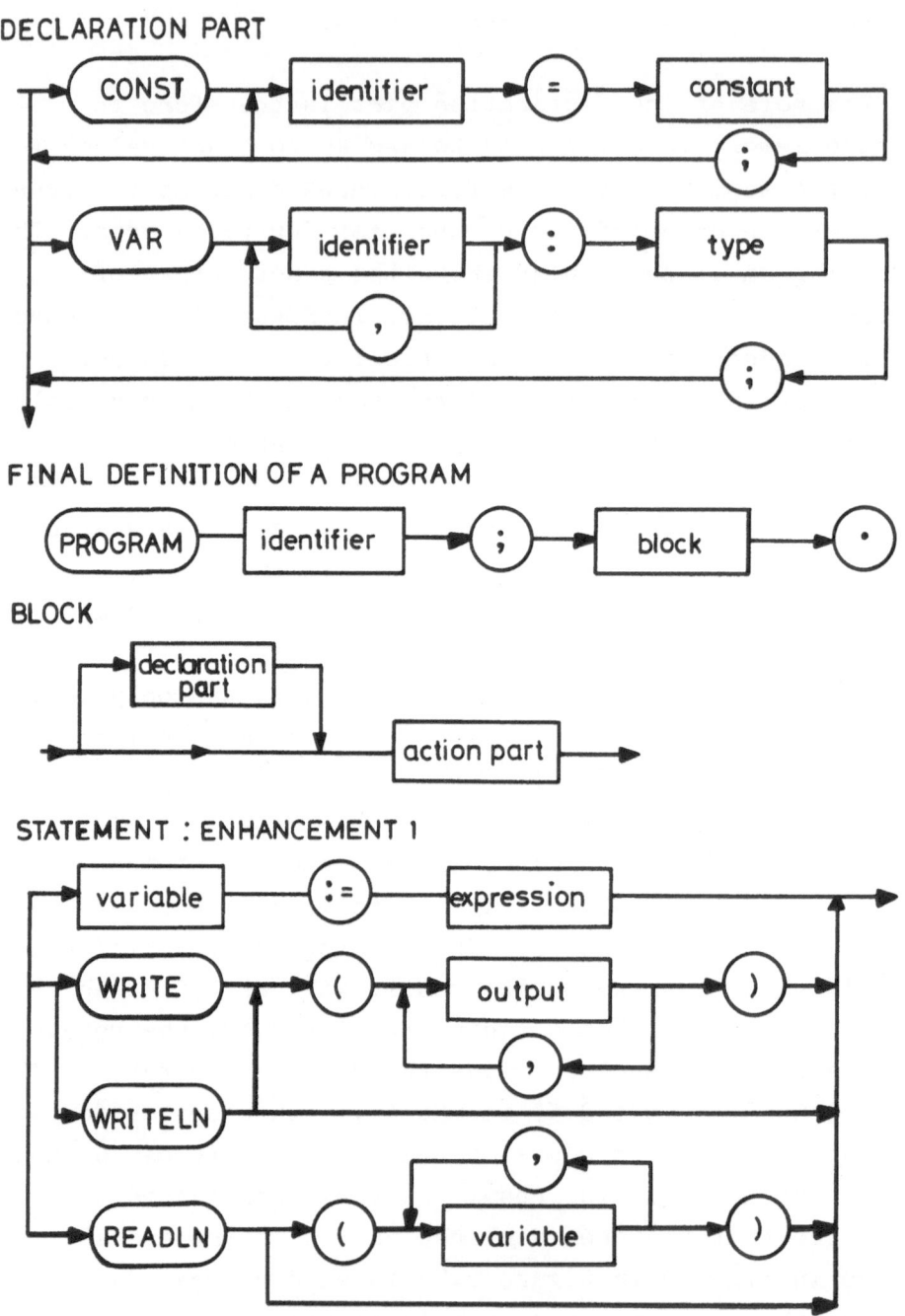

FINAL DEFINITION OF A PROGRAM

BLOCK

STATEMENT : ENHANCEMENT 1

Fig. 2.6. Syntax Diagrams for DECLARATION PART, PROGRAM, BLOCK and STATEMENT

The syntax diagrams in Figures 2.7 and 2.8 deal with the fine points of Pascal grammar that have been illustrated in programs PAY and TEMPERATURECONVERSION. Unfortunately the syntax diagrams fail to show that reals cannot be assigned to integers explicitly.

OUTPUT

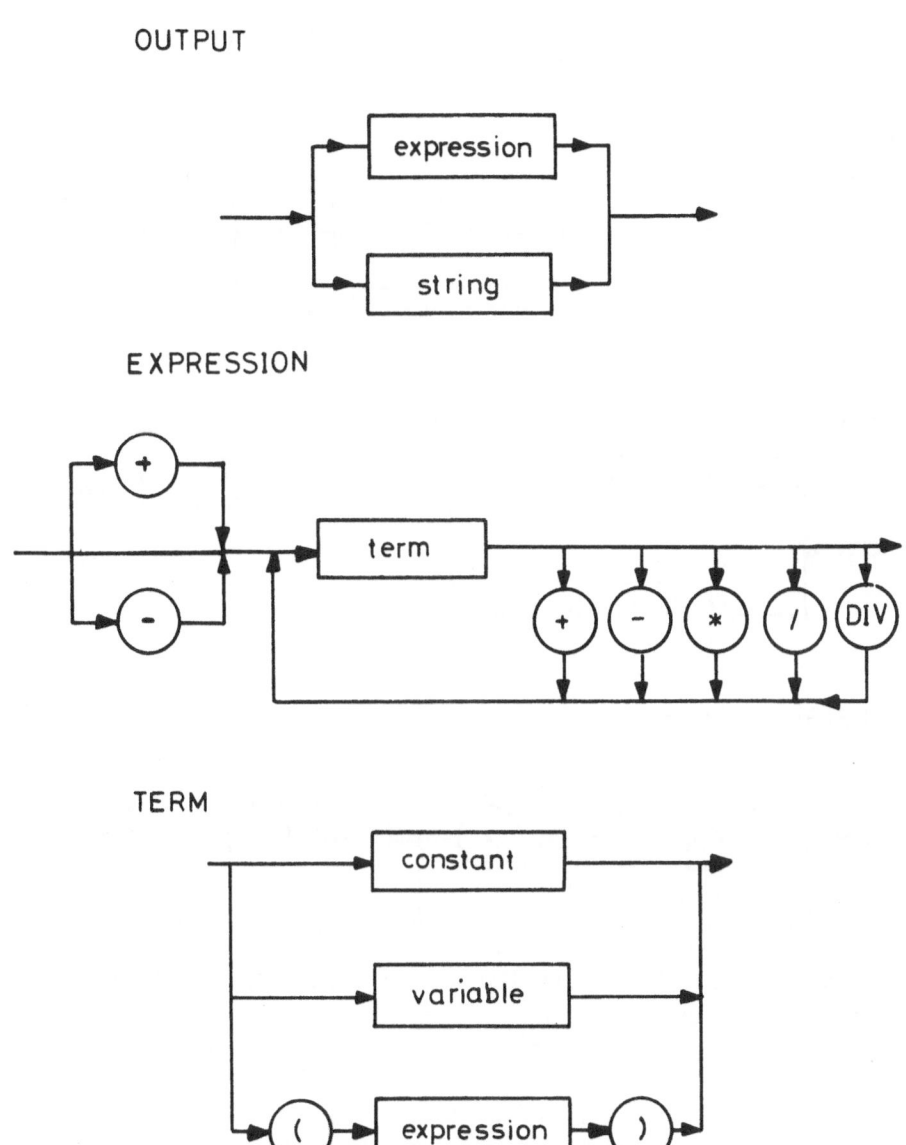

Fig. 2.7. Syntax Diagrams for OUTPUT, EXPRESSION and TERM

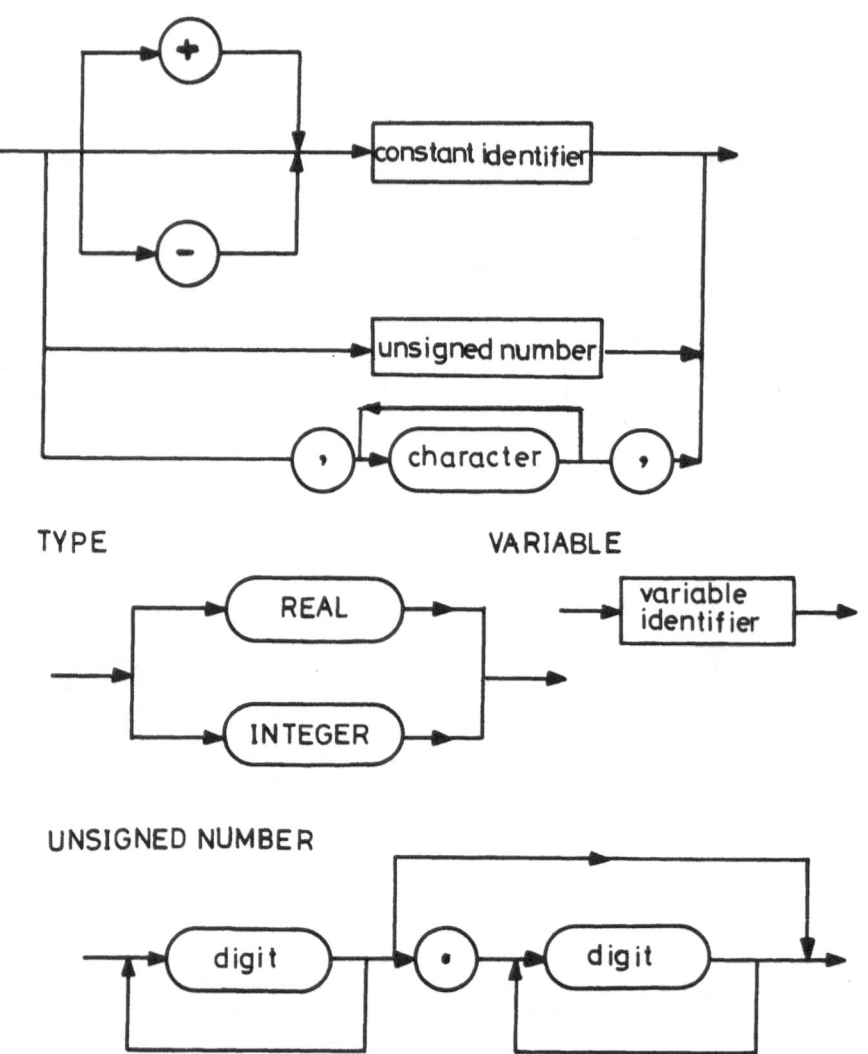

Fig. 2.8. Syntax Diagrams for CONSTANT, TYPE, VARIABLE and UNSIGNED NUMBER

Refining a problem

```
 1: PROGRAM WALKING ;
15: BEGIN
16:    LEFTFOOT ; RIGHTFOOT ;
17:    LEFTFOOT ; RIGHTFOOT ;
18:    LEFTFOOT
19: END.
```

Fig. 2.9. WALKING

Just as it allows for the introduction of variables
and constants, Pascal provides the facility to add what
amount to new instructions for the duration of the program.
Thus program WALKING in Figure 2.9 contains the
"instructions" LEFTFOOT and RIGHTFOOT. Of course these are
not standard Pascal instructions at all but are
self-contained segments of code called procedures which are
"called" in the action part of the main program, nd
declared in its declaration part. Figure 2.10 contains
possible definitions of LEFTFOOT and RIGHTFOOT.

```
 2: PROCEDURE LEFTFOOT ;
 3: BEGIN
 4:    WRITELN('TRAMP') ;
 5:    WRITELN ;
 6:    WRITELN
 7: END ; (* LEFTFOOT *)
 8: PROCEDURE RIGHTFOOT ;
 9: CONST SPACE = '    ' ;
10: BEGIN
11:    WRITELN(SPACE, 'TRAMP') ;
12:    WRITELN ;
13:    WRITELN
14: END ; (* RIGHTFOOT *)
```

Fig. 2.10. LEFTFOOT and RIGHTFOOT

One of the advantages of using procedures is that the
production of the main program is straightforward: it will
consist of procedure calls (using their descriptive names)
whose execution will be as desired and whose details can be
considered at another time. The production of the
procedures themselves is not difficult because each one
should accomplish only one task. (When the tasks get more

```
 1: PROGRAM WALKING ;
 2: PROCEDURE LEFTFOOT ;
 3: BEGIN
 4:   WRITELN('TRAMP') ;
 5:   WRITELN ;
 6:   WRITELN
 7: END ; (* LEFTFOOT *)
 8: PROCEDURE RIGHTFOOT ;
 9: CONST SPACE = '    ' ;
10: BEGIN
11:   WRITELN(SPACE, 'TRAMP') ;
12:   WRITELN ;
13:   WRITELN
14: END ; (* RIGHTFOOT *)
15: BEGIN
16:   LEFTFOOT ; RIGHTFOOT ;
17:   LEFTFOOT ; RIGHTFOOT ;
18:   LEFTFOOT
19: END.
```

Fig. 2.11. Final WALKING

DECLARATION PART:ENHANCEMENT 1

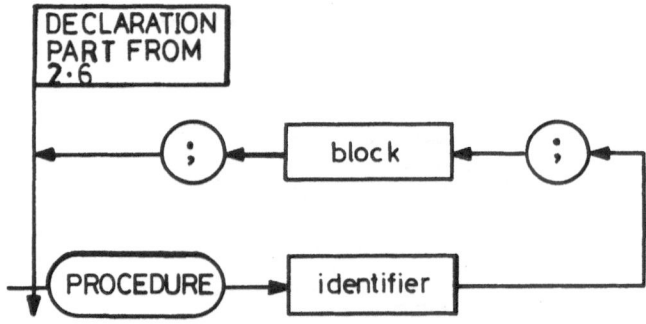

STATEMENT :ENHANCEMENT 2

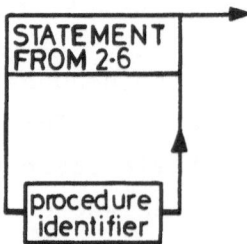

Fig. 2.12. Syntax Diagrams for DECLARATION PART
and STATEMENT

complicated than WALKING, the number of times they are
subdivided -- called stepwise refinement -- is increased.
Refinement stops when there is little point in further
subdivision.)

Looking at lines 2-14 in Figure 2.11 and the first
syntax diagram in Figure 2.12, it can be seen that a
procedure follows the same format as a program, with just
two differences:
 1. The title line is PROCEDURE identifier; rather
 than PROGRAM identifier;
 2. There is a semi-colon rather than a full stop
 at the end of a PROCEDURE
since a full stop is the signal to the compiler that the
whole program is completed. Like any other identifier,
before using a procedure identifier in the action part of a
program it must be declared (see Figure 2.11); that means
giving a full listing of the associated code.

Since procedures are very much like programs they too
can have declaration parts (see Figure 2.10 line 9). And
like whole programs, upon exit from a procedure, the items
declared in it become unavailable, because their memory
locations are released. Any identifier declared within a
procedure is said to be <u>local</u> to it. Identifiers in the
declaration part of the main program are said to be <u>global</u>
and can be used within any procedure. The one exception to
this rule is that a procedure can only call another
procedure if it has been previously defined.

Conclusion

Drawing all the various lines together, there emerge
three significant points:
 1. Pascal is a language which gives flexibility
 to the programmer without interfering with the

predictable format required for an efficient compiler.

2. The major means of achieving this in Pascal is through the separation of a program into declaration and action parts.

3. Programmer control over the declaration part offers freedom of specification of both variable names and types as well as giving powerful operational procedures that enable the straightforward coding of (often repetitive) tasks.

Exercise 1: Draw syntax diagrams for a comment.

Exercise 2: Write a program called PAYPACKET that (like PAY) asks for hours worked and which displays as well as the wage, the number of five pound notes required to make up the wage packet. Use integer rather than real variables and an overtime rate of 2.

Exercise 3: Write a program called MARCHING that prints out twice:

```
    LEFT
    LEFT
    LEFT
        RIGHT
    LEFT
```

This program should contain three procedures, called LEFT, RIGHT and QUICKSTEP. QUICKSTEP should call the other two procedures.

Chapter 3. Control Structures 1: Loops

In the last chapter, the procedure was presented as a means of performing the repetitive tasks so often required in computer programming. Some programs however have to repeat their procedures a large number of times, the precise figure often depending on conditions arising within the data or as a result of previous calculation and hence not known in advance. In order to deal with these requirements, a programming device known as the loop exists in almost all languages.

The function of a loop is to cause the execution of certain lines of code (the body) a certain number of times. Different types of loop may be distinguished by the way in which they decide how many repetitions (or iterations) are required. The process of deciding whether to repeat the body of the loop one more time or to continue with the rest of the program is called a test. Every loop therefore consists of a body and a test and is known as a control structure because it causes the program control or "flow" to differ from the normal sequential execution of program statements.

The most elementary type of loop is designed to execute the body a predefined number of times. This operation is controlled by an explicit counter variable and the test consists of comparing the value of the counter with the known finishing value. Depending on the outcome of the test, the counter is incremented (or sometimes

28

ENHANCED STATEMENT

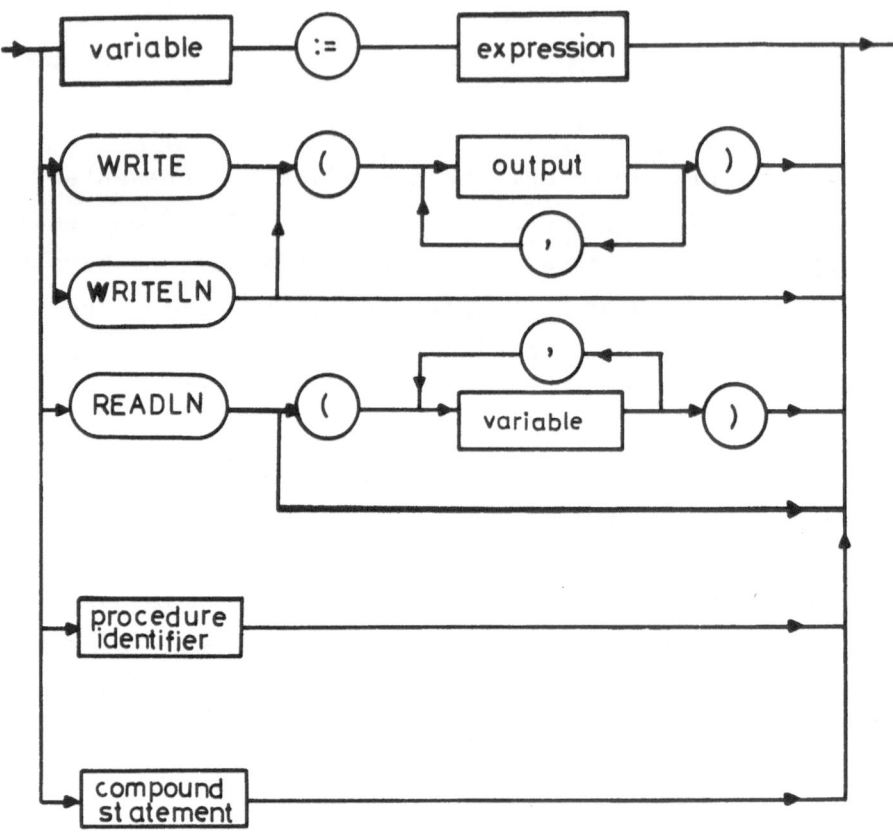

COMPOUND STATEMENT

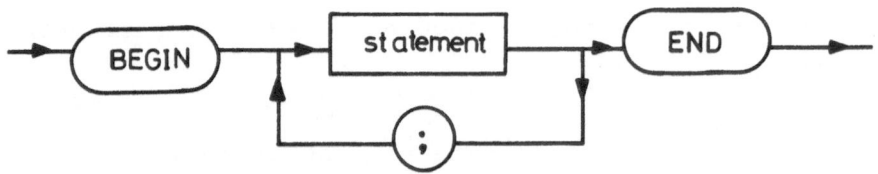

Fig. 3.1. Syntax Diagrams for STATEMENT

decremented) and the body is repeated, otherwise program
control passes to the code immediately beyond the loop.

In BASIC this structure is known as a FOR-NEXT loop, in
FORTRAN a DO loop, in Pascal the FOR-DO loop. In addition,
Pascal has two loops for executing the body an unknown (or
at least uncalculated) number of times. In these the test
depend on conditions arising within the body and a counter,
if used at all, is not an explicit part of the loop. In the
WHILE-DO loop, the test is made before the body is
commenced whereas in the REPEAT-UNTIL loop, the test comes
right at the end of the body. In the next few sections each
of the above will be described, defined and exemplified in
programs.

The body of a loop consists of either a single
statement (now expanded to include the compound statement,
as in the syntax diagram in Figure 3.1) or in certain
cases, a sequence of statements. When laying out a program
it is normal to indent the code between every BEGIN-END
pair. When the body of a loop does not contain a BEGIN-END
pair, by convention it is indented anyway, to emphasize
that it is controlled by a loop.

The FOR-DO Loop

Program ROLLOVER in Figure 3.2 illustrates a FOR-DO
loop in a fairly typical context. Procedure RESTOFVERSE
contains parts of the song which are repeated in each
verse. The loop, set up in line 11, ensures that the part
that changes (CROWDS) is correct for each verse. This
requires the special DOWNTO reserved word to make the
counter work backwards. Lines 13 and 14 actually produce
each verse and line 15 sends the program control back to
line 11 for the next verse -- and so on. Line 16 finishes

```
 1: PROGRAM ROLLOVER ;
 2: VAR CROWDS : INTEGER ;
 3: PROCEDURE RESTOFVERSE ;
 4: BEGIN
 5:     WRITELN(' IN A BED AND THE LITTLE ONE SAID') ;
 6:     WRITELN('',ROLLOVER, ROLLOVER''') ;
 7:     WRITELN('SO THEY ALL ROLLED OVER AND ONE FELL OUT.') ;
 8:     WRITELN
 9: END ; (* RESTOFVERSE *)
10: BEGIN (* MAINPROGRAM *)
11:     FOR CROWDS := 10 DOWNTO 2 DO
12:         BEGIN
13:             WRITE('THERE WERE ', CROWDS) ;
14:             RESTOFVERSE
15:         END ;
16:     WRITELN ('THERE WAS 1 IN THE BED AND HE SAID ''GOODNIGHT''.')
17: END.
```

Fig. 3.2. ROLLOVER

FOR-DO LOOP

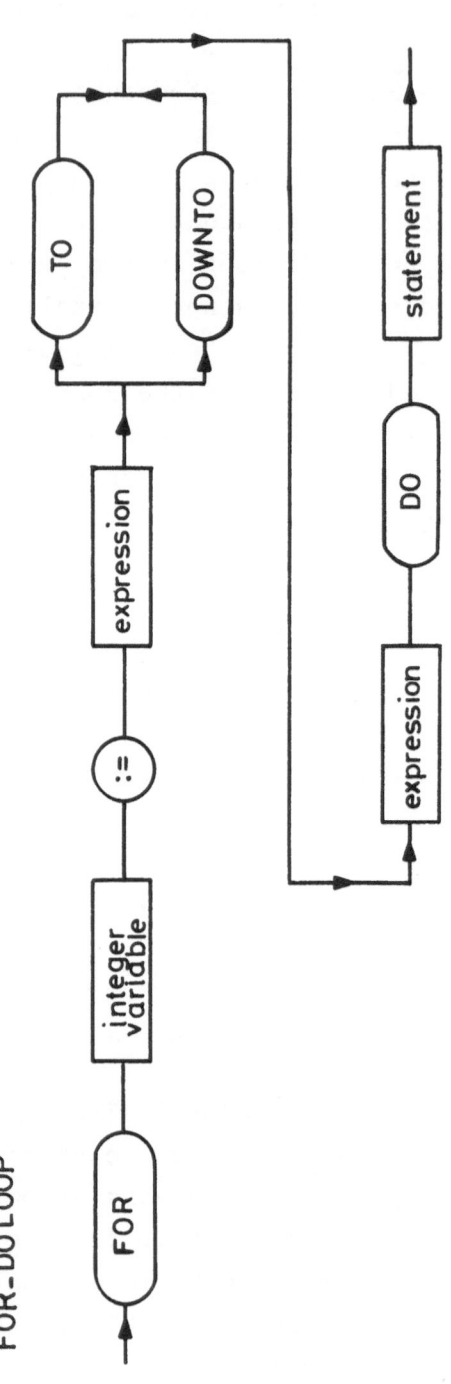

Fig. 3.3. Syntax Diagram for FOR-DO LOOP

off the song. Lines 12 to 15 provide an example of a
compound statement. Finally, note Pascal's solution to the
problem of printing a ' mark (line 6). Since the quote ' is
the text delimiter, the Pascal compiler searches for pairs
of quotes enclosing text. Two adjacent quotes will indicate
that the text is not to be terminated but rather that a
single quote is required for output.

The syntax diagram in Figure 3.3 shows the precise
structure of the FOR-DO loop. The different components
appear as:
    FOR (test) DO (body)
The counter is a variable (but not a REAL) and must
therefore, like any other variable, be declared explicitly
in the declaration part of the procedure which contains the
loop.

The starting and finishing expressions are evaluated
before the loop commences, rather than during each
iteration, so there is no loss of efficiency in using quite
complex expressions if required. (In contrast, in the
ALGOL languages, where expressions are evaluated on every
iteration, programmers learn to keep these simple.) The
counter increases or decreases (depending on whether TO or
DOWNTO, respectively, is used) by one step on each iteration.
In some languages, any step size is allowed, but the
restriction of the step size creates a loop-test requiring
the minimal number of machine-code instructions. If a
different step size is required, a "dummy" counter can be
constructed within the body of the loop, but on no account
should the value of the actual counter be changed inside
the loop (for obvious reasons). The FOR-DO loop test will
discontinue the loop when the value of the counter moves
beyond the finishing value (in the indicated direction).
This ensures not only that the body is executed the correct
number of times, but also, if the counter is accidentally

set up to move away from the finishing value, the body of
the loop will be skipped over entirely.

When the loop has finished the counter variable loses
any value it had (i.e. it becomes <u>undefined</u>). This feature
is included in Pascal as a safety measure to guard against
the tendency of some programmers to re-use a loop counter
at a later stage of the program, without assigning a new
value to it.

The Generalized Loop

Circumstances can often arise in programming where the
use of a fixed-limit FOR-DO loop is too restrictive to
allow for a fluent program style. As an example consider
the problem of entering a list of numbers from a keyboard
into a program. If the number of numbers to be entered is
unknown, there must be a way of telling the program when
the list has come to an end. This is usually done with a
"rogue" value -- a number which couldn't possibly be a part
of the list (e.g. -9999). When the program detects the
rogue value, this is an indication that the input list is
complete and further processing can continue.

It would be nice to place the item-by-item reading of
such a list in a loop, but if the length of the list is
unknown, then the only way of doing this with a FOR-DO loop
leads to awkward and error-prone code. Because
circumstances such as this arise quite frequently, Pascal
has a more generalized loop form. The distinguishing
feature of the generalized loop lies in the nature of its
test. Instead of a steady incrementation of a counter, the
test checks the validity of some relationship which may be
altered in the body of the loop. When the relationship
holds, one course of action is taken and when events within
the loop cause the relationship to change, a different

course of action is embarked upon. Quite clearly, only two possibilities exist -- the relationship holds or it doesn't (i.e. it is <u>true</u> or <u>false</u>). Such a relationship is called a <u>Boolean</u> expression after the English mathematician George Boole who first studied the algebra of such expressions.

The syntax diagram in Figure 3.4 fully defines the Boolean expression. Note that <> stands for "is not equal to". Consider a Boolean expression such as A=B. This expresses the relationship "A is equal to B" and the = is known as a <u>relational</u> <u>operator</u> as are all the other symbols shown in Figure 3.4. (Compare this with the <u>assignment</u> statement A:=B which reads "A becomes equal to B". Here := is an assignment operator and it is this distinction which enables one to write X:=X+1 in a program where it would make no sense in an equation.)

Pascal provides two versions of the generalized loop. In the first, the WHILE-DO loop, the test is made before the body is commenced, and iteration occurs as long as the Boolean expression is true. If the expression is false when the program first encounters the loop, the entire loop will be skipped. The syntax diagram in Figure 3.5 defines a WHILE-DO loop. As with a FOR-DO loop, the body must be a single statement, generally compound.

The program PERFECTSQUARE in Figure 3.6 illustrates the use of a WHILE-DO loop, which runs from lines 10 to 15, line 10 containing the test and the rest comprising the body. While this is not a very practical sort of guessing game, it does show the unlimited nature of the loop which will go on asking for new guesses until the right number turns up. It also shows the major danger of the generalized loop -- suppose the test never fails? The program will stay in the loop forever. For instance, suppose TARGET was 16 while CORRECT and GUESS were REAL

34

BOOLEAN EXPRESSION

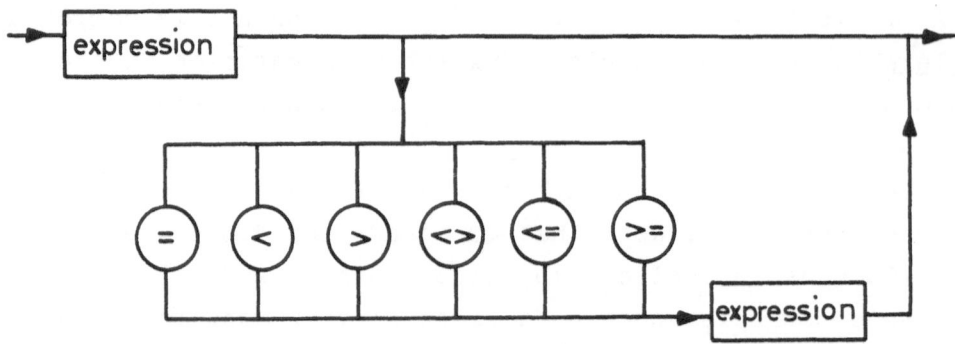

Fig. 3.4. Syntax Diagram for BOOLEAN EXPRESSION

WHILE-DO LOOP

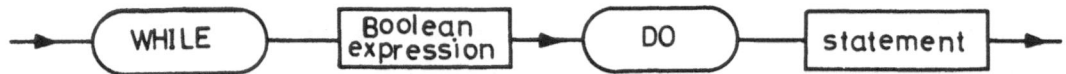

Fig. 3.5. Syntax Diagram for WHILE-DO LOOP

```
 1: PROGRAM PERFECTSQUARE ;
 2: VAR CORRECT, GUESS, TARGET : INTEGER ;
 3: BEGIN
 4:     WRITE('TYPE IN YOUR TARGET NUMBER -->') ;
 5:     READLN(TARGET) ;
 6:     CORRECT := TRUNC(SQRT(TARGET)) ;
 7:     WRITE('NOW GUESS THE LARGEST INTEGER YOU THINK HAS A SQUARE ' ,
 8:         'NOT LARGER THAN ' , TARGET , '-->') ;
 9:     READLN(GUESS) ;
10:     WHILE GUESS () CORRECT DO
11:     BEGIN
12:         WRITELN('NO THAT GIVES ' , GUESS*GUESS) ;
13:         WRITE('SO GUESS AGAIN -->') ;
14:         READLN(GUESS)
15:     END ;
16:     WRITELN('GOOD ', GUESS, ' HAS THE LARGEST PERFECT SQUARE '),
17:         ' NOT LARGER THAN ' , TARGET , ' . ')
18: END . (* PERFECTSQUARE *)
```

Fig. 3.6. PERFECTSQUARE

instead of INTEGER, and CORRECT became 3.99999 (as often
happens). Any integer value guessed could never pass the
test. This can happen quite easily especially when dealing
with the mathematical functions with which rounding errors
are associated. It is good programming practice to design
loop tests capable of dealing with worst case rounding
errors. In the above example ABS (GUESS-CORRECT) > 0.0001
would be a better test than a test for equality.

Examples of mathematical functions appear in line 6.
SQRT(A) is a REAL value representing the square root of A
while TRUNC(B) is the largest integer less than B (when B
is positive). In line 6 the above functions are nested so
that CORRECT is the square-root of the largest perfect square
less than TARGET. A list of all standard functions
available in Pascal appears in Appendix A.

The second generalized loop in Pascal is the
REPEAT-UNTIL loop defined in Figure 3.7. The test comes at
the end of the body and iteration occurs as long as the
condition is false. Pascal has two complementary loops to
allow for a fluent programming style. Sometimes it will seem
more natural to use a WHILE-DO loop and sometimes a
REPEAT-UNTIL will suggest itself. In the latter case,
however, the body will be executed at least once, whatever
state the Boolean expression is in, because the test comes
after the body. Program ANOTHERGO in Figure 3.8 illustrates
the use of a REPEAT-UNTIL loop running from lines 22 to 26.
Line 26 contains the test and the body lies above it.

The Pascal compiler needs to know where the loop body
stops and the rest of the program begins. It is for this
reason that the two DO loops restrict the programmer to a
body consisting of a single statement (usually compound).
Since there are reserved words at both the beginning and
the end of the REPEAT-UNTIL loop, it can contain more than

REPEAT_UNTIL LOOP

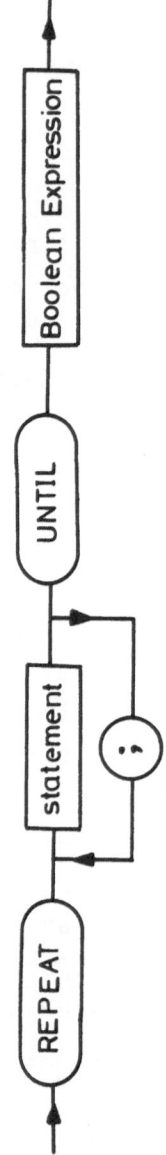

REPEAT — statement — UNTIL — Boolean Expression

Fig. 3.7. Syntax Diagram for REPEAT-UNTIL LOOP

```
1: PROGRAM ANOTHERGO ;
2: VAR ANSWER : CHAR ;
3: PROCEDURE PERFECTSQUARE ;
4: VAR CORRECT, GUESS, TARGET : INTEGER ;
5: BEGIN
6:     WRITE('TYPE IN YOUR TARGET NUMBER -->') ;
7:     READLN(TARGET) ;
8:     CORRECT := TRUNC(SQRT(TARGET)) ;
9:     WRITE('NOW GUESS THE LARGEST INTEGER YOU THINK HAS A SQUARE ',
10:     'NOT LARGER THAN ', TARGET , '-->') ) ;
11:     READLN(GUESS) ;
12:     WHILE GUESS <> CORRECT DO
13:     BEGIN
14:         WRITELN('NO THAT GIVES ', GUESS*GUESS) ;
15:         WRITE('SO GUESS AGAIN -->') ) ;
16:         READLN(GUESS)
17:     END ;
18:     WRITELN('GOOD ', GUESS, ' HAS THE LARGEST PERFECT SQUARE ',
19:     ' NOT LARGER THAN ', TARGET , ' . ')
20: END ; (* PERFECTSQUARE *)
21: BEGIN
22:     REPEAT
23:         PERFECTSQUARE ;
24:         WRITE('DO YOU WANT TO TRY ANOTHER TARGET --> ') ) ;
25:         READLN(ANSWER)
26:     UNTIL ANSWER = 'N'
27: END.
```

Fig. 3.8. ANOTHERGO

one statement in its body (c.f. syntax diagrams for the
different loops). This means that one tends not to find
BEGIN-END pairs following a REPEAT although the
indentation convention is observed nonetheless.

The program in Figure 3.6 has been converted into a
procedure for ANOTHERGO. This is a sensible way to develop
programs -- writing a small, self-contained section as a
separate program, testing it, and then incorporating it as
a procedure in some larger program. This theme will be
developed in more detail in the next section. Finally,
line 2 introduces a new data type, the character type CHAR
which consists of any single letter of the alphabet, digit
or normal keyboard punctuation mark. The variable ANSWER
can contain any one of these characters and can be compared
with actual characters enclosed in 'quotes' as in line 26.
Variables therefore can be declared as INTEGER, REAL or CHAR.

Each of the three control structures defined above is
an extension of the definition of a statement, since it
appears in the action part of a program.

Using Loops

As an everyday application of the use of loops,
consider the construction of a mortgage repayment table.
These are normally constructed by actuaries from formulae
which give the monthly payment incurred by a loan assuming
a fixed interest rate and where repayment occurs over a
fixed time period.

This reputedly boring occupation seems ideally suited
for rendering into machine soluble form, releasing the
actuary for more valuable tasks (like estimating the
insurance risks on a microcomputer). Instead of employing

the actuarial formula, however, the problem will be used to
illustrate a common programming technique which consists of
taking a guess at the likely value, working out the
implications, comparing the results with the required
outcome, improving the guess, working out the implications
again, and repeating this process until an acceptable answer
is reached. Clearly, the loop provides a means of
programming such an iterative solution -- although it's
unlikely to tempt any actuaries away from their formulae.

The approach we shall take in programming this problem
is known as "Top-Down Design". The Top-Down designer begins
by explicitly defining the problem, stating what results
are expected from what initial information. The task is
then coded by calling several procedures, each a distinct
subtask or module which contributes to the solution of the
total problem. Any consideration of the detail of these
modules is deferred to a later stage of the design. In due
course, each module will undergo the same treatment and
thus the problem devolves into a hierarchy of more-or-less
independent subproblems until a level is reached at which
only elementary programming functions are required. At this
point the final coding can be done quickly and accurately,
and the result should be a well-structured program.

Returning to the mortgage table program, the problem
definition could be:
    Given the interest rate and a time period for
    repayment, create a table showing the monthly
    payment due over a given range of loans. The
    input data required is therefore:
    1. interest rate (% p.a.)
    2. repayment period (years)
    3. maximum and minimum loans required (thousands
    of pounds).

The output should be a list of loans from minimum
to maximum in steps of 1000, showing monthly
repayments. The interest rate and repayment
period should also be displayed.

```
 1: PROGRAM REPAYMENTS ;
 2: VAR MIN, MAX, LOAN, REPAY : INTEGER ;
 4: PROCEDURE GETINPUTS;(*READ INTEREST RATE,NUM OF YEARS, MIN AND MAX LOANS*)


60: PROCEDURE PRINTHEADINGS ; (* PRINT OUT INTEREST RATE, NUMBER OF YEARS
61:                              AND TABLE HEADINGS *)
73: PROCEDURE CALCULATEREPAY ; (* WORK OUT MONTHLY REPAYMENTS *)
94: BEGIN (* MAIN PROGRAM *)
95:     GETINPUTS;
96:     PRINTHEADINGS ;
97:     LOAN := MIN ;
98:     WHILE LOAN <= MAX DO
99:     BEGIN
100:        CALCULATEREPAY ;
101:        WRITELN('   ', LOAN, '      ', REPAY) ;
102:        LOAN := LOAN + 1000
103:     END
104: END . (* REPAYMENTS *)
```

Fig. 3.9. REPAYMENTS

```
73: PROCEDURE CALCULATEREPAY ; (* WORK OUT MONTHLY REPAYMENTS *)
74: VAR TOTALMONTHS : INTEGER ;
75:     MONTHLYINTERESTRATE, AMOUNTDUE : REAL ;
76: PROCEDURE TRYREPAY ; (* WORK OUT THE ACTUAL AMOUNT A GIVEN
77:     REPAYMENT WILL ACTUALLY PAY OFF *)
83: BEGIN (* CALCULATEREPAY *)
84:     MONTHLYINTERESTRATE := INTERESTRATE/12 ;
85:     TOTALMONTHS := 12*YEARS ;
86:     REPAY := LOAN DIV TOTALMONTHS ;
87:     REPEAT
88:        AMOUNTDUE := LOAN ;
89:        REPAY := REPAY + 1 ;
90:        TRYREPAY
91:     UNTIL AMOUNTDUE<=0
92: END ; (* CALCULATEREPAY *)
```

Fig. 3.10. CALCULATEREPAY

The next stage is to decide on the method of solution
in order to code the main program. At this level the tasks
that must be accomplished include reading in the input
parameters, printing out the appropriate headings and, for
each loan from the minimum to the maximum requested,
calculating and printing the repayment amount.   The

calculations will have to be performed in a loop which will
stop when the maximum loan value is reached. In Figure 3.9,
the procedures named GETINPUTS and PRINTHEADINGS will
handle the initial part of the problem, and introduced a
WHILE-DO loop (lines 98-103) will control the calculation
and output of the table. Procedure CALCULATEREPAY will
actually perform the calculations.

   The declaration part of this first attempt includes
all identifiers used in the main program. These include
the integer variables MIN, MAX, LOAN and REPAY, together
with the procedures GETINPUTS, PRINTHEADINGS and
CALCULATEREPAY. Notice that these procedures have not been
fully defined at this stage but merely contain a comment
indicating what each will eventually do.

   Having completed the highest level of the program
design, the three procedures will be tackled in the same
way that the whole problem REPAYMENTS was approached. The
question arises as to which of the three should be dealt
with first. We prefer to start with the "Heart" of the
problem -- CALCULATEREPAY (Figure 3.10). The problem
definition of CALCULATEREPAY could be:

   Work out the monthly repayment as follows -- first
   guess an obviously low value and calculate how
   much that would pay off over the given time period,
   taking into account the interest charges. If
   there is still a debt by the end, the repayment
   value was not enough, so increase it and try
   again.   Continue until the repayment amount pays
   off the loan.
   Input data
   1. duration of loan
   2. interest rate
   3. amount of loan

Output data is the calculated monthly repayment
amount.

In the declaration part, the variables required in the
calculation will have to be declared only if they are local
to the procedure, since the global variables will already
have been declared. Thus a check should be made that the
input and output variables, YEARS, INTERESTRATE, LOAN and
REPAY appear in the variable declaration of the main
program. Some of these may be missing in a "first attempt"
version and so should be incorporated.

To start coding CALCULATEREPAY the first step is to
generate the working data from the input data. The
repayment period, for instance, is in years but is here
required in months as is the interest rate. Therefore two
new (local) variables TOTALMONTHS and MONTHLYINTERESTRATE
must be declared and calculated. Next, the initial estimate
should be made, in order to start the whole process off.
Since repayments will be increased to improve the "guess",
it is important to start with an estimate below the likely
value. A reasonable first estimate would be the amount one
would pay back interest-free. This is simple enough to
code at this stage as can be seen in line 86 of Figure 3.10.
(Note that DIV has been used since REPAY is an integer.
This program could be changed to give pounds and pence if
the user is willing to leave the program running to obtain
such accuracy.) Since the initial estimate must be too low,
the next step should be to add £1 to the repayment and test
whether that will pay off the loan.

The process of incrementing the repayment amount and
testing is repeated until a figure is reached which
actually does pay off the loan. This has been coded in the
REPEAT-UNTIL loop, lines 87 to 91, Figure 3.10, but, just
as this calculation was put off in the main program, so the

job of calculating how much a given value of REPAY would
actually pay off over the time-period is deferred to
procedure TRYREPAY, which is the next problem to be tackled
(Figure 3.11). The problem definition of TRYREPAY could be:

Evaluate how much a given value of REPAY would pay
off over the given duration of the mortgage using
the given interest rate, assuming monthly
payments and the compounding of interest.
Input data
1. monthly interest rate
2. duration of loan (months)
3. value of loan
4. value of repayment
Output data -- amount of debt remaining when time
period has elapsed.

What is owing at the end of one month? Suppose
AMOUNTDUE contains the amount due at the beginning of one
month and an amount REPAY is paid back. At the end of that
month, the amount due will be (AMOUNTDUE - REPAY) + interest
accrued during the month. This figure will become the
AMOUNTDUE for the next month; for N months, this
calculation should pass through N iterations. This is
coded in the FOR-DO loop, Figure 3.11, lines 80 and 81. The
only variable needed that has not been previously declared
is the loop counter, which is declared locally in line 78.
This completes the definition of TRYREPAY which, in turn,
completes the definition of procedure CALCULATEREPAY.

```
76: PROCEDURE TRYREPAY : (* WORK OUT THE ACTUAL AMOUNT A GIVEN
77:     REPAYMENT WILL ACTUALLY PAY OFF *)
78: VAR MONTH : INTEGER :
79: BEGIN (* CALCULATEREPAY *)
80:     FOR MONTH := 1 TO TOTALMONTHS DO
81:         AMOUNTDUE := (AMOUNTDUE - REPAY)*(1 + MONTHLYINTERESTRATE)
82: END : (* TRYREPAY *)
```

Fig. 3.11. TRYREPAY

```
 4: PROCEDURE GETINPUTS;(*READ INTEREST RATE,NUM OF YEARS, MIN AND MAX LOANS*)
 5: CONST IMIN = 2 ; IMAX =50 ;
 6:       YMIN = 5 ; YMAX = 35 ;
 7:       LMIN = 5 ; LMAX = 200 ;
 8:
 9: PROCEDURE GETINTEREST ; (* READS IN INTEREST RATE BETWEEN IMIN AND IMAX
10:                          AND CONVERTS IT TO A DECIMAL *)
20: PROCEDURE GETYEARS;(*READS DURATION OF LOAN BETWEEN YMIN AND YMAX YEARS*)
29: PROCEDURE GETMIN ; (* READS, IN THOUSANDS, THE MINIMUM LOAN VALUE BETWEEN
30:                       LMIN AND LMAX AND CONVERTS IT TO POUNDS *)
42: PROCEDURE GETMAX ; (* LIKE GETMIN, BUT FOR THE MAXIMAL LOAN VALUE *)
53: BEGIN (* GETINPUTS *)
54:     GETINTEREST ;
55:     GETYEARS ;
56:     GETMIN ;
57:     GETMAX
58: END ; (* GETINPUTS *)
```

Fig. 3.12. GETINPUTS

```
 9: PROCEDURE GETINTEREST ; (* READS IN INTEREST RATE BETWEEN IMIN AND IMAX
10:                          AND CONVERTS IT TO A DECIMAL *)
11: BEGIN
12:     WRITELN('TYPE IN THE RATE OF INTEREST AS A PERCENTAGE.') ;
13:     REPEAT
14:         WRITE('A NUMBER BETWEEN ' , IMIN, ' AND ', IMAX, '--)' ) ;
15:         READLN(INTERESTRATE)
16:     UNTIL (INTERESTRATE)=IMIN) AND (INTERESTRATE(=IMAX) ;
17:     INTERESTRATE := INTERESTRATE/100 ; (* % --) DECIMAL *)
18: END ;
19:
20: PROCEDURE GETYEARS;(*READS DURATION OF LOAN BETWEEN YMIN AND YMAX YEARS*)
21: BEGIN
22:     WRITELN('TYPE IN THE NUMBER OF YEARS FOR WHICH MORTGAGE WILL RUN. ') ;
23:     REPEAT
24:         WRITE('A NUMBER BETWEEN ', YMIN, ' AND ', YMAX, '--)') ;
25:         READLN(YEARS)
26:     UNTIL (YEARS)=YMIN) AND (YEARS(=YMAX)
27: END ; (* GETYEARS *)
28:
29: PROCEDURE GETMIN ; (* READS, IN THOUSANDS, THE MINIMUM LOAN VALUE BETWEEN
30:                       LMIN AND LMAX AND CONVERTS IT TO POUNDS *)
31: VAR LOANMIN : INTEGER ;
32: BEGIN
33:     WRITELN('TYPE IN THE SMALLEST MORTGAGE YOU ARE INTERESTED IN,',
34:         'IN THOUSANDS.') ;
35:     REPEAT
36:         WRITE('A NUMBER BETWEEN ', LMIN, ' AND ', LMAX, '--)') ;
37:         READLN(LOANMIN)
38:     UNTIL (LOANMIN)=LMIN) AND (LOANMIN(=LMAX) ;
39:     MIN := LOANMIN*1000
40: END ; (* GETMIN *)
41:
42: PROCEDURE GETMAX ; (* LIKE GETMIN, BUT FOR THE MAXIMAL LOAN VALUE *)
43: VAR LOANMAX : INTEGER ;
44: BEGIN
45:     WRITELN ('TYPE IN THE LARGEST MORTGAGE YOU ARE INTERESTED IN, ' ,
46:         'IN THOUSANDS.') ;
47:     REPEAT
48:         WRITE('A NUMBER BETWEEN ', MIN DIV 1000, ' AND ', LMAX, '--)') ;
49:         READLN(LOANMAX)
50:     UNTIL (LOANMAX )MIN DIV 1000) AND (LOANMAX (=LMAX) ;
51:     MAX := LOANMAX*1000
52: END ; (* GETMAX *)
```

Fig. 3.13. GETINTEREST

Having coded CALCULATEREPAY the information GETINPUTS must obtain is known. The problem definition could be: Read in interest rate, duration of loan and maximum and minimum loans (in thousands of pounds). Convert interest rate to a decimal (instead of percentage) and loan values to pounds. Output data

1. interest rate (decimal fraction)
2. duration of loan
3. minimum loan
4. maximum loan

An input procedure should usually check that the data it accepts is reasonable and unlikely to cause the program to crash. For instance, if the repayment period YEARS were zero, then TOTALMONTHS would also be zero. But TOTALMONTHS forms a denominator in CALCULATEREPAY, so that apart from zero being an unreasonable figure for YEARS it will also crash the program.

Figure 3.12 contains procedure GETINPUTS. In the action part the four procedures GETINTEREST, GETYEARS, GETMIN and GETMAX are called. The declaration part lays down limits within which the input data should fall (lines 5-7). If one of these should later on prove restricting, it will be easy to change the CONST declaration.

The four individual input procedures (Figure 3.13) are so similar that only one, GETINTEREST, need be considered in detail. Its problem definition could be: Output a message asking for the rate of interest. Check whether the response is within the range of reasonable values. Keep asking until an acceptable reply is received. Then convert this number from a percentage to a decimal fraction.

Input data
IMIN and IMAX -- limits of "reasonable" interest
rates (as a percentage).
Output data
INTERESTRATE -- actual required interest rate as a
decimal fraction.

A REPEAT-UNTIL loop (lines 13 to 16) is used to accept
input. The program remains in the loop until an acceptable
figure is entered. The other three input procedures are
developed in a similar fashion. Note that in procedure
GETMAX, the minimum value for a loan is not LMIN but MIN
DIV 1000 -- the actual lower limit obtained from GETMIN
(line 48). Finally, PRINTHEADINGS is tackled (Figure
3.14). Its problem definition could be:
Clear the screen, then print out a title followed
by the required interest-rate and the duration of
the loan. Skip several lines and print the
headings MORTGAGE (for the loan) and MONTHLY
REPAYMENTS.
Input data
1. yearly interest rate (%)
2. duration of loan (years)
Output Data -- This procedure simply produces the
headings.

The coding for this procedure appears in Figure 3.14.
The entire program can now be gathered together. In
Appendix B, REPAYMENTS can be seen with extra global
variables (INTERESTRATE and YEARS) incorporated into the
declaration part of the first attempt (Figure 3.9) and the
details of the different procedures filled in as they have
been designed.

46

```
60: PROCEDURE PRINTHEADINGS ; (* PRINT OUT INTEREST RATE, NUMBER OF YEARS
61:                                AND TABLE HEADINGS *)
62: CONST SPACE = '                    ' ;
63: BEGIN
64:     WRITELN ; WRITELN ;
65:     WRITELN(SPACE, '**MONTHLY MORTGAGE REPAYMENTS**') ;
66:     WRITELN(SPACE, '--------- -------- -------------') ;
67:     WRITELN ;
68:     WRITELN('INTEREST RATE=',100*INTERESTRATE,'% OVER ', YEARS, ' YEARS');
69:     WRITELN('    LOAN     REPAYMENTS') ;
70:     WRITELN('    ----     ----------')
71: END ; (* PRINTHEADINGS *)
```

Fig. 3.14. PRINTHEADINGS

Conclusion

    Loops control the repetition of a set of statements
within a program. Every language needs a loop -- Pascal has
three -- which enriches the language and makes it
versatile. Loops can be distinguished by the type and
position of the loop test relative to the loop body.

Exercise 1: Write a program to print out the song "Ten
Green Bottles".

Exercise 2: Computers (and calculators) are often tested
for accuracy by computing a range of nested mutually
inverse functions (e.g. $\exp(\ln(x))=x$). Write a program to
input a sequence of (positive) numbers (rogue values could
be 0 or less), in each case calculating $\exp(\ln(x))$ and
outputting this value, together with x and thence between
them before reading in the next one.

Exercise 3: Try rewriting the first attempt of PROGRAM
REPAYMENTS with a FOR-DO loop instead of a WHILE-DO loop.

Exercise 4: Adapt REPAYMENTS to produce a table showing the
15, 20, 25 and 30 year monthly repayment figures for a
given range of loans. The input should be the interest
rate and range of loans (and not the loan period) and the
output should be a table with 5 columns -- one for the
amount of the loan and one each for each repayment period.

Chapter 4. Data Structures 1:
Simple Data Types, Arrays and Sets

   During the execution of a program, data is stored as
bit patterns at addressable locations within memory. In
this form, however, it is very tiresome to access and even
more awkward to manipulate and so high-level languages
provide various devices for referencing specific memory
locations and for organising and interpreting the data
contained therein. In Pascal, perhaps the most striking
device is the incorporation of a distinct declaration part
which gives the programmer a chance to specify data storage
and access requirements, and the compiler a chance to
organise the memory in the machine to cope with the flow
of information, once the action part starts executing.

   In addition, Pascal provides for different types of
data (alphabetic, numeric, etc.) to be referenced by
arbitrary variable names and for different items of data to
be associated with one another in a variety of ways, either
out of logical necessity or for convenience. The
association of one data item with one or more other items
is known as a data structure and can be an extremely
powerful tool to the programmer. When data is badly
organised, the amount of additional processing required to
access and evaluate a given data element is increased,
lengthening the execution time and increasing the likelihood
of errors. Having a declaration part in a program forces
the programmer to devote time and energy to considering the
organisation of data -- and data thoughtfully and skilfully
organised can be manipulated more efficiently and reliably.

Most languages provide for one or more types of data
structure. Scientific languages must have good array
handling whereas any business language needs record and file
structures. Interactive languages should have good string
handling facilities.

While Pascal offers all of these, perhaps its most
powerful feature is the element of freedom offered in the
definition of any data type or structure. As a
programmer's skill develops, this freedom will be used with
increasing sophistication in the creation and use of highly
complex and efficient data structures. Clearly there have
to be some limits to the freedom of definition offered to
programmers and two of these limits are imposed by the
architecture of the hardware on which Pascal is to be
implemented. Firstly, the word-length (and bus width) of
the system dictates the size of the numbers which can be
held in a "natural" way, either as integers (two's
complement) or real numbers (floating point format).
Secondly, the particular character set which the system (or
terminal) will recognise, limits the number of characters
and symbols available to the programmer. For example,
curly brackets, the preferred comment delimiters are
frequently omitted from terminal keyboards and are hence
not available.

It is in recognition of these implementation-dependent
requirements that Pascal provides four basic <u>standard</u> <u>data</u>
<u>types</u> INTEGER, REAL, CHAR and BOOLEAN. The range, storage
characteristics and, in some cases, the position in memory
for variables declared as these types have been decided in
advance by whoever designed the processor, the data bus or
the Pascal compiler, and are not the responsibility of the
Pascal programmer. (In most Pascal implementations on
microcomputers, BOOLEAN's and CHAR's occupy one byte,
whereas INTEGER's need two bytes and REAL's use four.)

Subrange Types

The advantages of defining one's own data types are
twofold. Firstly, the particular form and structure of the
data has to be thought through in advance, which often
means that the problem becomes better understood and hence
more effectively programmed. Secondly, if the limits and
restrictions imposed on the data are known in advance, checks
can be built into the program to ensure that no particular
calculation or other process can go out of control.
Classic examples of unchecked data include inadvertently
dividing by zero (thus crashing the system) or sending a
customer a Final Demand on a bill of 0.00 pounds.

Both of these types of programming fault can be
avoided in Pascal by declaring a variable as falling within
a subrange of the available range of integers or sometimes
characters. (This does not apply to REALs). Suppose one is
writing a program to accumulate and store table-tennis
scores. No one can get a negative score, nor a score
greater than 21 so a sensible limitation on the integer
variables ASCORE and BSCORE would be declared as follows:
    VAR ASCORE, BSCORE : 0..21 ;
Now if anything goes wrong while this data is being input or
during a calculation, the program will stop and the system
will give an error message which draws attention to the
particular variable which has moved "out of range". The
next chapter will outline some explicit safeguards
available to the programmer faced with the prospect of
designing a program where data input is likely to contain
errors.

Similarly, in a program which deals with examination
grades, one might declare a character variable as follows:
    VAR GRADE : A..F ;

where A to E are the pass grades and F is a fail. Once
again, if something goes wrong and GRADE becomes corrupted,
the program will exit with an error message. It often
seems a nuisance having to think out reasonable subranges
for variables simply in order to give the program more ways
of crashing -- but the payoff is improved data integrity
and hence more reliable processing.

The syntax diagram for subrange definition is shown in
Figure 4.1 as a variation of the "simple type" definition.
This is employed in a program through the VAR declaration,
also shown in Figure 4.1. In a chapter largely about data
and the declaration part, it is difficult to provide
full-program examples which are truly illustrative.
Nevertheless, program CLASSAVERAGE in Figure 4.2 is an
attempt to show how subrange types can be used in a program
to calculate the average test mark of a class of students.
In line 3 COUNTER is declared within the range 0 to 50
which implies that the program won't work for classes with
more than 50 students. Line 2 shows that MARK must be less
than or equal to 100, which is reasonable when marks are
given as a percentage. If a teacher sets a test out of 50,
the program would still work as it stands -- but it would
be safer to amend line 2 to reflect the new maximum before
running the program. Note the -1 value which MARK can have
-- this is the rogue value to allow an exit from the loop
when all the data has been input. AVERAGE is declared as
REAL in line 5 because it is the result of a division (line
20). In line 7 the variables COUNTER and TOTALMARKS are
initialised -- i.e. set to zero in this case.

Many computer systems automatically set everything to
zero before the program starts anyway, but a good
programmer wouldn't depend on this, and in certain cases
the initial value need not be zero. Lines 8 and 9 give the
operator a brief description of what to do to get the data

a) Simple Type

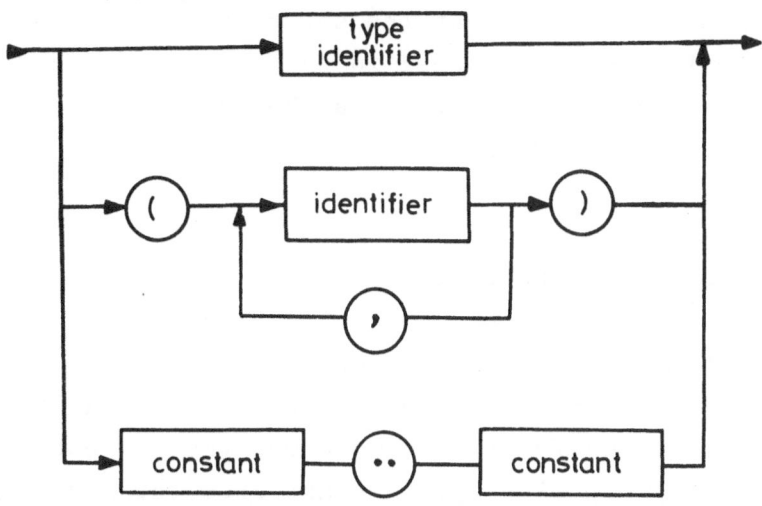

b) Variable Declaration

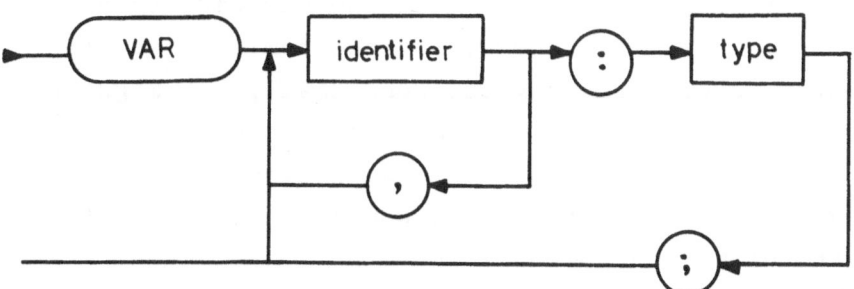

Fig. 4.1. Syntax Diagrams for SIMPLE TYPE and VARIABLE
DECLARATION

```
 1: PROGRAM CLASSAVERAGE ;
 2: VAR MARK : -1..100 ;
 3:     COUNTER : 0..50 ;
 4:     TOTALMARKS : REAL ;
 5:     AVERAGE : REAL ;
 6: BEGIN
 7:     COUNTER := 0 ; TOTALMARKS := 0 ;
 8:     WRITELN('TYPE EACH MARK AS REQUESTED,  ',
 9:             'TYPE -1 WHEN THE LIST IS COMPLETE.') ;
10:     WRITELN ;
11:     WRITE('MARK --) ') ;
12:     READLN(MARK) ;
13:     WHILE MARK)-1 DO
14:     BEGIN
15:         COUNTER := COUNTER + 1 ;
16:         TOTALMARKS := TOTALMARKS + MARK ;
17:         WRITE('MARK --) ') ;
18:         READLN(MARK)
19:     END ;
20:     AVERAGE := TOTALMARKS / COUNTER ;
21:     WRITE('THE AVERAGE OF THE MARKS IS ', AVERAGE)
22: END . (* CLASSAVERAGE *)
```

Fig. 4.2. CLASSAVERAGE

into the program. This is done in lines 12 to 19, and line
21 gives the answer. Note that the use of a WHILE-DO loop
forces the first datum to be read in before the loop has
been set up (lines 11 & 12). This can be avoided by slightly
different coding and more complex initialisation.

Scalar Types and Data Structuring

Anyone who has ever had to handle largish amounts of
information will know that in order to classify data it is
often necessary to codify it. Suppose one was collecting
information on a group of people. Apart from totally
individual data like names and addresses, there are usually
a variety of categories into which one may want to subdivide
the group e.g. sex, age group, socioeconomic class, part of
the country, etc. If the group were small, one might have
an entry as follows: Lady Godiva, female aged 22 years,
aristocrat of Coventry. However, if the group were larger,
with several hundred entries, it would be necessary to
codify the data. For example:

SEX:	MALE=0
	FEMALE=1
AGE GROUP:	16-25=1
	26-35=2
	36-45=3
	46-55=4 etc.
CLASS:	Aristocrat=1
	Professional=2
	White Collar=3
	Blue Collar=4
	Labourer=5.
REGION:	South East=1
	South West=2
	Midlands=3 etc.

and thus -- Lady Godiva,1,1,1,3.

This is quicker to write down and it becomes easier to
search through for particular features or characteristics
-- but it is easy to see how someone becomes "just a
number". In addition, there is a likelihood of making
mistakes whilst encoding or reinterpreting a previously
encoded datum, and these mistakes are difficult to spot.
Somehow,

       Lady Godiva, Male, etc.,

strikes the eye more than does

       Lady Godiva, 0,1,1,3.

The more categories there are, the more likely such encoding
errors become and the less readable each entry (and the
whole block of data) becomes.

The above remarks apply to most types of information
gathering and analysis activities, but when it comes to
programming, the temptation (and necessity) to use code
numbers as a shorthand is greatly increased. Firstly, the
memory (in the shape of the variable identifiers) can hold
numbers like 1 or 0 more compactly than words like MALE and
FEMALE. Secondly, these numbers can be manipulated much
faster and with less programming effort than strings of
characters, which require special routines to enable
searching and sorting rather than comparatively
straightforward arithmetic. However, the two problems of
encoding errors and poor readability (both of data and
program) still remain. In order to ensure against these, a
great deal of cross-checking between the data entries and
the code-lists has to be done. This is irritating and
time-consuming for the programmer and just the kind of job
the compiler should do.

In response to this sort of requirement, Pascal
provides a means of getting the machine to do all the
encoding and decoding, allowing the programmer to retain
descriptive names for the different categories of

classification. The trick is to allow the programmer to define new data types (called <u>scalar</u> types) which consist of a sequence of "values" whose names are just those categories the programmer wants to use. The TYPE declaration must appear before the VAR declaration in the declaration part so that a variable declared as belonging to one particular scalar type can take any of the values mentioned in the list. Lady Godiva and her friends could have been dealt with thus:

```
TYPE    GENDER=(MALE,FEMALE) ;
        AGEGROUP=(YOUNG,MATURE,MIDDLEAGED,ELDERLY) ;
        CLASS=(ARISTOCRAT,PROFESSIONAL,WHITECOLLAR,
            BLUECOLLAR,LABOURER) ;
        ORIGIN=(SOUTHEAST,SOUTHWEST,WALES,MIDLANDS,
            EASTANGLIA,NORTHEAST,NORTHWEST) ;
VAR     SEX : GENDER ;
        AGE : AGEGROUP ;
        GROUP,FAMILY,FRIENDS : CLASS ;
        PLACE,ADDRESS : ORIGIN ;
```

So SEX is a variable which can take a "value" of MALE or FEMALE -- and so on. Lady Godiva herself thus becomes:

```
LADY GODIVA,FEMALE,YOUNG,ARISTOCRAT,MIDLANDS
```

which presents no confusion to the writer (or reader) of the program. The Pascal compiler makes the switch to the number set whose precise values need never bother the programmer. Also instructions like:

```
WHILE ADDRESS=NORTHWEST DO
```

will pick out the relevant individuals and

```
FOR GROUP:=LABOURER DOWNTO ARISTOCRAT DO
```

will cycle through the loop taking each member of CLASS in turn.

The computer uses numbers for these operations, ensuring no loss of efficiency in execution, but the secret of the encoding and control of these numbers is locked in

the Pascal compiler and not accessible to the programmer.
The only disadvantage in this arrangement is that there is
no simple way to print out scalar values.

Two points need to be made here. Firstly, the
standard data type BOOLEAN is a special predefined scalar
type. It can take values FALSE and TRUE -- i.e. there is
an implied declaration of the form:
    TYPE BOOLEAN = (FALSE, TRUE);
in every declaration part of every program. The second
point is that the order of the elements in the list is
important. It is this that enables GROUP to be used as a
loop counter above. Two reserved words exist which allow
one to change position within a type list. These are SUCC
(for successor) and PRED (for predecessor) such that:
    SUCC(MATURE) is MIDDLEAGED and PRED(EASTANGLIA) is
    MIDLANDS,
in the example given above.

Program OLDMANRIVER in Figure 4.3 contains a
demonstration of a scalar type at work in a complete program.
The scalar type is WEEKDAY (line 2) while DAY (line 3) is a
variable which can take any value listed in line 2. Lines 5
to 10 and 12 to 16 define procedures used in the main
program, and it is the overall readability of the main
program (lines 18 to 22) that is the important feature.
(If you think that the output sounds more repetitive than
you remember, then you've probably not worked on a cotton
plantation.)

Sometimes the implied order in a scalar type list
becomes a nuisance because the programmer needs to connect
up the different categories in another way. Alternatively,
the programmer might need to use only a few numbers of the
list for one particular procedure -- these could be a
subrange or they could be dotted all over the list. This can

```
 1: PROGRAM OLDMANRIVER ;
 2: TYPE WEEKDAY = (MON, TUE, WED, THU, FRI) ;
 3: VAR DAY : WEEKDAY ;
 4:
 5: PROCEDURE WORK ;
 6: BEGIN
 7:     WRITELN('TOTE THAT BARGE') ;
 8:     WRITELN('LIFT THAT BALE') ;
 9:     WRITELN ;
10: END ; (* WORK *)
11:
12: PROCEDURE PLAY ;
13: BEGIN
14:     WRITELN('YOU GET A LITTLE DRUNK') ;
15:     WRITELN('AND YOU LANDS IN JAIL.') ;
16: END ; (* PLAY *)
17:
18: BEGIN (* MAIN PROGRAM *)
19:     FOR DAY := MON TO FRI DO
20:         WORK ;
21:     PLAY
22: END . (* OLDMANRIVER *)
```

Fig. 4.3. OLDMANRIVER

```
 1: PROGRAM MISSISSIPPI ;
 2: TYPE DAY = (MON, TUE, WED, THU, FRI, SAT, SUN) ;
 3:     WEEK = SET OF DAY ;
 4: VAR WEEKDAYS, WEEKEND : WEEK ;
 5:     TODAY : DAY ;
 6:
 7: PROCEDURE WORK ;
 8: BEGIN
 9:     WRITELN('TOTE THAT BARGE') ;
10:     WRITELN('LIFT THAT BALE') ;
11:     WRITELN
12: END ; (* WORK *)
13:
14: PROCEDURE PLAY ;
15: BEGIN
16:     WRITELN('YOU GET A LITTLE DRUNK') ;
17:     WRITELN('AND YOU LANDS IN JAIL. ')
18: END ; (* PLAY *)
19:
20: BEGIN (* MAIN PROGRAM *)
21:     WEEKDAYS :=[MON..FRI] ;
22:     WEEKEND :=[SAT,SUN] ;
23:     TODAY := MON ;
24:     WHILE TODAY IN WEEKDAYS DO
25:     BEGIN
26:         WORK ;
27:         TODAY := SUCC(TODAY)
28:     END ;
29:     TODAY := SUN ;
30:     WHILE TODAY IN WEEKEND DO
31:     BEGIN
32:         PLAY ;
33:         TODAY := PRED(TODAY)
34:     END
35: END . (* MISSISSIPPI *)
```

Fig. 4.4. MISSISSIPPI

happen with the standard data types. For instance, the full
set of examination grades should be A..F,O,U (O for
"ordinary" pass and U for "unclassified"). It is not
possible to specify this set of requirements in terms of
subranges and so Pascal provides the SET declaration as a
solution to the problem.

The way in which this works can best be seen by
looking at the sample program (PROGRAM MISSISSIPPI) in
Figure 4.4. Firstly, DAY is declared as a scalar type in
line 2, and the list of values (MON, etc.) is enumerated.
Then WEEK is declared as a SET OF the scalar type DAY (line
3) and finally the variables WEEKDAYS and WEEKEND are
declared to be of type WEEK (line 4). The action taken by
the Pascal compiler at this stage is as follows: for every
variable declared as of type WEEK, a structure is created
containing an element (of type BOOLEAN) for each value
appearing in the list DAY, i.e. WEEKDAYS -- 7 BOOLEAN
elements, etc. Then, when the assignment to these
variables is made (lines 21 and 22), the compiler checks
which elements of DAY should appear in WEEKDAYS and sets
each corresponding BOOLEAN variable to TRUE. The remaining
elements are set to FALSE so that
    WEEKDAYS contains (T,T,T,T,T,F,F) and
    WEEKEND contains (F,F,F,F,F,T,T).
Now a variable like TODAY which can take any single value
in the list DAY can either be a member of the set WEEKDAYS
or not, depending on the value assigned to it. This gives
a more control over these types of variables than would be
the case without sets since membership can be checked
through the set membership operator IN as illustrated in
lines 24 and 30. The improvement in readability should be
evident from the program as a whole, although this version
is a little more clumsy (and longwinded) than the last
version. (This is partly to demonstrate the application of
PRED and SUCC.)

Although not demonstrated in this simple example, sets in Pascal are manipulatable by means of the conventional set operations union (represented by +), intersection (*) and set difference (-).

Arrays

The variables WEEKDAYS and WEEKEND of the previous section represent a departure from all other variables so far defined since they contain information about several different items (i.e. whether or not they include each day of the week) rather than about one single item (like TODAY). Any linkage of more than one datum into some sort of organisation (like a set) is known as a data structure and the variables WEEKDAYS etc. are examples of a rudimentary form of data structure. In fact they consist of a series of TRUEs and FALSEs which have to be related back to the list of words (MON etc.) defined in the declaration part.

Another data structure which will be familiar to most programmers is the array which can be considered as a set of elements, all of the same type and each of which can be referenced by means of one or more indices. The prototype array has only one index and is often called a vector. This can be considered as a simple list of objects, (of the same data type). If one particular object needs to be accessed, it can be found via its index member which marks its position in the list, and since the program can go directly to this element (without searching through preceding members of the list), the array is considered to be a direct- access (or random-access) structure.

In Pascal, the array as a whole is given a variable name and is declared (in the case of a vector) as follows:

        VAR DAYS : ARRAY [1..12] OF INTEGER;
where DAYS is the array name and ARRAY [ ] OF forms the
"reserved word". Whatever appears in the brackets is the
index type -- this is a subrange of scalar type. The type
integer is never used because this would imply that the
precise size of the array would be decided in the action
part (when the integer would take on some value) rather
than in the declaration part (when the boundaries are more
clearly defined). The last word, in this case INTEGER,
defines the base type. The above declaration instructs the
compiler to set aside 12 successive integer locations
within memory. In the action part these will be referenced
in turn as DAYS [1], DAYS [2] etc., where DAYS [1] might
hold the number of days in January and so on.

        An alternative approach could be:
        TYPE MONTH=(JAN,FEB,MAR,APR,MAY,JUN,
                    JUL,AUG,SEP,OCT,NOV,DEC) ;
        VAR DAYS : ARRAY [MONTH] OF INTEGER ;
Here the array of DAYS has a previously declared scalar type
(i.e. MONTH) as an index type permitting statements of the
form DAYS[JAN] := 31, and thus offering improved
readability. A third alternative, which is useful when a
number of identical arrays is required, lies in declaring an
array type in the TYPE section and then, in the VAR section
declaring a list of variables of that type.

        An example of this technique can be seen in program
COUNTDOWN, Figure 4.5, where the type SHORTSTRING is
declared as a character array of four characters in length
(line 2). Then the six "words" are declared as being of
type SHORTSTRING (line 3). Lines 6 to 11 initialise the
array WORD. Strings are a standard method of dealing with
words and phrases (i.e. textual data) in a program, and UCSD
Pascal actually includes the string, with up to eighty
characters rather than four as a standard data type. The

```
1: PROGRAM COUNTDOWN ;
2: TYPE SHORTSTRING = PACKED ARRAY[1..4] OF CHAR ;
3: VAR WORD : ARRAY[1..6] OF SHORTSTRING ;
4:     I, J : 0..6 ;
5: BEGIN
6:     WORD[1] := 'OH  ' ;
7:     WORD[2] := 'PAT ' ;
8:     WORD[3] := 'LETS' ;
9:     WORD[4] := 'NOT ' ;
10:    WORD[5] := 'STOP' ;
11:    WORD[6] := 'HERE' ;
12:    FOR I := 6 DOWNTO 0 DO
13:    BEGIN
14:        FOR J := 1 TO I DO
15:            WRITE(' ', WORD[J] ) ;
16:        WRITELN('....') ;
17:        WRITELN ; WRITELN
18:    END
19: END . (* COUNTDOWN *)
```

Fig. 4.5. COUNTDOWN

TYPE

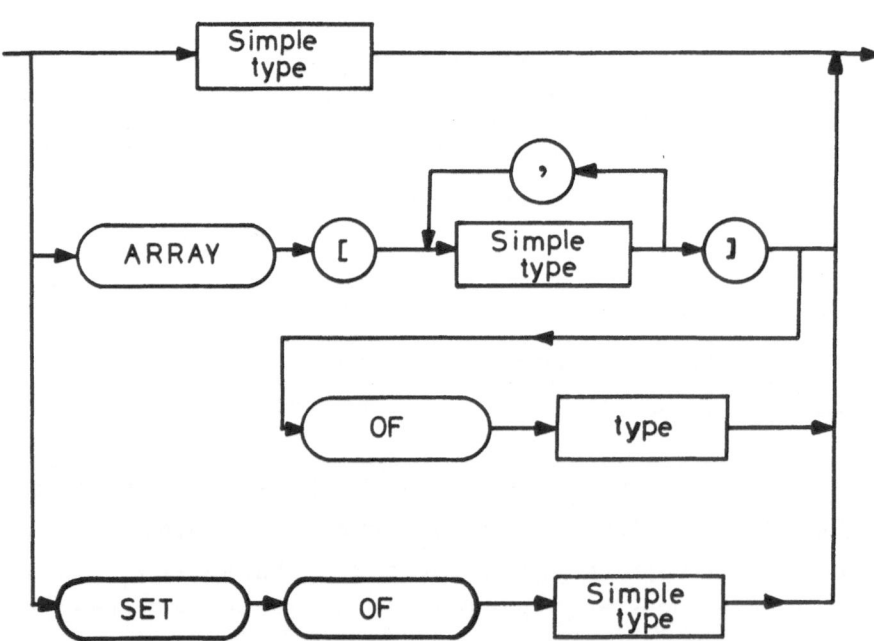

Fig. 4.6. Syntax Diagram for TYPE

applications of string variables and the associated string operations will be discussed in a later chapter.

The syntax diagram for a TYPE is shown in Figure 4.6, suitably amended to include both SET and ARRAY declarations. Likewise, the syntax diagram for a block in Figure 4.7 provides a convenient summary of the aspects of the declaration part dealt with so far. Note that any block can only have one CONST, TYPE and VAR statement although any number of PROCEDURE statements is allowed. This is reflected in the positions of the returning arrows on the main stalk of the indicated syntax diagram.

The last example of this chapter shows the use of a two dimensional array (Figure 4.8). The idea of the program is to output a sales graph of pairs of jeans sold in a shop in a day. The two dimensional array (QUANTITY) is declared as an "array of an array", although it could equally have been declared as
    QUANTITY: ARRAY [28..34, SIZE] of 0..40;
which looks more like the way it is referenced -- i.e.
QUANTITY [28,L] stands for the number of 28 inch waist, long leg jeans sold. The procedure INPUT serves to get the data into the program; in a suite of data-processing programs this data would normally be gathered as sales occurred so that the array would be prepared by some other program and passed to this program -- probably via a data file, rather than being created in this way.

Procedure DRAWGRAPH contains two procedures, HEADING (lines 26-31) and PRINTLINE (lines 33-39) which are called from within its main body. Note how PRINTLINE controls the size of each row as it turns up.

BLOCK

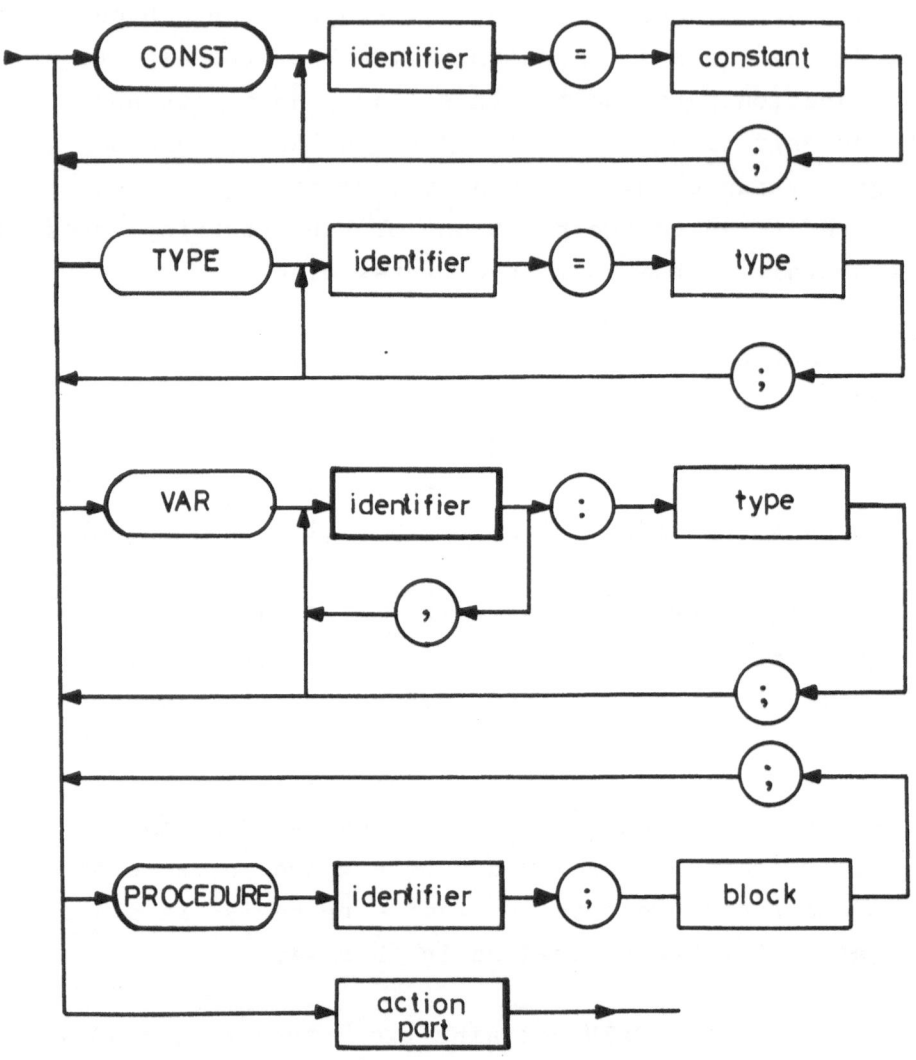

Fig. 4.7. Syntax Diagram for BLOCK

```
 1: PROGRAM JEANSGRAPH ;
 2:
 3: TYPE SIZE = (R, L, X) ;
 4:     ALFA = PACKED ARRAY[1..10] OF CHAR ;
 5: VAR WAIST : 28..34 ;
 6:     LENGTH : SIZE ;
 7:     LEG   : ARRAY[SIZE] OF ALFA ;
 8:     QUANTITY : ARRAY[28..34] OF ARRAY[SIZE] OF 0..40 ;
 9:
10: PROCEDURE INPUT ;
11: BEGIN
12:     WRITELN('PLEASE TYPE IN THE NUMBER OF JEANS OF EACH SIZE SOLD.') ;
13:     FOR WAIST := 28 TO 34 DO
14:     BEGIN
15:         WRITELN('WAIST ', WAIST) ;
16:         FOR LENGTH := R TO X DO
17:         BEGIN
18:             WRITE('LEG ', LEG[LENGTH], '--) ' ) ;
19:             READLN(QUANTITY[WAIST, LENGTH] )
20:         END
21:     END
22: END ; (* INPUT *)
23:
24: PROCEDURE DRAWGRAPH ;
25: CONST TAB = '          ' ;
26: PROCEDURE HEADING ;
27: BEGIN
28:     WRITELN(TAB, TAB, 'TODAY''S JEANS SALES ') ;
29:     WRITELN(TAB, TAB, '-------- ----- -----') ;
30:     WRITELN ; WRITELN
31: END ; (* HEADING *)
32:
33: PROCEDURE PRINTLINE ;
34: VAR I : INTEGER ;
35: BEGIN
36:     FOR I := 1 TO QUANTITY[WAIST, LENGTH] DO
37:         WRITE('*') ;
38:     WRITELN
39: END ; (* PRINTLINE *)
40:
41: BEGIN (* DRAWGRAPH *)
42:     HEADING ;
43:     FOR WAIST := 34 DOWNTO 28 DO
44:     BEGIN
45:         WRITELN(WAIST) ;
46:         FOR LENGTH := R TO X DO
47:         BEGIN
48:             WRITE(TAB, LEG[LENGTH] ) ;
49:             PRINTLINE
50:         END ;
51:         WRITELN
52:     END
53: END ; (* DRAWGRAPH *)
54:
55: BEGIN (* MAIN PROGRAM *)
56:     LEG[R] := 'REGULAR   :' ;
57:     LEG[L] := 'LONG      :' ;
58:     LEG[X] := 'EXTRALONG:' ;
59:     INPUT ;
60:     DRAWGRAPH
61: END .
```

Fig. 4.8. JEANSGRAPH

64

Conclusion

This chapter has expounded the basic Pascal philosophy
of data handling, which is to permit data items to be
associated with one another in a wide variety of ways
(through codes, lists, structures, etc.) but at the same
time to provide a set of built-in checks to help maintain
control. The next chapter will continue with more explicit
control mechanisms for manipulating both program and data
flow in the action part.

Exercise 1: Rewrite CLASSAVERAGE using a REPEAT-UNTIL loop.

Exercise 2: Replace lines 6-11 in COUNTDOWN with a
procedure which reads in any 6-word Expression, one word at
a time, from the keyboard.

Exercise 3: Tidy up DRAWGRAPH, using type declarations for
all the subranges and eliminating the empty lines between
rows in the output.

Exercise 4: Rewrite the program to output in columns up and
down the page.

Chapter 5. Control Structures 2: Branches

One of the most powerful features of the computer both as an information processor and as a control machine is its ability to detect differing conditions in the data or varying situations within the process and to respond to these, often in a sophisticated and complex way. When analyzed, this activity reduces to the capacity (of a program) to pose a question, to use the available data to establish the correct answer and then to act on that answer.

This particular feature exists in most programming languages and goes under the name of a conditional branch or just a conditional. Before looking at what Pascal provides in the way of such control structures, it is as well to define the constituent elements. The outcome of a conditional is always one particular course of action chosen from a set of options laid down in the program. The function of the conditional is to select the appropriate course depending on some circumstance. So the format is:

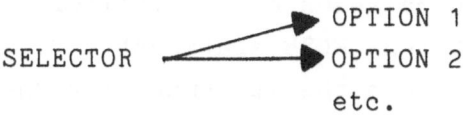

```
                          ➤ OPTION 1
    SELECTOR  ━━━━━━━━━━━➤ OPTION 2
                            etc.
```

Clearly the options are simply sections of code which perform the different actions required. The difficult part is setting up the selection to get the right option in the first place.

Single and Double Branches

In the simplest kind of branch, the programmer may
wish a piece of code to be executed only if some condition
holds, and the program to continue once this code is
completed. If the condition doesn't hold, the program
continues directly anyway. In Pascal this circumstance is
handled by means of the IF-THEN statement which takes the
following form:

IF expression THEN statement;

The expression, defined in Figure 5.1, takes a Boolean
value (i.e.TRUE or FALSE) which explains how it behaves as
the selector. When the expression is TRUE, the statement
following THEN will be executed. Otherwise program control
will pass directly to the statement immediately after the
";", which is the next instruction in the program. This
type of conditional can be viewed as a "single" branch
because there is only one optional statement open to the
selector.

An enhancement of this type of conditional is the
"double" branch where the selector directs program control
to alternative sections of code (depending on whether TRUE
or FALSE). At the completion of either alternative,
program control passes to the same point in the program --
namely the statement immediately following the conditional.
In Pascal this is dealt with by means of the following:

IF expression THEN statement ELSE statement ;

Note that there is no ";" between the statement governed by
THEN and the reserved word ELSE. It is a frequent error
amongst programmers new to Pascal to insert a separator
here, with erroneous results.

At this point the possibility of a highly ambiguous
circumstance arises. Consider

```
IF expression THEN
                    IF expression THEN statement
             ELSE statement    and
IF expression THEN
                    IF expression THEN statement
                    ELSE statement.
```

From the layout, it is obvious that, in the first case, the
ELSE clause "belongs" to the first IF (i.e. it forms an
alternative course of action to the first THEN), while in
the second layout, the ELSE clause belongs to the second
IF. The compiler, however, has no recourse to the layout
but must rely on the ";" statement separator to divide the
different statements. However, there can be no separators
on this occasion and in consequence there is no way for the
compiler to resolve the different logic implicit in the two
fragments. As a result, it is necessary to build in a
default -- i.e. when this circumstance arises, the compiler
always opts for one possibility -- and in the case of
Pascal, it is the second fragment above which reflects the
default.

  Figure 5.2 gives the syntax diagrams for the IF
statement, and Figure 5.3 consists of a sample program which
illustrates its use. When writing a program which is
likely to be used by other people, particularly if data
input is to be handled by inexperienced or unskilled
operators, it is advisable to accept all input in ordinary
character strings, checking on the validity and sorting out
the different data types within the program. If the user
makes a mistake, the program will detect it and ask for the
input again, instead of crashing the processor.
Considering that some such programs may run for hours (or
even continuously) and may accept simultaneous input from
many terminals (e.g. an airline bookings system), it is
unnecessary to give further stress to the advantages of
this technique.

Program READINTEGER (Figure 5.3) is an example of the
sort of routine one would use for inputting positive
integers up to a fixed maximum length. The maximum number
of digits allowed in any particular implementation of
Pascal will depend on the hardware being used so the
program specifies INTSIZE as a CONST which can be tailored
to different machines (line 2). The technique lies in
reading the number in character form and translating each
digit into numeric form.

The program reads the integer into a character string
TEMPNUM in procedure GETNUMBER, lines 16-25. Note the test
(line 24) checks for "EOLN" (i.e. carriage return) or for
integers which exceed the maximum length. The central ploy
of the program can be seen in procedure TESTDIGIT. Every
keyboard character has an associated numeric value such
that the value for 'A' is less than that for 'B' and '0' 's
value is less than '1' 's value which in turn is less than
'2' 's value. ORD is a standard function whose argument
is a character and whose result is the numeric value
associated with that character. On a system that uses ASCII
codes ORD('0')=48, ORD('1')=49 etc. If one wants to turn a
numeric character X into its numeric value then ORD(X) -
ORD('0') will be the number desired. Each element of
TESTNUM is treated in this fashion and compared with the
counter of a loop running from 0 - 9 (lines 29 - 31). If
the nth comparison is successful then n is the digit sought
(line 31).   The IF statement allows this to occur without
any action being taken for an unsuccessful comparison. In
the main body of the program, DIGIT is used not only to
hold each digit as it is "peeled" off the input string but
also as the selector (line 42) in the IF statement since a
value of -1 means that the last character under scrutiny
wasn't a digit at all. The two courses of action (i.e.
updating the number or signalling an error) are laid out in
lines 43 and 44.

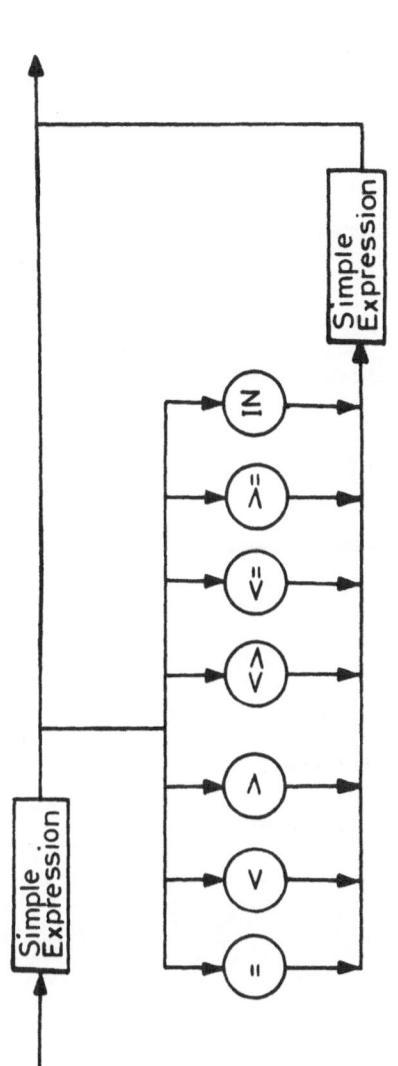

Fig. 5.1. Syntax Diagram for EXPRESSION

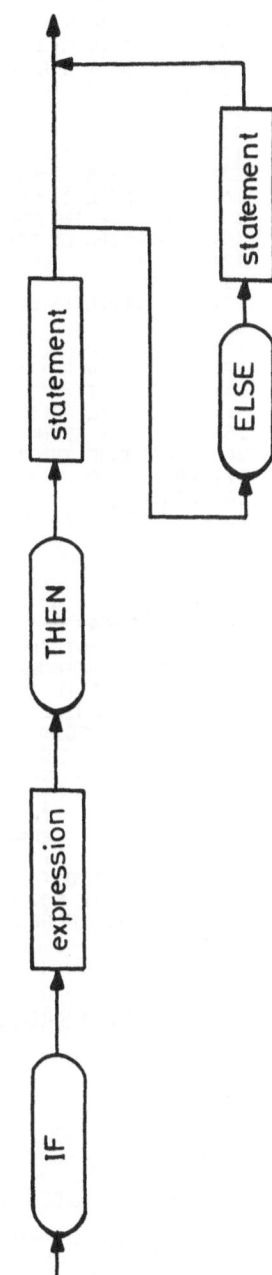

Fig. 5.2. Syntax Diagram for IF-THEN-ELSE

```
 1: PROGRAM READINTEGER ;
 2: CONST INTSIZE = 4 ;
 3: VAR TEMPNUM : ARRAY [1..9] OF CHAR ;
 4:     I : 0..9 ;
 5:     DIGIT : -1..9 ;
 6:     NUMBER : INTEGER ;
 7:     CORRECT : BOOLEAN ;
 8: PROCEDURE INITIALISE ;
 9: VAR I : 1..9;
10: BEGIN
11:     FOR I := 1 TO 9 DO
12:         TEMPNUM[I] := ' ' ;
13:     NUMBER := 0 ;
14:     CORRECT := TRUE
15: END ; (* INITIALISE *)
16: PROCEDURE GETNUMBER ;
17: VAR I : 1..9 ;
18: BEGIN
19:     WRITE('NOW TYPE IN YOUR NUMBER PLEASE --> ') ;
20:     I := 1 ;
21:     REPEAT
22:         READ(TEMPNUM[I]) ;
23:         I := I + 1 ;
24:     UNTIL EOLN OR (I=INTSIZE)
25: END ; (* GETNUMBER *)
26: PROCEDURE TESTDIGIT ;
27: VAR J : 0..9 ;
28: BEGIN
29:     FOR J := 0 TO 9 DO
30:         IF J = ORD (TEMPNUM[I]) - ORD ('0')
31:         THEN DIGIT := J
32: END ; (* TESTDIGIT *)
33: BEGIN (* READINTEGER *)
34:     REPEAT
35:         INITIALISE ;
36:         GETNUMBER ;
37:         I := 1 ;
38:         WHILE TEMPNUM[I] <> ' ' DO
39:         BEGIN
40:             DIGIT := -1 ;
41:             TESTDIGIT ;
42:             IF DIGIT = -1
43:             THEN CORRECT := FALSE
44:             ELSE NUMBER := 10*NUMBER + DIGIT ;
45:             I := I + 1
46:         END ;
47:         IF NOT CORRECT THEN WRITELN('TRY AGAIN')
48:     UNTIL CORRECT
49: END .
50:
```

Fig. 5.3. READINTEGER

Multiple Branching

Frequently, just having two options at some particular
point in a program is not enough, since it is necessary for
the program to split many ways. Perhaps the most explicit
example of this requirement can be seen in the handling of
a menu of the type found in many "business" packages. Take
the example in Figure 5.4 where the relation between the

```
 1: PROGRAM SALESLEDGER ;
 2: VAR SELECTION : INTEGER ;
 3: PROCEDURE MENU ;
 4: BEGIN
 5:     WRITELN('0.   FINISH') ;
 6:     WRITELN('1.   LIST ALL SALES') ;
 7:     WRITELN('2.   MONITOR SALES BY STOCK CODE') ;
 8:     WRITELN('3.   INVOICE SEARCH') ;
 9:     WRITELN('4.   AMEND LEDGER FILES') ;
10:     WRITELN('5.   TOTAL ALL SALES')
11: END ; (* MENU *)
12: PROCEDURE LIST ; (* LISTS ALL SALES FROM AND TO GIVEN DATES *)
13: BEGIN
14: END ; (* LIST *)
15: PROCEDURE STOCKCODE ; (* DISPLAYS RECORDS USING STOCK CODE AS KEY *)
16: BEGIN
17: END ; (* STOCKCODE *)
18: PROCEDURE INVOICE ; (* DISPLAYS RECORDS USING INVOICE NUMBER AS KEY *)
19: BEGIN
20: END ; (* INVOICE *)
21: PROCEDURE AMEND ; (* FOR ALTERING FILES *)
22: BEGIN
23: END ; (* AMEND *)
24: PROCEDURE TOTAL ; (* TOTALS SALES ON SEVERAL KEYS *)
25: BEGIN
26: END ; (* TOTAL *)
27: BEGIN (* MAIN PROGRAM *)
28:     REPEAT
29:         MENU ;
30:         WRITE('PLEASE TYPE IN YOUR SELECTION -->') ;
31:         READLN(SELECTION) ;
32:         IF SELECTION = 1
33:         THEN LIST
34:         ELSE IF SELECTION = 2
35:             THEN STOCKCODE
36:             ELSE IF SELECTION = 3
37:             THEN INVOICE
38:             ELSE IF SELECTION = 4
39:                 THEN AMEND
40:                 ELSE IF SELECTION = 5
41:                     THEN TOTAL
42:                     ELSE WRITELN('GOODBYE')
43:     UNTIL (SELECTION<1) OR (SELECTION>5)
44: END . (* MESSY WASN'T IT? *)
```

Fig. 5.4. SALESLEDGER

options in MENU and the procedures listed below is obvious.
However, in order to get the right item in the menu, the
main program has to go through the jumble of IF's from
lines 32 to 42.

It is for occasions like these that the Pascal CASE
statement has been defined (most other languages have an
equivalent facility). Figure 5.5 shows the syntax diagram
for the CASE statement. The format is as follows:

CASE selector OF options END;

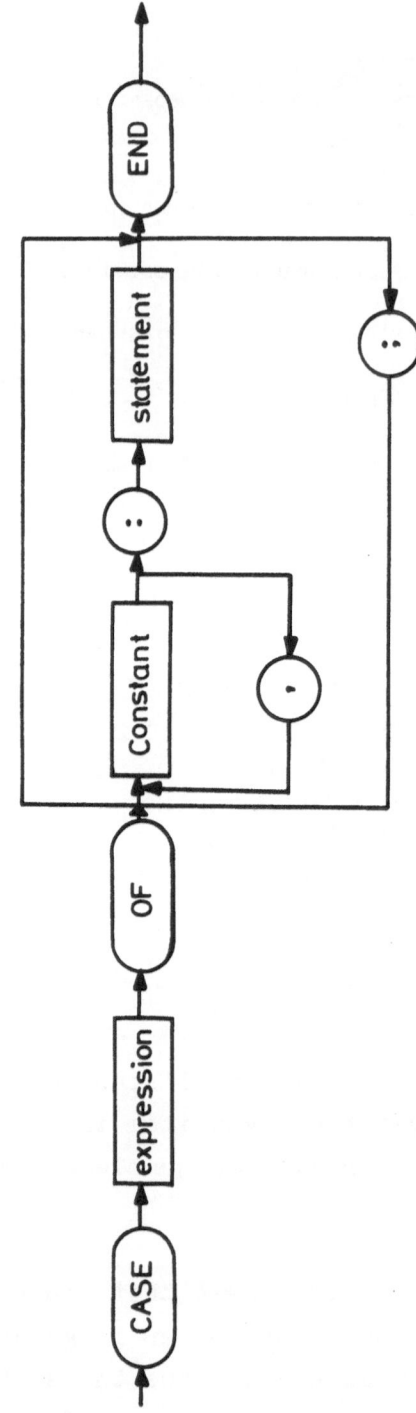

Fig. 5.5. Syntax Diagram for CASE

72

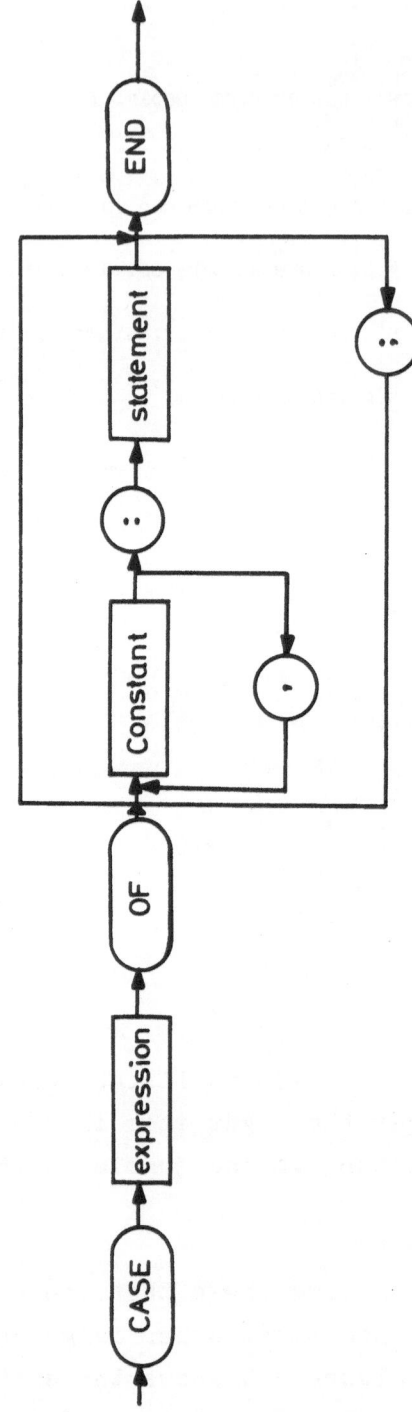

Fig. 5.5. Syntax Diagram for CASE

```
1: PROGRAM SALESLEDGER ;
2: VAR SELECTION : INTEGER ;
3:     ACCEPTABLE : SET OF 0..5 ;
4: PROCEDURE MENU ;
5: BEGIN
6:     WRITELN('0.   FINISH') ;
7:     WRITELN('1.   LIST ALL SALES') ;
8:     WRITELN('2.   MONITOR SALES BY STOCK CODE') ;
9:     WRITELN('3.   INVOICE SEARCH') ;
10:    WRITELN('4.   AMEND LEDGER FILES') ;
11:    WRITELN('5.   TOTAL ALL SALES')
12: END ; (* MENU *)
13: PROCEDURE LIST ; (* LISTS ALL SALES FROM AND TO GIVEN DATES *)
14: BEGIN
15: END ; (* LIST *)
16: PROCEDURE STOCKCODE ; (* DISPLAYS RECORDS USING STOCK CODE AS KEY *)
17: BEGIN
18: END ; (* STOCKCODE *)
19: PROCEDURE INVOICE ; (* DISPLAYS RECORDS USING INVOICE NUMBER AS KEY *)
20: BEGIN
21: END ; (* INVOICE *)
22: PROCEDURE AMEND ; (* FOR ALTERING FILES *)
23: BEGIN
24: END ; (* AMEND *)
25: PROCEDURE TOTAL ; (* TOTALS SALES ON SEVERAL KEYS *)
26: BEGIN
27: END ; (* TOTAL *)
28: BEGIN (* MAIN PROGRAM *)
29:     ACCEPTABLE := [0, 1, 2, 3, 4, 5] ;
30:     REPEAT
31:         MENU ;
32:         WRITE('PLEASE TYPE IN YOUR SELECTION -->') ;
33:         READLN(SELECTION) ;
34:         IF NOT(SELECTION IN ACCEPTABLE)
35:         THEN SELECTION := 0 ;
36:         CASE SELECTION OF
37:             0 : WRITELN('GOODBYE') ;
38:             1 : LIST ;
39:             2 : STOCKCODE ;
40:             3 : INVOICE ;
41:             4 : AMEND ;
42:             5 : TOTAL
43:         END (* CASE *)
44:     UNTIL SELECTION = 0
45: END .
```

Fig. 5.6. SALESLEDGER

Note that the value taken by the selector must be one of the
items in the list of constants which label the different
options.   The outcome is undefined wherever this is not
true -- so it is advisable to build a test into the
program to ensure that the selector is within the
permissible range.   Figure 5.6 shows the way in which a CASE
statement is used to tidy up SALESLEDGER. Lines 37 to 42
lay out the options and SELECTION acts as the selector.
However, before SELECTION is "allowed into" the CASE a check
is made (lines 34 and 35) to ensure that it will make a

successful selection (i.e. that it holds one of the values
specified in line 3).

Note the use of the statement separator ";" within the
CASE statement (Figures 5.5 and 5.6), since a semi-colon
between the last option and the END which finishes the
CASE statement will result in a compilation error.
Finally, the CASE statement is the only instance in Pascal
where the reserved word END appears unmatched by a
corresponding BEGIN. It is normal to add (* CASE *)
afterwards (line 43) to bring this fact to the attention of
the reader.

Sample program -- Othello

In this section a full program is developed, in order
illustrate not only the control structures of this chapter
but also some of the data structures introduced in the last.
Instead of describing the details of this program in the
text, the readability of the Pascal coding will be
exploited. For instance, anyone unfamiliar with the rules
of the game of OTHELLO should consult the text output in
procedure INSTRUCTIONS (Figure 5.7).

When tackling a program in this way, the approach
should be to look at the data structures defined in the
beginning, in conjunction with the body of the main program
(Figure 5.8) to try to deduce the programming strategy.
Often the choice of data structures will dictate specific
programming tactics within the program. A look at the TYPE
statements (lines 3 to 6) will show that a board game is to
be played and this is confirmed by the presence of the
array BOARD with scalar indices and elements limited to
FIRST, SECOND, and EMPTY.

In the main program the outer REPEAT-UNTIL loop (lines 365 to 388) allows players as many games as they like. It contains procedures to get each game started and to give the score when finished together with an inner WHILE-DO loop, (lines 367 to 385) which controls a single game. Note the use of BOOLEANS (GAMEOVER, NOMORE, LEGAL and PASS) to make the control structures (both loops and conditionals) obvious and easy to read. During the game, MOVER keeps tabs on whose move it is (lines 380 to 382) and COUNTER monitors the number of successful moves made (lines 378 and 383). After a move has been input (procedure GETMOVE, Figure 5.9) accepted (CHECKMOVE, Figure 5.10) and made (FLIPS, Figure 5.11), COUNTER and MOVER are altered to reflect the state of the game.

The core of the program lies in the "move" mechanism described by these three procedures. GETMOVE gets the player's move from the keyboard and determines whether the characters input refer to (any) square on the board. This constitutes a check for validity. Note the use of the set RANGE (line 189) to guarantee that the CASE selector in DETAILEDCHECK (lines 151 to 163) will find one of the options. Note also that the move can be typed in, in either order -- i.e. "4A" will work as well as "A4".

CHECKMOVE checks on the legality of the move by "looking" in every direction (lines 258 to 270) to see if a winning sequence of "target" squares exists (i.e. a sequence of the opponent's counters followed by one of the player's own counters). Procedure CHOOSESQUARE handles the different sequences (CASE statement, lines 208 to 238) while CHECKIT has the job of tallying up a FLIPCOUNTER for each direction (line 244). Note that CHECKMOVE looks in all directions, even when the move is known to be legal. This ensures that FLIPCOUNTER is set for each direction so that the business of making the actual move (FLIPS, line 273 to

```
30: PROCEDURE INSTRUCTIONS ; (* PRINTS OUT RULES OF OTHELLO *)
31: PROCEDURE SCREEN1 ;
32: BEGIN
33:     WRITELN('OTHELLO IS A BOARD GAME PLAYED BETWEEN TWO PLAYERS. EACH ') ;
34:     WRITELN('PLAYER HAS A DIFFERENT COLOURED COUNTER. THE PLAYERS START') ;
35:     WRITELN('WITH TWO COUNTERS.EACH IN THE CENTRAL FOUR SQUARES OF THE') ;
36:     WRITELN('BOARD. THE FIRST PLAYER MUST PLACE A COUNTER IN AN EMPTY') ;
37:     WRITELN('SQUARE ADJACENT TO AN OCCUPIED SQUARE IN SUCH A WAY THAT ') ;
38:     WRITELN('AT LEAST ONE OF THE OPPENENT''S COUNTERS LIES BETWEEN THE ') ;
39:     WRITELN('CURRENT COUNTER AND ANOTHER OF HIS COUNTERS IN A STRAIGHT ') ;
40:     WRITELN('LINE DRAWN HORIZONTALLY, VERTICALLY, OR DIAGONALLY ACROSS') ;
41:     WRITELN('THE BOARD. ALL OF THE OPPONENTS COUNTERS SO ''SANDWICHED''') ;
42:     WRITELN('BECOME CAPTURED. THAT IS THEY CHANGE COLOUR.') ;
43:     WRITELN
44: END ; (* SCREEN1 *)
45: PROCEDURE SCREEN2 ;
46: BEGIN
47:     WRITELN('AS THE NUMBER OF COUNTERS BUILDS UP MORE AND MORE HAVE TO') ;
48:     WRITELN('BE SWAPPED IN EACH MOVE, SO OTHELLO IS CLEARLY A TEDIOUS') ;
49:     WRITELN('GAME TO PLAY BY HAND.THIS IMPLEMENTATION USES ''O'' AND ') ;
50:     WRITELN('''X'' TO REPRESENT THE DIFFERENT COLOURS AND EMPLOYS A') ;
51:     WRITELN('STANDARD A-H, 1-8 CHESSBOARD CONVENTION.THE PLAYER WITH') ;
52:     WRITELN('THE GREATER NUMBER OF COUNTERS AT THE END OF THE GAME') ;
53:     WRITELN('WINS.A PLAYER MAY BE FORCED TO PASS IF NO EMPTY SQUARE') ;
54:     WRITELN('EXISTS WHICH IS ADJACENT TO AN OPPONENT''S SQUARE') ;
55:     WRITELN('IN A LINE CONTAINING ONE OF HIS OWN.') ;
56:     WRITELN;
57: END ; (* SCREEN2 *)
58:
59: BEGIN (* INSTRUCTIONS *)
60:     SCREEN1 ;
61:     WRITE ('PLEASE PRESS RETURN TO SEE THE REST OF THE INSTRUCTIONS.') ;
62:     READLN ;
63:     SCREEN2 ;
64:     WRITE('PLEASE PRESS RETURN WHEN YOU ARE READY TO PLAY.') ;
65:     READLN
66: END ; (* INSTRUCTIONS *)
```

Fig. 5.7. INSTRUCTIONS

325) is fairly straightforward, requiring a call to
NEXTSQUARE, lines 278 through 311 (which is an identical
procedure to CHOOSESQUARE) to choose the next square.

Conclusion

        Conditionals provide a means of decision making
within a program, the particular form used depending on
whether a single (IF-THEN), double (IF-THEN-ELSE) or
multiple (CASE-OF) branch is required. Appendix B contains
a full listing of Program OTHELLO.

Exercise 1: Enhance   READINTEGER to cater for negative as
well as positive integers.

```
  1: PROGRAM OTHELLO ;
  2: CONST SCREENHEIGHT = 16 ;
  3: TYPE ROWNUM = '1'..'8' ;
  4:      COLCHAR = 'A'..'H' ;
  5:      DIR = (N, NE, E, SE, S, SW, W, NW) ;
  6:      MOVE = (FIRST, SECOND, EMPTY) ;
  7: VAR NOUGHT, CROSS : ARRAY[1..10] OF CHAR ;
  8:      BOARD : ARRAY[ROWNUM, COLCHAR] OF MOVE ;
  9:      MOVER, TARGET : MOVE ;
 10:      COUNTER : 0..60 ;
 11:      ROWNOW : ROWNUM ;
 12:      COLNOW : COLCHAR ;
 13:      ANSWER : CHAR ;
 14:      LEGAL, GAMEOVER, NOMORE, PASS, FINISHED : BOOLEAN ;
 15:      DIRECTION : DIR ;
 16:      FLIPCOUNTER : ARRAY[DIR] OF 0..8 ;

360: BEGIN (* MAIN PROGRAM *)
361:     WRITE('DO YOU WANT TO READ THE INSTRUCTIONS? TYPE Y OR N--)') ;
362:     READLN(ANSWER) ;
363:     IF ANSWER = 'Y' THEN  INSTRUCTIONS ;
364:     IDENTIFY ;
365:     REPEAT
366:     STARTGAME ;
367:         WHILE NOT GAMEOVER DO
368:         BEGIN
369:             REPEAT
370:                 PRINTBOARD ;
371:                 GETMOVE ;
372:                 IF PASS THEN LEGAL := TRUE ELSE CHECKMOVE
373:             UNTIL LEGAL ;
374:             IF NOT PASS
375:             THEN
376:             BEGIN
377:                 FLIPS ;
378:                 COUNTER := COUNTER + 1
379:             END ;
380:             IF MOVER = FIRST
381:             THEN MOVER := SECOND
382:             ELSE MOVER := FIRST ;
383:             IF COUNTER = 60
384:             THEN GAMEOVER := TRUE
385:         END ;
386:         GIVESCORE ;
387:         ANOTHERGO
388:     UNTIL NOMORE
389: END.
```

Fig. 5.8. OTHELLO

Exercise 2: Write a program to count the occurence of each letter of the alphabet and total of all non-alphabetic characters in a piece of text. Use a CASE statement.

Exercise 3: The situation can arise in OTHELLO where it is impossible for either player to move (i.e. two consecutive PASSES). The current program does not cater for this -- adapt it.

```
134: PROCEDURE GETMOVE ; (* REQUESTS AND VALIDATES MOVE *)
135: VAR CORRECT : BOOLEAN ;
136:
137: PROCEDURE ASKFORMOVE ; (* REQUESTS APPROPRIATE MOVE *)
138: BEGIN
139:     WRITELN ;
140:     IF MOVER = FIRST
141:     THEN BEGIN WRITECROSS ; WRITE('''S MOVE --) ') END
142:     ELSE BEGIN WRITENOUGHT ; WRITE(' ''S MOVE --) ') END
143: END ; (* ASKFORMOVE *)
144:
145: PROCEDURE GETINPUT ;
146: VAR COLIN, ROWIN : BOOLEAN ;
147:     RANGE : SET OF CHAR ;
148:     RESPONSE : ARRAY[1..2] OF CHAR ;
149:     I : 1..2 ;
150:
151: PROCEDURE DETAILEDCHECK ; (* TESTS FOR AND ACCEPTS LEGAL MOVE *)
152: BEGIN
153:     FOR I := 1 TO 2 DO
154:         CASE RESPONSE[I] OF
155:             '1','2','3','4','5','6','7','8' : BEGIN
156:                                                  ROWNOW := RESPONSE[I] ;
157:                                                  ROWIN := TRUE
158:                                              END ;
159:             'A','B','C','D','E','F','G','H' : BEGIN
160:                                                  COLNOW := RESPONSE[I] ;
161:                                                  COLIN := TRUE
162:                                              END
163:         END ; (* CASE *)
164:         IF COLIN AND ROWIN
165:         THEN
166:         BEGIN
167:             IF BOARD[ROWNOW, COLNOW] = EMPTY
168:             THEN CORRECT := TRUE
169:             ELSE WRITELN('BAD MOVE - TRY AGAIN')
170:         END
171:         ELSE WRITELN( 'BAD MOVE - TRY AGAIN')
172: END ; (* DETAILED CHECK *)
173:
174: BEGIN (* GETINPUT *)
175:     COLIN := FALSE ;
176:     ROWIN := FALSE ;
177:     PASS := FALSE ;
178:     CORRECT := FALSE ;
179:     RANGE :=['1','2','3','4','5','6','7','8',
180:             'A','B','C','D','E','F','G','H','P'] ;
181:     READ(RESPONSE[1]) ; READ(RESPONSE[2]) ;
182:     IF RESPONSE[1]='P'
183:     THEN
184:     BEGIN
185:         CORRECT := TRUE ;
186:         PASS := TRUE
187:     END
188:     ELSE
189:         IF (RESPONSE[1] IN RANGE) AND (RESPONSE[2] IN RANGE)
190:         THEN DETAILEDCHECK
191:         ELSE WRITELN('IMPOSSIBLE MOVE - TRY AGAIN')
192: END ; (* GETINPUT *)
193:
194: BEGIN (* GETMOVE *)
195:     ASKFORMOVE ;
196:     REPEAT
197:         GETINPUT
198:     UNTIL CORRECT
199: END ; (* GETMOVE *)
```

Fig. 5.9. GETMOVE

```
202: PROCEDURE CHECKMOVE ;
203: VAR ROW : ROWNUM ;
204:     COL : COLCHAR ;
205:
206: PROCEDURE CHOOSESQUARE ; (* CHOOSE NEXT SQUARE FOR EXAMINATION *)
207: BEGIN
208:     CASE DIRECTION OF
209:         N : IF ROW='1' THEN FINISHED := TRUE ELSE ROW := PRED(ROW) ;
210:         NE : IF (ROW='1') OR (COL='H') THEN FINISHED := TRUE
211:                                       ELSE
212:                                       BEGIN
213:                                           ROW := PRED(ROW) ;
214:                                           COL := SUCC(COL)
215:                                       END ;
216:         E : IF COL = 'H' THEN FINISHED := TRUE
217:                          ELSE COL := SUCC(COL) ;
218:         SE : IF (ROW = '8') OR (COL = 'H') THEN FINISHED := TRUE
219:                 ELSE
220:                 BEGIN
221:                     ROW := SUCC(ROW) ;
222:                     COL := SUCC(COL)
223:                 END ;
224:         S : IF ROW = '8' THEN FINISHED := TRUE ELSE ROW := SUCC(ROW) ;
225:         SW : IF (ROW = '8') OR (COL = 'A') THEN FINISHED := TRUE
226:                                           ELSE
227:                                           BEGIN
228:                                               ROW := SUCC(ROW) ;
229:                                               COL := PRED(COL)
230:                                           END ;
231:         W : IF COL = 'A' THEN FINISHED := TRUE ELSE COL := PRED(COL) ;
232:         NW : IF (ROW = '1') OR (COL ='A') THEN FINISHED := TRUE
233:                                          ELSE
234:                                          BEGIN
235:                                              ROW := PRED(ROW) ;
236:                                              COL := PRED(COL)
237:                                          END
238:     END (* CASE *)
239: END ; (* CHOOSESQUARE *)
240:
241: PROCEDURE CHECKIT ; (* EXAMINE SQUARE *)
242: BEGIN
243:     IF BOARD[ROW, COL] = TARGET
244:     THEN FLIPCOUNTER[DIRECTION] := FLIPCOUNTER[DIRECTION] + 1
245:     ELSE
246:     BEGIN
247:         FINISHED := TRUE ;
248:         IF BOARD[ROW, COL] = MOVER
249:         THEN BEGIN IF FLIPCOUNTER[DIRECTION] > 0 THEN LEGAL := TRUE END
250:         ELSE FLIPCOUNTER[DIRECTION] := 0 (* EMPTY *)
251:     END
252: END ; (* CHECKIT *)
253: BEGIN (* CHECKMOVE *)
254:     LEGAL := FALSE ;
255:     IF MOVER = FIRST
256:     THEN TARGET := SECOND
257:     ELSE TARGET := FIRST ;
258:     FOR DIRECTION := N TO NW DO
259:     BEGIN
260:         FINISHED := FALSE ;
261:         FLIPCOUNTER[DIRECTION] := 0 ;
262:         ROW := ROWNOW ;
263:         COL := COLNOW ;
264:         REPEAT
265:             CHOOSESQUARE ;
266:             IF FINISHED (** EDGE REACHED **)
267:             THEN FLIPCOUNTER[DIRECTION] := 0
268:             ELSE CHECKIT
269:         UNTIL FINISHED
270:     END
271: END ; (* CHECKMOVE *)
```

Fig. 5.10. CHECKMOVE

```
273: PROCEDURE FLIPS ;
274: VAR I : INTEGER ;
275:     ROW : ROWNUM ;
276:     COL : COLCHAR ;
277:
278: PROCEDURE NEXTSQUARE ; (* CHOOSE NEXT SQUARE FOR EXAMINATION *)
279: BEGIN
280:     CASE DIRECTION OF
281:         N : IF ROW='1' THEN FINISHED := TRUE ELSE ROW := PRED(ROW) ;
282:         NE : IF (ROW='1') OR (COL='H') THEN FINISHED := TRUE
283:                                             ELSE
284:                                             BEGIN
285:                                                 ROW := PRED(ROW) ;
286:                                                 COL := SUCC(COL)
287:                                             END ;
288:         E : IF COL = 'H' THEN FINISHED := TRUE
289:                     ELSE COL := SUCC(COL) ;
290:         SE : IF (ROW = '8') OR (COL = 'H') THEN FINISHED := TRUE
291:                 ELSE
292:                 BEGIN
293:                     ROW := SUCC(ROW) ;
294:                     COL := SUCC(COL)
295:                 END ;
296:         S : IF ROW = '8' THEN FINISHED := TRUE ELSE ROW := SUCC(ROW) ;
297:         SW : IF (ROW = '8') OR (COL = 'A') THEN FINISHED := TRUE
298:                                             ELSE
299:                                             BEGIN
300:                                                 ROW := SUCC(ROW) ;
301:                                                 COL := PRED(COL)
302:                                             END ;
303:         W : IF COL = 'A' THEN FINISHED := TRUE ELSE COL := PRED(COL) ;
304:         NW : IF (ROW = '1') OR (COL ='A') THEN FINISHED := TRUE
305:                                             ELSE
306:                                             BEGIN
307:                                                 ROW := PRED(ROW) ;
308:                                                 COL := PRED(COL)
309:                                             END
310:     END (* CASE *)
311: END ; (* NEXTSQUARE *)
312:
313: BEGIN
314:     BOARD[ROWNOW, COLNOW] := MOVER ;
315:     FOR DIRECTION := N TO NW DO
316:     BEGIN
317:         ROW := ROWNOW ;
318:         COL := COLNOW ;
319:         FOR I := 1 TO FLIPCOUNTER[DIRECTION] DO
320:         BEGIN
321:             NEXTSQUARE ;
322:             BOARD[ROW, COL] := MOVER
323:         END
324:     END
325: END ; (* FLIPS *)
```

Fig. 5.11. FLIPS

Chapter 6. Data Structures 2: Records and Files

Computers have traditionally been employed in the fields of scientific research (number crunching) and business data-processing. The different requirements of these two types of user have produced opposing specialisms amongst computer professionals; conflicting designs and configurations of both hardware and software; and, most importantly from our point of view, programming languages with differing facilities and capabilities. Scientific languages tend to standardize on specialized and sophisticated mathematical functions and to ignore non-standard and bulk data handling features which are consequently provided (with greater or lesser degrees of effectiveness) by the individual implementors of the language. This reflects perfectly reasonably the general format of a mathematical problem where complex operations need to be performed on a relatively restricted amount of data.

Commercial languages, however, often don't provide sophisticated or even convenient mathematical functions since their processing tends to consist of more routine operations but with much larger quantities of data. This is not to suggest that a good sorting algorithm is not every bit as complex as, say, a fast Fourier transform module, but while the latter operates on the supplied data to produce completely different data, the former works with data, reordering it but not actually changing or producing any values. In any case, in a typical data-processing

problem, the quantity of supplied data is generally so
large that no more than a small fraction can fit into the
machine at one time so that the organizational problems
associated with containing this data in machine-readable
form and of making it available to the program in a
controlled and ordered manner dominate these commercial
languages.

While the data is being manipulated within the machine
it is often grouped together in structures called records.
Loosely, a record is a number of data items, usually of
different types, which need to be associated in some way,
probably because they all pertain to a single entity. A
second record would contain the corresponding information,
in the same format, pertaining to another entity, and so
on. An entry in a telephone directory, i.e. Name, Address,
Telephone No., is a simple example of a record.

A file is a data structure external to the program and
usually consists of a collection of records. The
characteristics of any particular file will depend not only
on the size and number of the records it is to contain, but
also on the medium on which the file is being stored.
Magnetic tape files are called sequential files because
records are stored in sequence and can only be accessed as
such -- i.e. starting at the beginning and dealing with
each record in turn. Clearly, quite a bit of complicated
programming has to be done at system level to control the
tape drive and the motion of data through the read/write
tape heads. This software can usually be initiated by
fairly simple calls embedded in the programming language.
Wirth's standard Pascal provides a set of these sequential
file-handling facilities.

Pascal, however, was designed when discs were
considered as a sort of extension of the main memory in
large computer systems and were too expensive to be a

TYPE :

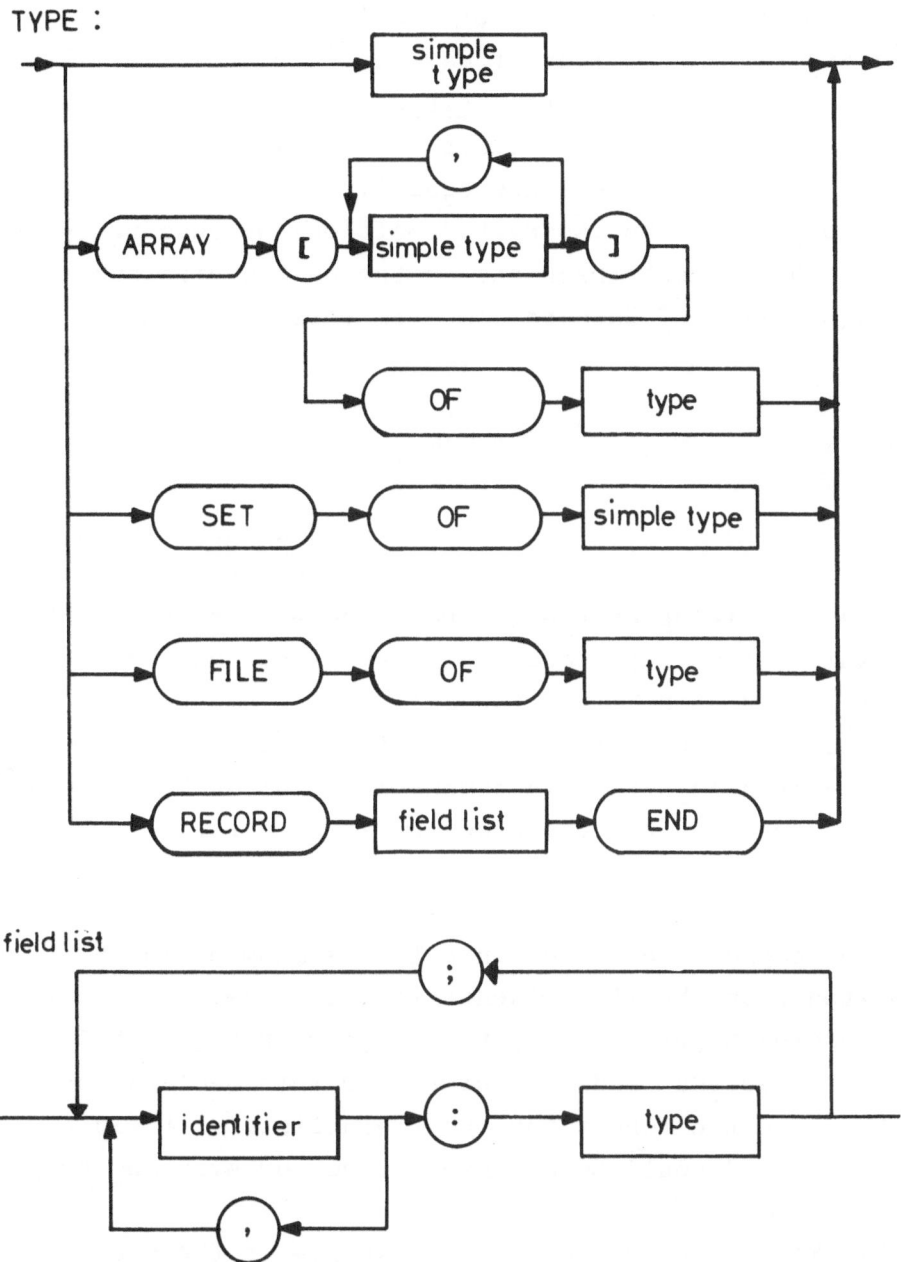

field list

Fig. 6.1. Syntax Diagrams for TYPE and FIELD LIST

suitable medium for data file storage. The advent of small
hard disc packs and reliable floppy disc subsystems has
put this medium within reach of small system users, and
most micro implementations of Pascal incorporate facilities
for handling and manipulating direct-access files. These
are so named because the data is stored over the whole disc
surface so that all items are equally accessible directly.
System software is necessary to position the read/write
heads at the correct track and sector on the disc and to
control the flow of data to and from this location.

Records

The record was defined in the previous section as a
grouping of associated data items. These data items are
known as the fields of the record. There is no restriction
as to which data type each field may be so that the
structure is distinct from the array where all elements must
be of the same type. In addition, individual fields are
not directly accessible via computable indices like array
elements, but must be referenced by a fixed field
identifier.

The record is declared in a TYPE statement in which is
stipulated both the field identifiers and their
corresponding types. The syntax diagram in Figure 6.1
shows the reserved words required for this declaration,
together with the format for the field list. A field
within a record could be another record, or even an array.

FIRSTILL in Figure 6.2 is an example of the uses of
records in a program. The program represents a cash
register for a small shop which sells printers and
stationery for microcomputers. A tally is kept of every

sale so that, in addition to producing a slip for the customer, a daily summary can be output at closing time. The record type STOCK is declared in lines 2 to 8 with the field list laid out in lines 3 to 7. The field NAME is declared as a PACKED ARRAY. Packing is a device whereby elements of a particular structured data type are packed into the smallest amount of memory needed -- e.g. a bit for a BOOLEAN, a byte for a CHAR etc. Every time a particular element is referenced, special software will be invoked to unpack the element from the structure and to pack it back after use, so that space is saved at the expense of a certain processing overhead. PACKED RECORDs and ARRAYs of BOOLEAN, CHAR or small integer subrange elements often save worthwhile storage space. However, it is left to programmer to decide whether a PACKED structure will be more efficient than its unpacked equivalent. (Two standard procedures PACK and UNPACK are provided to allow data to be moved from one type of structure to the other dynamically within the program although it is unusual to find these implemented on a microcomputer translator.) The PACKED ARRAY OF CHAR is formally defined as a STRING which will be dealt with at some length in the next chapter.

In line 10, array ITEM is declared as of type STOCK which implies that 5 records will be set aside in memory for this data structure. Each record can be referenced by a different value of the array index. Line 15 and the rest of procedure SETUP (lines 13-29) provide illustrations of the method by which individual fields within a record are referenced. The record name and the field name, separated by a ".", must both be supplied, and lines 15 to 19 refer to the same field in different records. Lines 22 and 23 on the other hand refer to different fields in the same record (selected by I). The instruction in line 24 clears the screen. Lines 25 to 27 reflect today's uncertain

```
 1: PROGRAM FIRSTILL ;
 2: TYPE STOCK = RECORD
 3:     NUMBER : INTEGER ;
 4:     NAME : PACKED ARRAY[1..24] OF CHAR ;
 5:     PRICE : REAL ;
 6:     QUANTITY : INTEGER ;
 7:     VAT : 0..100
 8:   END ; (* RECORD *)
 9: VAR ANSWER : CHAR ;
10:     ITEM : ARRAY[0..4]OF STOCK ;
11:     ACCEPTABLE : SET OF 'A'..'Z' ;
12:     I := -1..4 ;
13: PROCEDURE SETUP ;
14: BEGIN
15:     ITEM[0].NAME := 'DAISY BELL PRINTER        ' ;
16:     ITEM[1].NAME := 'MICRO DOT MATRIX PRINTER' ;
17:     ITEM[2].NAME := 'NCR PAPER                 ' ;
18:     ITEM[3].NAME := 'CONSTAT PAPER             ' ;
19:     ITEM[4].NAME := 'CARBON RIBBON             ' ;
20:     FOR I := 0 TO 4 DO
21:     BEGIN
22:         ITEM[I].NUMBER := I ;
23:         ITEM[I].QUANTITY := 0 ;
24:         PAGE (OUTPUT) ;
25:         WRITELN('PLEASE TYPE IN TODAY''S PRICE FOR ', ITEM[I].NAME) ;
26:         WRITE('FOLLOWED BY THE VAT RATE AS A % --)') ;
27:         READ (ITEM[I].PRICE) ; READLN (ITEM[I].VAT)
28:     END
29: END ; (* SETUP *)
30:
31: PROCEDURE HELP ;
32: BEGIN
33:     PAGE (OUTPUT) ;
34:     WRITELN('TYPE H TO SEE THIS DISPLAY.') ;
35:     WRITELN('     T TO PRODUCE A TILL SLIP.') ;
36:     WRITELN('     S TO PRODUCE A SUMMARY OF THE DAY''S TRANSACTIONS.') ;
37:     WRITELN('     E TO EXIT FROM THIS PROGRAM.') ;
38:     WRITELN ; WRITELN ;
39:     WRITE ('WHEN PRODUCING A TILL SLIP TYPE EACH ITEM NUMBER FINISHING ') ;
40:     WRITELN('WITH A -1.') ;
41:     WRITE ('HIT THE RETURN KEY TO CONTINUE.') ;
42:     READLN
43: END ; (* HELP *)
44: PROCEDURE TILLSLIP ;
45: VAR TOTAL, TAX : REAL ; NUM : INTEGER ;
46: BEGIN
47:     TOTAL := 0 ;
48:     TAX := 0 ;
49:     READLN (NUM) ;
50:     WHILE (NUM > -1) AND (NUM < 5) DO
51:     BEGIN
52:         WRITELN (ITEM[NUM].NAME, '     ', ITEM[NUM].PRICE) ;
53:         ITEM[NUM].QUANTITY := ITEM[NUM].QUANTITY + 1 ;
54:         TOTAL := TOTAL + ITEM[NUM].PRICE ;
55:         TAX := TAX + 0.01*ITEM[NUM].VAT ;
56:         READLN (NUM)
57:     END ;
58:     WRITELN ;
59:     WRITELN('VAT            ', TAX) ;
60:     WRITELN('TOTAL          ', TOTAL + TAX) ;
61:     READLN
62: END ; (* TILLSLIP *)
63:
64: PROCEDURE SUMMARY ;
65: CONST TAB = '          ' ;
66: VAR TOTAL, TAX : REAL ;
67: BEGIN
68:     TOTAL := 0 ;
69:     TAX := 0 ;
70:     WRITELN('NAME                          QTY SOLD           AMOUNT') ;
```

```
71:      FOR I := 0 TO 4 DO
72:      BEGIN
73:          WRITELN(ITEM[I].NAME, TAB, ITEM[I].QUANTITY, TAB,
74:              ITEM[I].QUANTITY*ITEM[I].PRICE) ;
75:          TAX := TAX + 0.01*ITEM[I].VAT*ITEM[I].QUANTITY ;
76:          TOTAL := TOTAL + ITEM[I].PRICE * ITEM[I].QUANTITY ;
77:      END ;
78:      WRITELN ; WRITELN ;
79:      WRITELN ('SUBTOTAL = ', TOTAL) ;
80:      WRITELN ('VAT = ', TAX) ;
81:      WRITELN ('TOTAL = ', TOTAL + TAX) ;
82:      READLN
83: END ; (* SUMMARY *)
84: BEGIN (* MAIN PROGRAM *)
85:      SETUP ;
86:      ACCEPTABLE := ['E', 'H', 'S', 'T'] ;
87:      WRITELN ('TYPE H FOR HELP.') ;
88:      REPEAT
89:          READLN (ANSWER) ;
90:          IF NOT (ANSWER IN ACCEPTABLE) THEN ANSWER := 'H' ;
91:          CASE ANSWER OF
92:              'E' : WRITELN ('GOOD BYE ') ;
93:              'H' : HELP ;
94:              'S' : SUMMARY ;
95:              'T' : TILLSLIP
96:          END (* CASE *)
97:      UNTIL ANSWER = 'E'
98: END .
```

Fig. 6.2. FIRSTILL

commercial climate by offering the user an opportunity to
input altered prices and tax rates.

Procedure HELP (lines 31-43) reveals the
menu-driven nature of the program, since each of the
different functions may be selected by entering a single
character at tne keyboard. The most important key to
remember, especially for an inexperienced teller, is "H"
which executes HELP itself. The two procedures TILLSLIP
(lines 44-62) and SUMMARY (lines 64-83) show how record
fields can be manipulated like ordinary variables although
the referencing scheme makes them appear a bit long-winded.
This can be avoided by means of the WITH statement whose
syntax diagram is given in Figure 6.3. The "variable" box
consists of the record identifier and the compiler
automatically appends it to any field identifier it finds in
the "statement" box so that the record name is taken as a
default for the duration of the statement. This is
illustrated in the new version of SUMMARY appearing in
Figure 6.4, lines 10 to 15.

88

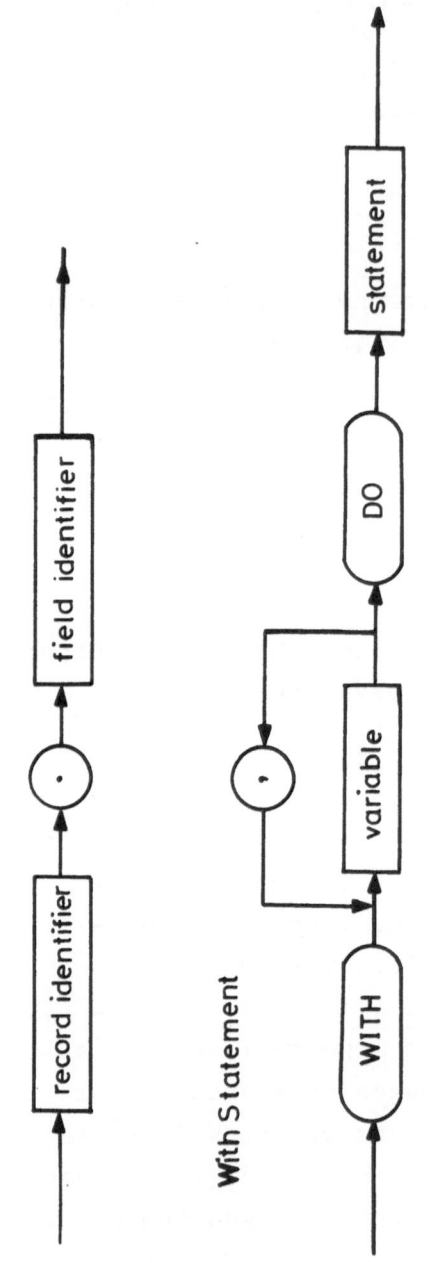

"Normal" Reference

With Statement

Field Referencing

Fig. 6.3. Syntax Diagram for FIELD REFERENCING

```
 1: PROCEDURE SUMMARY ;
 2: CONST TAB = '                ' ;
 3: VAR TOTAL, TAX : REAL ;
 4: BEGIN
 5:     TOTAL := 0 ;
 6:     TAX := 0 ;
 7:     PAGE (OUTPUT) ;
 8:     WRITELN ('NAME                    QUANTITY SOLD        AMOUNT') ;
 9:     FOR I := 0 TO 4 DO
10:         WITH ITEM[I] DO
11:         BEGIN
12:             WRITELN(NAME, TAB, QUANTITY, TAB, QUANTITY*PRICE) ;
13:             TAX := TAX + 0.01*VAT*QUANTITY ;
14:             TOTAL := TOTAL + QUANTITY*PRICE
15:         END ; (* WITH *)
16:     WRITELN ; WRITELN ;
17:     WRITELN ('SUBTOTAL = ', TOTAL) ;
18:     WRITELN ('VAT = ' , TAX) ;
19:     WRITELN ('TOTAL = ', TOTAL + TAX) ;
20:     READLN
21: END ; (* SUMMARY *)
```

Fig. 6.4. SUMMARY

Files

One of the essential characteristics of a file is that
it is external to the program as a whole. Only a small
portion of the data is accessible to the program at any one
time and although it is possible to have a file of arrays,
say, it will be assumed in this section that a typical
file contains records and is a sequential file--a sequence
of records in strict order. When a file is accessed
therefore, the "unit" in which the program must deal with
the data is one record.

A file is declared by means of a type statement as
shown in the syntax diagram of Figure 6.1. The "type"
referred to in the declaration will be a record which will
have been declared earlier on in the declaration part.
When the compiler encounters the file declaration, it notes
the file identifier and establishes the correct I/O channel
(and peripheral) on which the file is to be found. In
addition, the compiler creates a structure in the
program's data area in main memory of exactly the type (i.e.

record) previously defined. This structure is known as the
file window or buffer variable and is referenced with:
                    file identifier^.

     During execution of the ensuing program, any reference
to "file identifier^" will involve those memory locations
set aside for that structure. It is the job of the
programmer, however, to ensure that the contents of these
locations are in fact the fields of the record under
consideration. For this purpose there are a number of
file-handling operators available. These enable the
programmer to manipulate the peripheral on which the file
is stored and so access the data needed. The file-handling
operators are:
     RESET (filename) -- This statement is used to open
     an existing file for the purpose of reading data
     out of the file. On execution, the file is
     opened and the first record is read into the
     buffer variable.
     REWRITE (filename) -- This statement is used to
     open a new file for the purpose of writing data
     to the file (or to open an existing file for the
     purpose of overwriting the current contents). On
     execution, the file is simply opened -- no actual
     writing is done.
     GET (filename) -- Used to read the record from the
     file. On execution, the file window is advanced
     to the next record and its contents are assigned
     to the buffer variable.
     PUT (filename) -- Used to write one record to the
     file. On execution, the contents of the buffer
     variable are appended to the end of the file --
     i.e. this becomes the last record of the file.

     During the course of file operations, an additional
control element is maintained. This is a Boolean variable

called EOF (for "end-of-file") which is a FALSE until the file window reaches the last record. Each of the file operations described above makes reference to EOF in one way or another, as follows:

RESET -- sets EOF to FALSE provided a file exists.

REWRITE -- sets EOF to TRUE.

GET -- tests for EOF=FALSE before execution.

PUT -- tests for EOF=TRUE before execution.

This makes it impossible to write a record accidentally into the middle of a file.

When a program is written in which a file is to be accessed, the user will often want to run several different sets of data through the program and these will normally be held under different file names. Inside the program, however, the file is declared as a single filename with associated buffer variable, etc.

The solution to this problem is to regard the filename within the program as an identifier (symbolic name) which provides enough information to the compiler to set up the buffer variable and then to find some means of associating this identifier with the actual name of the datafile to be accessed at runtime. Wirth gives no details in the User Manual of how this is to be done, stipulating only that identifiers for external files are to be contained in the program heading, thus

PROGRAM name (filename1, filename 2, etc.) ;

This does not solve the problem, however, since it takes no account of the actual filenames at all.

Most microcomputer implementations seem to ignore this and instead require that the matching of the actual filename with the symbolic file identifier occur when the

file is opened -- i.e. in a RESET or REWRITE statement as
follows:

    RESET   (filename, actualfile)   (UCSD)
    REWRITE

    RESET   (actualfile, filename)   (PASCAL/Z)
    REWRITE

        Of course, this will not solve the problem
entirely since the compiler still requires the details of
"actualfile". However, this can be avoided by declaring
actualfile as a PACKED ARRAY OF CHAR (STRING) and reading
the actual filename into the program at runtime. For the
remainder of this book, the UCSD syntax for RESET and
REWRITE will be used.

        PROGRAM BIGTILL in Figure 6.5 is an expanded version
of FIRSTILL. In FIRSTILL the data was input at the
beginning of each program run. This may be acceptable for
a shop that sells five items, but for one that sells fifty
it would be a tedious and time consuming process. BIGTILL
differs from FIRSTILL in that the records are held on disc
in a file (called RECORDS.DATA), loaded into memory at the
start of each day's transactions and copied back at the end
of each day. Throughout the day the records are held in
memory in array ITEM.

    In FIRSTILL, PROCEDURE SUMMARY produced the day's
results. In BIGTILL results are produced weekly by
PROCEDURE WEEK (lines 104 through 120). Because it is
important to know what should be in the till at the end of
each day, PROCEDURE DAYSTILL (lines 96 through 102) is
provided. DAYTOTAL (line 221) and DAYTAX (line 222) keep
tabs of the shop's money and the government's money
respectively.

Upon starting up the execution of the program the user is asked if there is an old file (line 223). If the answer is yes, PROCEDURE SETUP (lines 19 through 32) opens the file (line 23) and gets the first record. Note that RESET takes two parameters -- the identifier STOCKFILE and the string RECORDS.DATA (which actually appears in the system directly). The second parameter is required by UCSD Pascal but is not required in Wirth's Pascal. In lines 24 through 29 each record is read, one at a time, from the STOCKFILE into ITEM. The loop is terminated when the End of File marker is reached (line 24). Line 30 contains another reserved word, CLOSE, that is needed in UCSD Pascal. In this version of Pascal files must be closed before the next RESET or REWRITE can occur. CLOSE(X) deletes X as well as closing it while CLOSE(X, LOCK) retains X in the directory.

If the user does not have a file, then PROCEDURE INITIALISE (lines 34 through 59) is called. In line 39 the STOCKFILE is opened for writing. For each record, the FOR-DO loop (lines 40-56) reads each field into a record STOCKFILE^ and then writes this record (line 55) to STOCKFILE. Since this process does not put the informtion into ITEM it is necessary to call SETUP (line 58) to read the new discfile into memory.

PROCEDURE WRITEFILE (lines 61 through 71) opens the STOCKFILE for writing (line 64) and then in the FOR DO loop (lines 65 through 69) assigns each element of the array ITEM into the file window STOCKFILE^ so that it can be written to the file (line 68). In fact, line 67 (and line 26) shows one of the major advantages of having a record data structure. Assignment of one record to another of the same type can be done in one statement even if the fields of the record contain records, sets and arrays.

```
 1: PROGRAM BIGTILL ;
 2: CONST MAX = 100 ;
 3: TYPE STOCK = RECORD
 4:     NUMBER : INTEGER ;
 5:     NAME : STRING[25] ; (* UCSD ONLY *)
 6:     PRICE : REAL ;
 7:     TOTQUANTITY : INTEGER ;
 8:     QUANTITYSOLD : INTEGER ;
 9:     REORDERLEVEL : INTEGER ;
10:     VAT : 0..100
11:   END ; (* RECORD *)
12: VAR ANSWER, OLD : CHAR ;
13:     ITEM : ARRAY[1..MAX] OF STOCK ;
14:     STOCKFILE : FILE OF STOCK ;
15:     ACCEPTABLE : SET OF 'A'..'Z' ;
16:     DAYTAX, DAYTOTAL : REAL ;
17:     TOTNUM : INTEGER ;
18:
19: PROCEDURE SETUP ;
20: VAR I : INTEGER ;
21: BEGIN
22:     I := 1 ;
23:     RESET (STOCKFILE, 'RECORDS.DATA') ;
24:     WHILE NOT EOF (STOCKFILE) DO
25:     BEGIN
26:         ITEM[I] := STOCKFILE↑ ;
27:         I := I + 1 ;
28:         GET (STOCKFILE)
29:     END ;
30:     CLOSE (STOCKFILE, LOCK) ;
31:     TOTNUM := I - 1
32: END ; (* SETUP *)
33:
34: PROCEDURE INITIALISE ;
35: VAR I, NUM : INTEGER ;
36: BEGIN
37:     WRITE ('HOW MANY DIFFERNT ITEMS WILL BE SOLD --> ') ;
38:     READLN (TOTNUM) ;
39:     REWRITE (STOCKFILE, 'RECORDS.DATA') ;
40:     FOR I := 1 TO TOTNUM DO
41:         WITH STOCKFILE↑ DO
42:         BEGIN
43:             NUMBER := I ;
44:             WRITE('NAME --> ') ;
45:             READLN (NAME) ;
46:             WRITE ('PRICE --> ') ;
47:             READLN (PRICE) ;
48:             WRITE ('STOCKLEVEL --> ') ;
49:             READLN (TOTQUANTITY) ;
50:             QUANTITYSOLD := 0 ;
51:             WRITE ('REORDER LEVEL --> ') ;
52:             READLN (REORDERLEVEL) ;
53:             WRITE ('VAT AS A % --> ') ;
54:             READLN (VAT) ;
55:             PUT (STOCKFILE)
56:         END ; (* WITH *)
57:         CLOSE (STOCKFILE, LOCK) ;
58:         SETUP
59: END ; (* INITIALISE *)
60:
61: PROCEDURE WRITEFILE ;
62: VAR I : INTEGER ;
63: BEGIN
64:     REWRITE (STOCKFILE, 'RECORDS.DATA') ;
65:     FOR I := 1 TO TOTNUM DO
66:     BEGIN
67:         STOCKFILE↑ := ITEM[I] ;
68:         PUT (STOCKFILE)
69:     END ;
70:     CLOSE (STOCKFILE, LOCK)
```

```
71: END ; (* WRITEFILE *)
72: PROCEDURE TILLSLIP ;
73: VAR TOTAL, TAX : REAL ; NUM : INTEGER ;
74: BEGIN
75:     TOTAL := 0 ;
76:     TAX := 0 ;
77:     READLN (NUM) ;
78:     WHILE (NUM)0) AND (NUM(=TOTNUM) DO
79:         WITH ITEM[NUM] DO
80:         BEGIN
81:             WRITELN(NAME, ' ', PRICE) ;
82:             TOTQUANTITY := TOTQUANTITY - 1 ;
83:             QUANTITYSOLD := QUANTITYSOLD + 1 ;
84:             TOTAL := TOTAL + PRICE ;
85:             TAX := TAX + 0.01*VAT*PRICE ;
86:             READLN (NUM)
87:         END (* WITH *) ;
88:         DAYTAX := DAYTAX + TAX ;
89:         DAYTOTAL := DAYTOTAL + TOTAL ;
90:         WRITELN ;
91:         WRITELN ('VAT      ', TAX) ;
92:         WRITELN ('TOTAL    ', TOTAL + TAX) ;
93:         READLN
94: END ; (* TILLSLIP *)
95:
96: PROCEDURE DAYSTILL ;
97: BEGIN
98:     WRITELN ('SUBTOTAL = ' , DAYTOTAL) ;
99:     WRITELN ('VAT =      ', DAYTAX) ;
100:    WRITELN ('TOTAL =    ', DAYTOTAL + DAYTAX) ;
101:    READLN
102: END ; (* DAYSTILL *)
103:
104: PROCEDURE WEEK ;
105: VAR I : INTEGER ;
106: BEGIN
107:    WRITELN('NUMBER  NAME        PRICE      STOCK   SOLD  REORDER  VAT');
108:    FOR I := 1 TO TOTNUM DO
109:        WITH ITEM[I] DO
110:        BEGIN
111:            WRITE(NUMBER,'       ',NAME,'          ',PRICE,'        ') ;
112:            WRITE(TOTQUANTITY, '     ',QUANTITYSOLD) ;
113:            IF REORDERLEVEL)TOTQUANTITY - QUANTITYSOLD
114:            THEN WRITE ('       Y      ')
115:            ELSE WRITE ('       N      ') ;
116:            WRITELN (VAT) ;
117:            QUANTITYSOLD := 0
118:        END ; (* WITH *)
119:    READLN
120: END ; (* WEEK *)
121:
122: PROCEDURE AMENDFILE ;
123: VAR NUM, FIELD : INTEGER ; CONT : CHAR ;
124: PROCEDURE RECMENU ;
125: BEGIN
126:    WRITELN('TYPE 0 FOR NO CHANGES.') ;
127:    WRITELN('     1 TO ALTER A NAME.') ;
128:    WRITELN('     2 TO ALTER A PRICE.') ;
129:    WRITELN('     3 TO ALTER A CURRENT STOCK LEVEL.') ;
130:    WRITELN('     4 TO ALTER A WEEKLY SALES LEVEL.') ;
131:    WRITELN('     5 TO ALTER A REORDERING LEVEL.') ;
132:    WRITELN('     6 TO ALTER A VAT RATE.') ;
133:    READLN
134: END ; (* RECMENU *)
135:
136: PROCEDURE NOCHANGE ;
137: BEGIN
138:    WRITELN (' NO CHANGES MADE. ') ; READLN
139: END ; (* NOCHANGE *)
140: PROCEDURE NAMECHANGE ;
```

```
141: BEGIN
142:     WRITELN ('OLD NAME --) ', ITEMINUMI.NAME) ;
143:     WRITE ('NEW NAME --) ') ;
144:     READLN (ITEMCNUM].NAME)
145: END ; (* NAMECHANGE *)
146:
147: PROCEDURE PRICECHANGE ;
148: BEGIN
149:     WRITELN ('OLD PRICE --) ', ITEMINUMI.PRICE) ;
150:     WRITE ('NEW PRICE --) ') ;
151:     READLN (ITEMCNUM].PRICE)
152: END ; (* PRICECHANGE *)
153:
154: PROCEDURE TOTCHANGE ;
155: BEGIN
156:     WRITELN ('OLD STOCK LEVEL --) ', ITEMINUMI.TOTQUANTITY) ;
157:     WRITE ('NEW STOCK LEVEL --) ') ;
158:     READLN (ITEMCNUM].TOTQUANTITY)
159: END ; (* TOTCHANGE *)
160:
161: PROCEDURE SOLDCHANGE ;
162: BEGIN
163:     WRITELN ('NUMBER SOLD --) ', ITEMCNUM].QUANTITYSOLD) ;
164:     WRITE ('NEW NUMBER SOLD --) ') ;
165:     READLN (ITEMCNUM].QUANTITYSOLD)
166: END ; (* SOLDCHANGE *)
167:
168: PROCEDURE ORDERCHANGE ;
169: BEGIN
170:     WRITELN ('OLD REORDERING LEVEL --) ', ITEMCNUM].REORDERLEVEL) ;
171:     WRITE ('NEW REORDERING LEVEL --) ') ;
172:     READLN (ITEMCNUM].REORDERLEVEL)
173: END ; (* ORDERCHANGE *)
174: PROCEDURE VATCHANGE ;
175: BEGIN
176:     WRITELN ('OLD VAT RATE --) ', ITEMINUMI.VAT) ;
177:     WRITE ('NEW VAT RATE --) ') ;
178:     READLN (ITEMCNUM].VAT)
179: END ; (* VATCHANGE *)
180: BEGIN (* AMENDFILE *)
181:     REPEAT
182:         REPEAT
183:             WRITE ('RECORD NUMBER --) ') ;
184:             READLN (NUM)
185:         UNTIL (NUM)0) AND (NUM(=TOTNUM) ;
186:         WITH ITEMCNUM] DO
187:         BEGIN
188:             RECMENU ;
189:             READLN (FIELD) ;
190:             IF (FIELD)6) OR (FIELD(0) THEN FIELD := 0 ;
191:             CASE FIELD OF
192:                 0 : NOCHANGE ;
193:                 1 : MAMECHANGE ;
194:                 2 : PRICECHANGE ;
195:                 3 : TOTCHANGE ;
196:                 4 : SOLDCHANGE ;
197:                 5 : ORDERCHANGE ;
198:                 6 : VATCHANGE
199:             END (* CASE *)
200:         END (* WITH *) ;
201:         WRITE ('MORE CHANGES, TYPE Y OR N --) ') ;
202:         READLN (CONT)
203:     UNTIL CONT = 'N' ;
204:     WRITEFILE (* DONE TO MINIMIZE EFFECTS OF A SYSTEM CRASH *)
205: END ; (* AMENDFILE *)
206:
207: PROCEDURE HELP ;
208: BEGIN
209:     PAGE (OUTPUT) ;
210:     WRITELN ('TYPE H TO SEE THIS DISPLAY') ;
```

```
211:      WRITELN ('      T TO PRODUCE A TILL SLIP') ;
212:      WRITELN ('      D TO PRODUCE THE DAY''S TILL TOTALS') ;
213:      WRITELN ('      W TO PRODUCE A SUMMARY OF THE WEEK''S SALES') ;
214:      WRITELN ('      E TO EXIT FROM THIS PROGRAM') ;
215:      WRITELN ('      A TO ALTER THE STOCKFILE') ;
216:      READLN
217: END ; (* HELP *)
218:
219: BEGIN (* MAIN PROGRAM *)
220:      ACCEPTABLE := ['A', 'D', 'E', 'H', 'W', 'T'] ;
221:      DAYTOTAL := 0 ;
222:      DAYTAX := 0 ;
223:      WRITE ('DOES A FILE ALREADY EXIST? TYPE Y OR N --> ') ;
224:      READLN (OLD ) ;
225:      IF OLD = 'Y'
226:      THEN SETUP
227:      ELSE INITIALISE ;
228:      WRITELN ('TYPE H FOR HELP.') ;
229:      REPEAT
230:         READLN (ANSWER) ;
231:         IF NOT (ANSWER IN ACCEPTABLE) THEN ANSWER := 'H' ;
232:         CASE ANSWER OF
233:            'A' : AMENDFILE ;
234:            'D' : DAYSTILL ;
235:            'E' : BEGIN WRITEFILE ; WRITELN (' GOOD BYE ') END ;
236:            'H' : HELP ;
237:            'T' : TILLSLIP ;
238:            'W' : WEEK
239:         END (* CASE *)
240:      UNTIL ANSWER = 'E'
241: END .
```

Fig. 6.5. BIGTILL

PROCEDURE AMENDFILE (lines 122 through 205) allows the
user to alter any of the information in array ITEM. This
allows for the correction of mistakes made, as well as for
the changing of stockfile levels when stock comes into the
shop or "walks". In line 204 PROCEDURE WRITEFILE is called
to make the changes permanent. It isn't essential to do
this, since before exiting from the program for the day,
the file is written to disc (line 235); this is a
precaution to prevent the loss of data if the system
crashes.

Compared with handling ordinary variables, the
business of file-accessing is clearly rather awkward in
programming terms. In particular, where large files of
textual materials are concerned, Pascal supports a number
of specialized features. These will be dealt with in
Chapter 8.

Direct Access File Handling

Up to this section all the examples have dealt with
sets of data that could be completely held in main memory
while processing occurred. With memory prices decreasing
generally and the new 16-bit micros with their enormous
address spaces coming on the market, many applications will
actually be able to keep their data in main memory in this
way. However, if one isn't planning to purchase a Z8000
with a megabyte of RAM there probably will come a time when
the amount of data required is too large for the memory
available. In this case files are kept on disc (or tape)
and only the record currently being processed will be in
memory. As access speeds on disc are very much slower than
those of main memory, every effort has to be made to minimize
access time.

When data is held in main memory, the data can be
updated during each transaction. When the data is held in
sequential files, however, such alteration is more
complicated. The file must be copied over into a new file,
one record at a time. When the record to be altered is
reached, it is brought into memory, amended and then
written out into the new file. The rest of the file is then
transferred as before. Although this technique ensures
that the data being accessed is always up-to-date, the
delay between transactions would be of the order of minutes
for any reasonably sized file. In consequence, sequential
files are not usually updated in this way. Instead, a
secondary file with the update information is established
and all alterations over some period (e.g. a day) are
collected. At the end of the period the master file is
updated. Unfortunately, as this period drags on, the
master file becomes progressively more inaccurate and in
some applications (e.g. airline reservation systems) such
out-of-date information is completely unacceptable,

although in the till program, the name, price and VAT
rating of the stock are likely to be constant over long
periods of time.

If Pascal is to gain acceptance as a viable language
for data processing, it will have to offer the more
convenient direct-access facilities associated with
disc-based backing store rather than the current standard
tape-oriented sequential access methods. Most
implementations of Pascal on microcomputers include a
facility for directly accessing files. This section
discusses the UCSD implementation of these features which,
although non-standard, are widely available on micros.

SEEK is a UCSD reserved word that will search out an
individual record from a disc file. SEEK requires two
parameters, the first being the file identifier, and the
second, an integer representing the record number to which
the window must be moved. The first record of a UCSD
direct-access file is number 0.

If STOCKFILE in program BIGTILL became so large that
the internal array ITEM could not fit into the available
memory, several changes would be necessary in the program.
With only one record present in memory, the array ITEM
would become superfluous. Procedure TILLSLIP in Figure 6.6
is a rewrite of the version in Figure 6.5. Line 9 locates
the required record while line 10 reads it into the window
STOCKFILE^. STOCKFILE in line 11 corresponds to the array
element in line 79 of Figure 6.5. After the information
has been accessed and altered (lines 13-17) the amended
record is copied back into STOCKFILE. Line 18 is necessary
because a GET moves the window forward one record, so that
PUT in line 19 would otherwise overwrite the (NUM + 1)th
record rather than the NUMth.

```
 1: PROCEDURE TILLSLIP ;
 2: VAR TOTAL, TAX : REAL ; NUM : INTEGER ;
 3: BEGIN
 4:     TOTAL := 0 ;
 5:     TAX := 0 ;
 6:     READLN (NUM) ;
 7:     WHILE NUM > -1 DO
 8:     BEGIN
 9:         SEEK (STOCKFILE, NUM) ;
10:         GET (STOCKFILE) ;
11:         WITH STOCKFILE↑ DO
12:         BEGIN
13:             WRITELN (NAME, '   ', PRICE) ;
14:             QUANTITYSOLD := QUANTITYSOLD + 1 ;
15:             TOTQUANTITY := TOTQUANTITY - 1 ;
16:             TOTAL := TOTAL + PRICE ;
17:             TAX := TAX + 0.01*VAT ;
18:             SEEK (STOCKFILE, NUM) ;
19:             PUT (STOCKFILE) ;
20:             READLN (NUM)
21:         END (* WITH *)
22:     END
23: END . (* TILLSLIP *)
```

Fig. 6.6. TILLSLIP

Conclusion

    Different methods of file-access and their relation to
the different media on which the information is stored have
been discussed. It would be misleading to pretend that
"normal" data processing programs are as trivial as the
examples discussed here, but it is hoped that they have
been sufficiently realistic at least to illustrate the
concepts involved.

Exercise 1: Rewrite FIRSTILL using WITH statements where
appropriate.

Exercise 2: Rewrite BIGTILL for a direct access master file.

Chapter 7. Procedures and Functions

Introduction

Throughout this series, procedures have been used to
break programming problems into collections of interlinked
but self-contained modules. This chapter seeks to examine
the different means of interlinking such modules and
thereby to analyze the different roles which they play in
modular program design.

If something has to be done several times within a
program, perhaps under different conditions or within
different contexts, it can either be coded over and over
again, whenever it is required (see CHECKMOVE in PROGRAM
OTHELLO) or it can be coded once only and initiated from
those points in the rest of the program where it is needed.
In consequence, even the most elementary assembly languages
usually provide some method of dividing a program into
modules (or subroutines) and of interrupting the normal
linear program flow by a subroutine call to some piece of
code remote from the section currently being executed.
However, it is one thing for a programmer to use such a
facility as a convenience, when the occasion arises, and
entirely another deliberately to design a program as a
hierarchy of interdependent subroutines each with a
specific, limited role within the whole program task.

The advantages of this approach to program writing
emerge from a consideration of the process of producing and
running a program in general. Firstly the task is

hierarchically divided and subdivided into successively more
detailed modules each of which has a well-defined, yet
limited goal. If the goal is well- defined, the subroutine
will be easy to code correctly. If the goal is limited,
the subroutine will be more likely to produce the correct
results and in addition makes the logical structure of the
whole program simpler. Secondly, execution errors will
pinpoint the subroutines within which they occur so that
debugging a program fragmented in this manner is reduced to
debugging one or two offending subroutines. Thirdly,
features of the program which depend on special machine,
peripheral or operating system characteristics are likely
to be concentrated into a few subroutines which can be
adapted to another computer environment without disturbing
the rest of the program. Likewise, when transferring to a
machine with limited memory, overlaying (i.e. the splitting
of a program so that only a portion is resident in memory
at any given time) is greatly assisted if the program is
modular.

        Finally, designing programs in this way imposes a
discipline on the programmer which reflects itself in a
logical and consistent approach to programming problems.
This means that programs are easier to read and understand
by other people. In block-structured languages which are
designed to exploit this philosophy (and of which Pascal is
a member) the program consists of a number of procedures,
within which may be nested other procedures, all controlled
from the main program block. Variables declared within a
procedure are local to the procedure and have no value
outside the scope of that procedure.

        Several important points arise from a
consideration of the technical mechanisms necessary to
achieve a satisfactory transfer of control from procedure

to procedure. It is fairly simple to call a procedure -- the procedure name is associated with the address of the first statement of the procedure so that, when the procedure is called, this address can be loaded into the program counter and processing can continue. However, getting back to the calling point when the procedure has finished is more difficult since the actual execution of the procedure will have altered the "state" of the processor. For instance, for processing to continue after the called procedure has finished, the address of the statement immediately following that which initiated the procedure (the return address) has to be loaded into the program counter.

However, the procedure could have been called from anywhere within the program and so could not contain in advance the point control is supposed to return to. Therefore, during the execution of the called procedure, the return address must be stored somewhere out of reach of the current procedure but available immediately it has finished. Likewise any other special conditions which hold at the moment of the procedure call (e.g. the contents of some or all of the processor registers) must be preserved before the procedure is called and must be reinstated at the point of return.

In order to guarantee the preservation of this information, most modern processor architectures and language implementations provide the processor with a run-time stack for use as immediate working space during program execution. The essential feature of the stack is that only the element most recently pushed onto the stack is accessible to the processor and anything further down the stack is consequently "safe" from interference. The processor communicates with the stack through a stack pointer which contains the first free address above the top

(i.e. latest) element on the stack. The processor can
access the last element by popping it off the stack (and
decrementing the stack pointer) or can push another element
onto the stack (and increment the stack pointer). Every
operation which uses the stack must ensure that everything
it pushes onto the stack is popped off before it finishes.
In this way when a procedure exits, it will leave the stack
in exactly the state in which it found it. If the return
address therefore was pushed onto the stack before the
procedure was called, it can now be popped off, loaded into
the program counter and processing can continue.

The region of the stack above the return address
becomes the current procedure's private working space
within which the local variables can be established and
intermediate results can be stored. This region, together
with the return address, is known as a stack frame. The
diagram in Figure 7.1 shows a representation of a stack
when a nested procedure is being executed. The current
procedure can access any variables in the stack although
when it exits its own local variables will be popped off
the stack and hence lost.

Procedures that Perform a Job

The fact that the current procedure can access any
variable on the stack and not just its own local variables
is something of a mixed blessing. On the plus side, the
current procedure will often require data from procedures
further down the stack and it is convenient, in assignment
statements and the like, to be able to refer to these
variables in a straightforward way. On the minus side
however, the further down the stack these variables are
declared, the more searching and manipulation is required

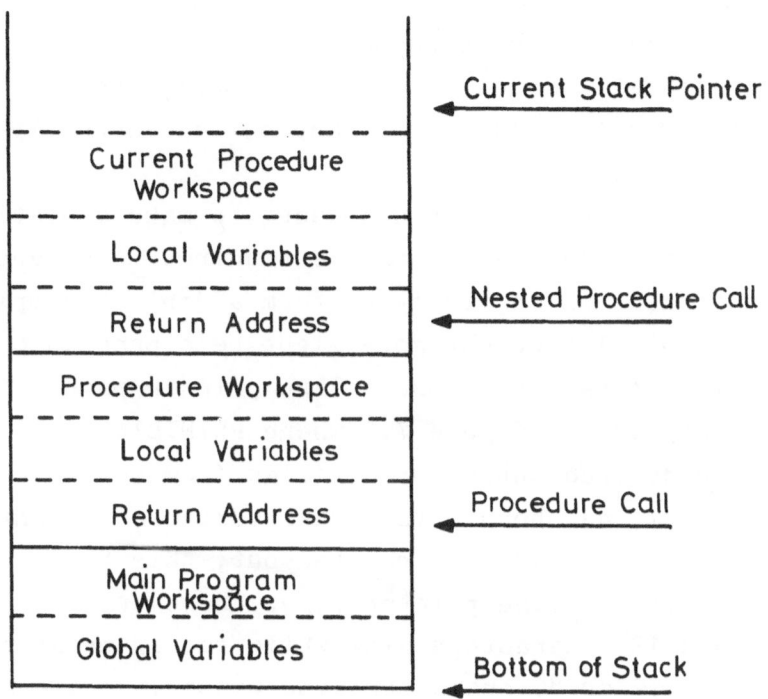

Fig. 7.1. The Stack

```
 1: --
 2: --
 3: PROCEDURE PRINTLINE ;
 4: VAR I : INTEGER ;
 5: BEGIN
 6:     FOR I := 1 TO 120 DO
 7:         WRITE('-') ;
 8:     WRITELN
 9: END ;
10: BEGIN (* MAIN PROGRAM *)
11: --
12: --
13: --
14: IF LINENUM<60 THEN PRINTEXT
15:                 ELSE PRINTLINE ;
16: --
17: --
18: --
```

Fig. 7.2. PRINTLINE

for each access. In addition, an assignment made to one of
these non-local variables will stand even after the current
procedure exits. This is known as a side-effect and is all
very well if deliberately done by the programemr but a
difficult error to trace if it happens inadvertently.

    As a consequence it is necessary to make a distinction
between those procedures which are required to produce a
result and those which merely perform a job. A simple
example of this latter category might be a procedure to
print a line of dashes across a line printer page. Such a
procedure appears in Figure 7.2 where PRINTLINE will
produce the desired output when called from some other part
of the program, as shown. The local variable I counts the
number of dashes -- 120 are printed out, this being the
width of a typical line printer page. However, some line
printers are 132 characters wide while matrix printers may
have 40, 64, 72 or 80 character line widths, so if
PRINTLINE were to be part of a package designed to run on a
variety of systems, something would have to be done to
customize the package to an individual user's system. One
approach would be to go through the code changing every
occurence of 120 to the desired value.

    This, of course, is time consuming, prone to errors of
omission and not a serious option, particularly when an
alternative is simply to create an integer variable (say
LINEWIDTH) which the user is asked to set at the beginning
of the program. All output can thence be customized to the
terminal merely by referencing LINEWIDTH (e.g. line 6,
Figure 7.2 would read:

FOR I := 1 TO LINEWIDTH DO).

Since LINEWIDTH is a global variable it appears at the
bottom of the stack and so is accessible to any procedure
which is subsequently called. Provided the procedure only

```
 1: PROGRAM SIDEFFECT ;
 2: VAR HEIGHT : ARRAY [1..10] OF INTEGER ;
 3:     I : INTEGER ;
 4: --
 5: --
 6: (* PROCEDURE TO FILL HEIGHT *)
 7: --
 8: --
 9: PROCEDURE LINEOUT1;
10: BEGIN
11:     WHILE HEIGHT[I]>0 DO
12:     BEGIN
13:         WRITE('H');
14:         HEIGHT[I]:=HEIGHT[I]-1
15:     END;
16:     WRITELN
17: END;
18: --
19: --
20: BEGIN (* MAIN PROGRAM *)
21: --
22: --
23:     WRITELN('RESULTS HISTOGRAM:');
24:     FOR I:=1 TO 10 DO
25:     BEGIN
26:         IF I<10 THEN WRITE(' ');
27:         WRITE(I,'    !');
28:         LINEOUT1
29:     END;
30: --

***----------------------------------------------***

31: PROGRAM CALLBYVALUE ;
32: VAR HEIGHT : ARRAY[1..10] OF INTEGERS ;
33:     I : INTEGER ;
34: --
35: --
36: (* PROCEDURE TO FILL HEIGHT *)
37: --
38: --
39: PROCEDURE LINEOUT2(J: INTEGER) ;
40: BEGIN
41:     WHILE J>0 DO
42:     BEGIN
43:         WRITE('H') ;
44:         J=J-1
45:     END ;
46:     WRITELN
47: END ;
48: --
49: --
50: BEGIN (* MAIN PROGRAM *)
51: --
52: --
53:     WRITELN('RESULTS HISTOGRAM') ;
54:     FOR I := 1 TO 10 DO
55:     BEGIN
56:         IF I<10 THEN WRITE(' ') ;
57:         WRITE(I, '    !') ;
58:         LINEOUT2(HEIGHT[I])
59:     END ;
60: --
61: --
```

Fig. 7.3. SIDEFFECT and CALLBYVALUE

uses such non-local variables and doesn't change their
values, this is a reasonably satisfactory way of allowing a
procedure to communicate with external data.

Suppose, however, that one wished to write a procedure
to produce a histogram, the data for which was stored in a
ten element array HEIGHT. Figure 7.3 shows two methods of
programming such a procedure. In program SIDEFFECT,
procedure LINEOUT1 references the global array elements of
HEIGHT and the global integer I. Consequently, each time an
element is needed, a search must be made, down to the
bottom of the stack, first to find the value of I and then
to get the contents of the array. This must occur for ten
iterations. In a large program where the arrays,
procedures and hence the stack itself can be expected to be
much larger, the inefficiency of this method becomes
amplified.

The second version of the program in Figure 7.3 is
intended to show how specific values may be passed to a
procedure when it is called. This implies that the called
procedure will make its own local copy of the value in its
own work space at the top of the stack. Thus the call in
line 58 passes the actual parameter value (i.e. the
appropriate element of HEIGHT) to procedure LINEOUT2 which
uses the local formal parameter J to reference that value.
Every time J is accessed it can be found at the top of the
stack so the search is shorter than the corresponding
search in program SIDEFFECT. LINEOUT2 alters the value of J
as it proceeds but this change does not affect the contents
of the array since, when LINEOUT2 exits all its work space
(including the current value of J) is returned to the free
space above the top of the stack.

This technique of passing useful external values to a
procedure for use in its own work space is known as a

call-by-value. The formal definition is shown in the
syntax diagram in Figure 7.4. Note that formal parameters
may be of any type and that more than one may be passed.

Procedures which Produce Results

Using a procedure with parameters that are
called by value is quite satisfactory unless the results
computed by the procedure are required, on return, by the
calling procedure or program. If a single result is
required and if it is of a standard scalar type (i.e.
INTEGER, REAL, BOOLEAN or CHAR) then Pascal provides a
special type of procedure called a function. A number of
standard functions exist in the language including:

EOLN,ODD(X)	-BOOLEAN functions
TRUNC(X),ROUND(X)	-INTEGER functions
SIN(X),SQRT(X)	-REAL functions
CHR(X)	-CHAR function

A complete list of these can be found in Appendix A.

The syntax diagram for user-defined functions is given
in Figure 7.6. For other types of procedure, the procedure
call is a complete statement consisting of the procedure
identifier followed by the list of actual parameters. In
contrast, since the result returned by a function is a single
standard type, the function call can be made implicitly by
using the function name directly in the statement within
which the returned result is required. Thus

    REPEAT

    --

    --

    UNTIL EOLN

where EOLN represents a function call returning a result of
TRUE or FALSE; and

    WRITE(SIN(X))

110

Procedure
Declaration

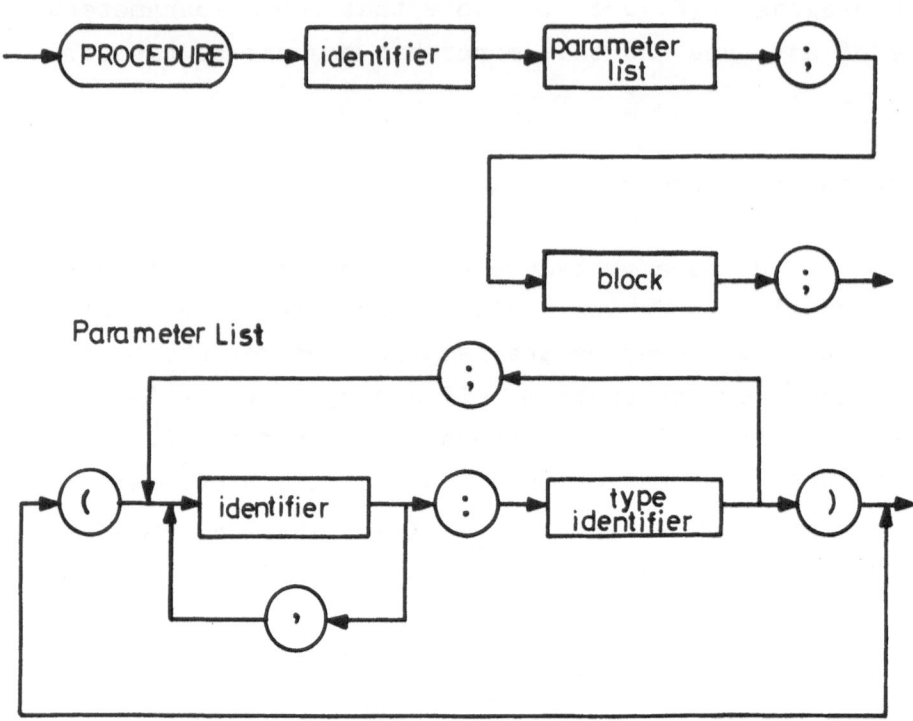

Fig. 7.4. Syntax Diagram for PROCEDURE DECLARATION and
PARAMETER LIST

```
1: --
2: VAR EVEN : BOOLEAN ;
3: PROCEDURE PROCEVEN(VAL : INTEGER) ;
4: BEGIN
5:     EVEN := 2*(VAL DIV 2)=VAL
6: END ;
7: --
8: --
9: BEGIN (* MAIN PROGRAM *)
10: --
11: --
12:     PROCEVEN(VAL) ;
13:     IF EVEN THEN ....
14: --
15: --
***----------------------------------------------***
16: --
17: FUNCTION EVEN(VAL : INTEGER) : BOOLEAN ;
18: BEGIN
19:     EVEN := 2*(VAL DIV 2)=VAL
20: END ;
21: --
22: --
23: BEGIN (* MAIN PROGRAM *)
24: --
25: --
26:     IF EVEN(VAL) THEN...
27: --
28: --
```

Fig. 7.5. PROCEVEN and EVEN

111

Procedure and Function Declarations

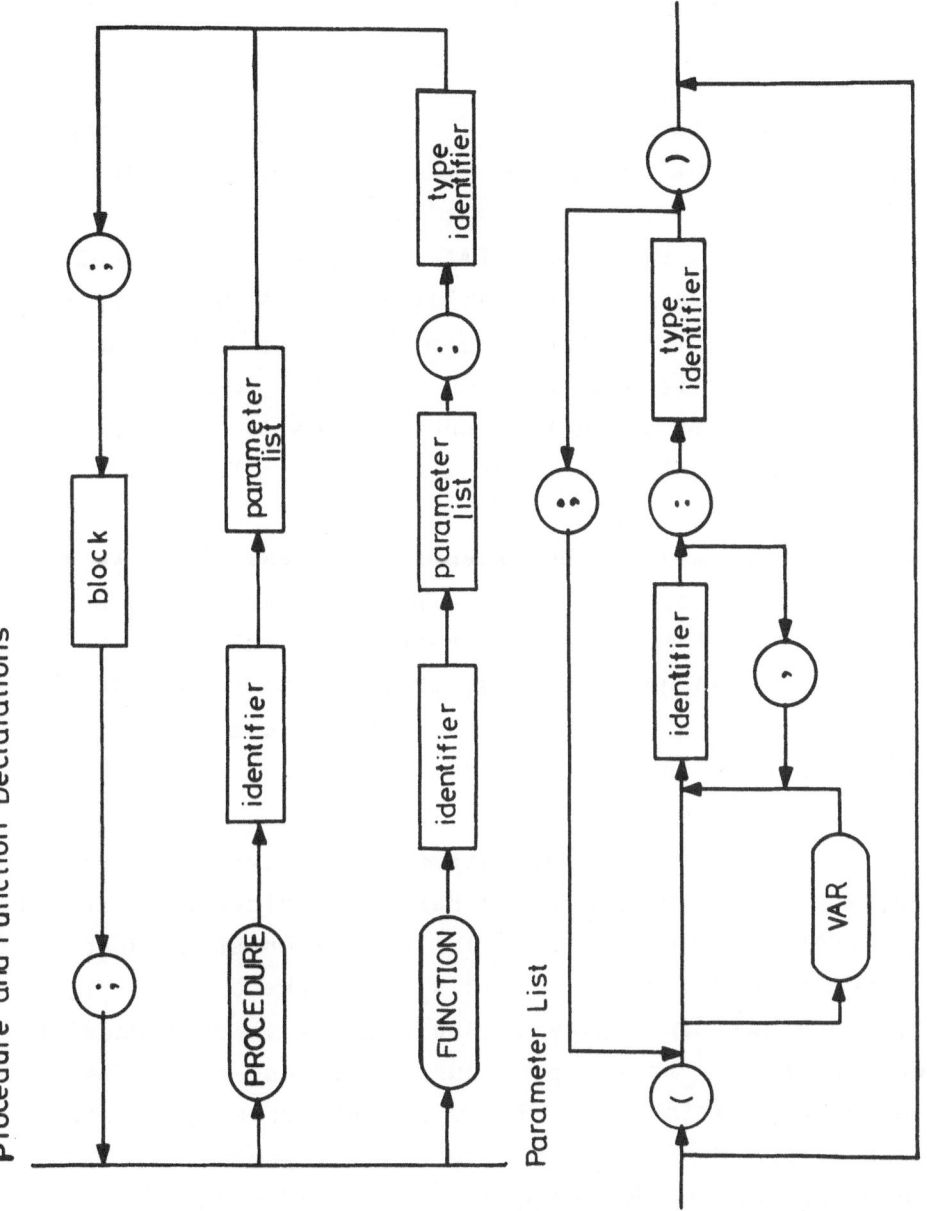

Parameter List

Fig. 7.6. Syntax Diagrams for PROCEDURE and FUNCTION DECLARATIONS

where the SIN function returns the result which is printed
out. User-defined functions can be referenced in exactly
the same way and the standard functions can even be
overridden within a program by a user- defined function of
the same name.

Compare the two segments of code in Figure 7.5, which
represent different approaches to the same task -- to
determine whether a given integer is even or not. When
PROCEVEN is used a global BOOLEAN variable must be declared.
This is set to TRUE or FALSE within PROCEVEN depending on
the nature of the indicated integer. In the second case,
the function EVEN is set to TRUE or FALSE. This is made
possible in line 17 where the function itself is declared
as a BOOLEAN (see also the syntax diagram in Figure 7.6).
In both cases the integer VAL is passed and in both cases
an assignment is made to the identifier EVEN. This is an
important feature of functions -- an assignment must be
made to the function identifier before control returns to
the calling procedure. Finally, the concise nature of the
function call (line 26) should be compared with the more
unwieldly version in lines 12 and 13.

Functions, for all their attractions, can still only
return single scalar values, so Pascal provides a different
means of returning multiple scalar values or structured
data types (arrays, records, etc.) While the ordinary type
of procedure call is employed, the call-by-value mechanism
can only pass data to the procedure. A second mechanism
exists whereby variables declared in the formal parameter
list are marked for return to the calling procedure. The
method of so marking parameters consists of preceding each
variable name (or sequence of variable names) to be
returned with the reserved word VAR, as shown in the syntax
diagram in Figure 7.6. These are consequently known as
variable parameters in contrast to the value parameters

defined in the previous section. The calling mechanism is often referred to as a call-by-reference.

The action taken by the compiler to achieve this two-way passing of data is quite complex. Provision must be made so that references to the formal parameter in the current procedure can be connected back to the actual parameter in the stack area of the calling procedure. Although the compiler must make these arrangements, the connections are made at run-time since the compiler does not always "know" where the actual parameter is. The classic example of this circumstance occurs when the actual parameter is an array element. Which particular array element is passed depends on the array indices whose values are not known to the compiler. Before the called procedure is activated therefore, the required array element must be identified and connected with the formal parameter name at the top of the stack.

As an example of a procedure using the call-by-reference approach, compare the two segments of code in Figure 7.7. Both are designed to achieve the exchange (or swapping) of the values of two REALs. Procedure BADSWAP achieves this by side- effect and requires two global REALs A and B to be declared in the main program. If any other REALs (apart from A and B) need to be swapped, then their values must be assigned to A and B before BADSWAP is called and retrieved once control has returned to the calling procedure (lines 15 to 19). In contrast, procedure SWAP contains the variable parameters A and B and any two REALs in the calling procedure can be passed and returned directly (line 36). Note that there is no reference to the variables A and B in the calling procedure declaration which implies that procedure SWAP could be inserted into any number of different programs without demanding that any external code be changed.

```
 1: --
 2: VAR A, B : REAL ;
 3:     MATRIX : ARRAY[1..50] OF REAL ;
 4: PROCEDURE BADSWAP ;
 5: VAR TEMP : REAL ;
 6: BEGIN
 7:     TEMP := A ;
 8:     A := B ;
 9:     B := TEMP
10: END ;
11:
12: BEGIN (* MAIN PROGRAM *)
13: --
14: --
15:     A := MATRIX[I] ;
16:     B := MATRIX[K] ;
17:     BADSWAP ;
18:     MATRIX[I] := A ;
19:     MATRIX[K] := B ;
20: --
21: --
***--------------------------------------------***
22: --
23: VAR MATRIX : ARRAY[1..50] OF REAL ;
24: --
25: PROCEDURE SWAP(VAR A, B : REAL) ;
26: VAR TEMP : REAL ;
27: BEGIN
28:     TEMP := A ;
29:     A := B ;
30:     B := TEMP
31: END ;
32:
33: BEGIN (* MAIN PROGRAM *)
34: --
35: --
36:     SWAP(MATRIX[I], MATRIX[K]) ;
37: --
38: --
```

Fig. 7.7. BADSWAP and SWAP

In this fashion it would be possible for a programmer
to build up a library of useful procedures which can
operate independently of the calling program. Provided
that there is a direct type correspondence between the
actual and the formal parameters, the programmer need never
think about the precise role of each variable in the
procedure. However, while this technique may be more
convenient, it is not usually more efficient than passing
parameters by value due to the connection activity required
to link formal and actual parameters. An exception occurs
when a large data structure is required in a called
procedure. The time (and space) taken in creating a fresh

copy at the top of the stack will often outweigh the time
lost in searching out those elements required in the
procedure.

String Handling

The next chapter will be concerned with the
development of a text formatting program in the course of
which a large amount of string manipulation will be
required. In preparation for this program, Figure 7.8
contains a set of functions and procedures which provide
basic string handling facilities. The UCSD Pascal system
provides a similar set of functions and procedures to
facilitate this kind of programming. However, UCSD has
had to define an extra data type the STRING (which is a
PACKED ARRAY OF CHAR) so that the function calling (and
returning) mechanism will work. Since this text is
concerned merely with using Pascal compilers and not
writing them, we must be content with a more pedestrian set
of procedures.

In particular, it will be necessary to write procedures
to mimic the UCSD string functions and these string
handling functions and procedures will be unable to cope
with literal strings (e.g. LENGTH ('HI THERE') will cause a
compiling error.) Note also that the declaration of STRING
in Figure 7.8 (line 3) will be rejected by any UCSD type
compiler for which STRING is a standard function.

The UCSD string functions and procedures are defined as
follows:

    1. FUNCTION LENGTH (STRING): INTEGER -- returns
the number of characters in the string STRING.

    2. FUNCTIONS POS (STRING, SOURCE): INTEGER --
returns the position of substring STRING in

```
1: PROGRAM STRINGS ;
2: CONST MAXLINE = 80 ;
3: TYPE STRING = ARRAY[1..MAXLINE] OF CHAR ;
4: (* VARIABLES AS NEEDED IN THE MAIN PROGRAM *)
5: FUNCTION LENGTH (S : STRING) : INTEGER ;
6: VAR TEMP : 1..MAXLINE ;
7: BEGIN
8:      TEMP := MAXLINE ;
9:      FOUND := FALSE ;
10:     WHILE (TEMP>0) AND NOT FOUND DO
11:          IF S[TEMP] = ' '
12:          THEN TEMP := TEMP - 1
13:          ELSE FOUND := TRUE ;
14:     LENGTH := TEMP
15: END ; (* LENGTH *)
16:
17: FUNCTION POSITION(PATTERN, SOURCE : STRING) : INTEGER ;
18: VAR I, J : INTEGER ;
19:     FOUND : BOOLEAN ;
20: BEGIN
21:     J := 0 ;
22:     REPEAT
23:          FOUND := TRUE ;
24:          FOR I := 1 TO LENGTH (PATTERN) DO
25:               IF PATTERN[I] <> SOURCE[J+I] THEN FOUND := FALSE ;
26:          J := J + 1
27:     UNTIL FOUND OF (J)LENGTH(SOURCE)) ;
28:     IF FOUND THEN POSITION := J ELSE POSITION := 0
29: END ; (* POSITION *)
30:
31: PROCEDURE STREAD (VAR S : STRING) ;
32: VAR I, J : 1..MAXLINE ;
33: BEGIN
34:     I := 1 ;
35:     REPEAT
36:          READ(S[I]) ;
37:          I := I + 1
38:     UNTIL EOLN ;
39:     FOR J := I TO MAXLINE DO
40:          S[J] := ' '
41: END ; (* STREAD *)
42:
43: PROCEDURE STWRITE ( S : STRING) ;
44: VAR I, J : 1..MAXLINE ;
45: BEGIN
46:     IF LENGTH(S) > 0
47:     THEN FOR I := 1 TO LENGTH(S) DO
48:               WRITE(S[I])
49: END ; (* STWRITE *)
50:
51: PROCEDURE CONCAT(S1, S2 : STRING ; VAR DESTINATION : STRING) ;
52: VAR I, L1, L2 : 1..MAXLINE ;
53: BEGIN
54:     L1 := LENGTH (S1) ; L2 := LENGTH (S2) ;
55:     IF (L1 + L2) > MAXLINE
56:     THEN WRITELN('STRINGS TOO LONG')
57:     ELSE
58:     BEGIN
59:          FOR I := 1 TO L1 DO
60:               DESTINATION[I] := S1[I] ;
61:          FOR I := 1 TO L2 DO
62:               DESTINATION[L1 + I] := S2[I]
63:     END
64: END ; (* CONCAT *)
65:
66: PROCEDURE COPY(SOURCE:STRING; VAR DESTINATION:STRING; INDEX,SIZE:INTEGER) ;
67: VAR I, J : 1..MAXLINE ;
68: BEGIN
69:     FOR I := 1 TO SIZE DO
70:     BEGIN
```

```
71:            J := INDEX + I - 1 ;
72:            DESTINATION[I] := SOURCE[J]
73:      END ;
74:      FOR I := SIZE + 1 TO MAXLINE DO
75:            DESTINATION[I] := ' '
76: END ; (* COPY *)
77:
78: PROCEDURE DELETE (VAR DESTINATION : STRING ; INDEX, SIZE : INTEGER) ;
79: VAR I : 0..MAXLINE ;
80: BEGIN
81:      FOR I := INDEX + SIZE TO MAXLINE DO
82:      BEGIN
83:            DESTINATION[I-SIZE] := DESTINATION[I] ;
84:            DESTINATION[I] := ' '
85:      END ;
86:      FOR I := 0 TO SIZE - 1 DO DESTINATION[MAXLINE - I] := ' '
87: END ; (* DELETE *)
88:
89: PROCEDURE INSERT (SOURCE:STRING; VAR DESTINATION:STRING ; INDEX:INTEGER) ;
90: VAR I, SIZE : 1..MAXLINE ;
91: BEGIN
92:      SIZE := LENGTH(SOURCE) ;
93:      IF SIZE + LENGTH(DESTINATION) > MAXLINE
94:      THEN WRITELN('STRING OVERFLOW -- INSERTION NOT MADE')
95:      ELSE
96:      BEGIN
97:         IF LENGTH(DESTINATION) >= INDEX
98:         THEN FOR I := LENGTH(DESTINATION) DOWNTO INDEX DO
99:                 DESTINATION[I+SIZE] := DESTINATION[I] ;
100:        FOR I := 1 TO SIZE DO
101:             DESTINATION[INDEX + (I-1)] := SOURCE[I]
102:      END
103: END ; (* INSERT *)
104:
105: BEGIN (* MAIN PROGRAM *)
106: END .
```

Fig. 7.8. STRINGS

string SOURCE. If more than one occurence exists,
POS will return the position of the first
occurrence. If no occurence exists, POS will
return 0.

3.   FUNCTION CONCAT (SOURCE1, SOURCE2,..): STRING
-- returns a string which is the concatenation of
the set of strings passed in the parameter list
taken in order. Note that the replacement
version in Figure 7.8 is a procedure rather than
a function and only concatenates a pair of strings.

4. FUNCTION COPY (SOURCE, INDEX, SIZE): STRING --
returns a string containing the substring of
length SIZE starting at position INDEX in STRING.

5. PROCEDURE DELETE (DESTINATION, INDEX, SIZE) --
deletes SIZE characters from the string
DESTINATION starting at position INDEX.

6. PROCEDURE INSERT (SOURCE, DESTINATION, INDEX)
-- inserts substring SOURCE into string
DESTINATION starting at position INDEX.

In addition, Figure 7.8 contains two procedures to read and
write strings (STREAD and STWRITE). This is managed at
system level in UCSD Pascal so that READ and WRITE under
UCSD will accept strings as parameters.

Conclusion

Procedures can be distinguished by the manner in
which data is passed between the calling and the called
procedure, and by the nature of the data which is passed.
Passing machanisms include the side effect, the call-by-
value and the call-by-reference. When a procedure needs to
return a single result of a standard scalar type, the use
of a FUNCTION is appropriate.

Exercise 1: Write a procedure which will cause the line
printer to skip "n" lines and which is called by the
statement NEWLINE (N).

Exercise 2: Write a program to read in a positive integer
less than 10,000 and print out the value in words, e.g.:
    input   1705
    output   ONE THOUSAND SEVEN HUNDRED AND FIVE
Use a function to extract the digits from the number, one at
a time starting with the thousands, and a variable
parameter to convert the digit into a word. Anything from
10 to 99 will need special treatment, especially up to 19.
Use CONCAT to put the output string together.

Chapter 8. Top-Down Design

In this chapter a large-scale programming problem, the production of a text-formatting program, is tackled from scratch, as a demonstration of how a program can be constructed from the top down.

Textfiles

Before embarking on a specification for a text formatting program and discussing the programming strategies associated with a top-down implementation it will be necessary to consider the provision Pascal makes for the control and manipulation of textual data. During execution, the program may need access to a variety of external media. For example, on discs or magnetic tapes the program will access a <u>file</u>. As described in Chapter 6, the key features of a file are that it <u>is</u> external to the program; that its components are all of the same, predefined data type; and that the program communicates with the file by means of a <u>buffer</u> <u>variable</u> and the reserved words GET and PUT. By contrast, when the program communicates with a terminal or line printer, the reserved words READLN and WRITELN are used to manage input or output in lines.

Clearly the disc (or tape) file is merely a form of storage for the program (perhaps an inconveniently slow but permanent form of memory), while the terminal is the primary means of communication with the human user. The <u>textfile</u> exists as a compromise between these two "media":

it is stored on and accessed from a disc, yet it is set up
for output on a VDU or line printer. It can contain all
the <u>printable</u> characters recognised by the terminal
together with a non-printable "control" character, used to
separate one line of text from another, and called the <u>line</u>
<u>separator</u>. In ASCII, the line separator is actually a pair
of control characters -- carriage return and line feed.

A declaration of the form
VAR ROUGHCOPY : TEXT
has the effect of declaring ROUGHCOPY as a textfile via the
standard type TEXT predefined as a FILE OF CHAR. Since
this will be a file of characters, the buffer variable
(ROUGHCOPY^) will be of type CHAR and access may occur by
means of GET and PUT operations. However, in a textfile
there are likely to be a large number of characters to
manipulate so that Wirth provides, as a shorthand, the
standard procedures:
READ (FILEID, CHARBUF),
which has the effect of
CHARBUF:=FILEID^ ; GET (FILEID)
and
WRITE (FILEID, CHARBUF),
which has the effect of
FILEID^:=CHARBUF ; PUT (FILEID)
where FILEID is a declared file identifier and CHARBUF
stands for "character buffer".

This still only deals with one character at a time, and
only with textfiles. Note also that in the case of READ,
the FILEID^ buffer contains the next character to be read
(as a result of the GET operation) while CHARBUF contains
the character of immediate interest. When the GET
operation encounters the line separator character, FILEID^
becomes blank and the Boolean EOLN (FILEID) is set to TRUE.

This is done in order to help the programmer to deal with the line-nature of the textfile. A following READ would just transfer the blank in FILEID^ to CHARBUF before advancing the file window but this is undesirable and liable to lead to errors.

   As a consequence, a second standard procedure, READLN (FILEID), exists whose function is to move the pointer beyond the line separator and clear EOLN (i.e. make it FALSE again) without placing the (spurious) blank in CHARBUF. After a READLN, FILEID^ will contain the first character of the next line and the program is thus ready for succeeding READs. If the READLN is called before all the characters on the line have been read, the pointer will skip to the beginning of the next line anyway. In a similar fashion, WRITE (FILEID, CHARBUF) transfers a character to an output file and WRITELN (FILEID) will append a line separator.

   This scheme is sufficiently useful in general programming that a non-standard extension, sanctioned by Wirth in his "Report", has been developed to allow more generalized READ and WRITE procedures. The first enhancement concerns the type of the variable permitted in a READ or WRITE call. In general, any variable of type INTEGER or REAL may be specified. The interesting point here is that the file type must still be a textfile so that some sort of conversion must be done (implicitly) between the character string in the textfile and the number in the program.   Incidentally, variables of type Boolean may also appear in WRITE or WRITELN statements in which case TRUE or FALSE will appear in the output file -- although the reader is unlikely to find this feature implemented on a micro system yet.

The second extension allows more than one variable to appear in a READ or WRITE statement. Thus

    READLN (FILEID, VAR1, VAR2, VAR3)

is equivalent to

    READ (FILEID, VAR1); READ (FILEID, VAR2);

    READ (FILEID, VAR3); READLN (FILEID)

which represents a considerable compression.

On large main-frame implementations of Pascal, the mode of operation is usually non-interactive and communication with a program would be through two standard textfiles called INPUT and OUTPUT which are regarded as defaults so that their identifiers need not be specified. Thus

WRITELN	refers to		WRITELN(OUTPUT)
READLN	"	"	READLN(INPUT)
EOLN	"	"	EOLN(INPUT)
EOF	"	"	EOF(INPUT)
READ(VAR)	"	"	READ(INPUT, VAR)
WRITE(VAR)	"	"	WRITE(OUTPUT, VAR)

Note that the declaration

    VAR INPUT, OUTPUT : TEXT,

and the statements

    RESET (INPUT) ;   REWRITE (OUTPUT)

are implicitly assumed and must never explicitly appear in a program. Readers with access to micro-based Pascal systems are more fortunate in that access is interactive so that the "file" INPUT refers directly to the terminal keyboard while OUTPUT refers to the VDU screen or teletype roll. This brings the formal definitions of Pascal input/output procedures into line with the syntax which has been employed in examples in the previous chapters.

Note that Wirth's definition of RESET(FILEID) not only opens a textfile FILEID for reading but also loads the first character into FILEID^, while READ(FILEID, CH) assigns to CH the contents of FILEID^ and then GETs another character into FILEID^. Using these definitions for INPUT in an interactive environment causes all programs to hang until a character is typed in. When RESET(INPUT) is called implicitly at the beginning of program execution, there is nothing to load into INPUT^. So, in virtually all micro implementations of Pascal, RESET(INPUT) only opens INPUT and doesn't attempt to fill INPUT^. READ expects INPUT^ to be filled and so Wirth's definition of READ(INPUT, CH) is reversed; i.e.

GET(INPUT); CH := INPUT^.

```
 1: PROCEDURE FREADLN (VAR INFILE : TEXT ; VAR BUFFER : STRING) ;
 2: (* READLN INTO BUFFER FROM INFILE *)
 3: VAR I, J : INTEGER ;
 4: BEGIN
 5:     REPEAT (* BLANK LINES *)
 6:         READLN (INFILE) ;
 7:         I := 1 ;
 8:         REPEAT
 9:             READ (INFILE, BUFFER[I]) ;
10:             I := I + 1
11:         UNTIL EOLN (INFILE)
12:     UNTIL EOF(INFILE) OR (LENGTH(BUFFER))>0) ;
13:     FOR J := I TO MAXLINE DO BUFFER[I] := ' '
14: END ; (* FREADLN *)
15: PROCEDURE FWRITELN (VAR OUTFILE : TEXT ; BUFFER : STRING) ;
16: (* WRITELN BUFFER TO OUTFILE *)
17: VAR I, J : 1..MAXLINE ;
18: BEGIN
19:     FOR I := 1 TO LENGTH(BUFFER) DO WRITE (OUTFILE, BUFFER[I])
20:     WRITELN (OUTFILE)
21: END ; (* FWRITELN *)
```

Fig. 8.1. FREADLN and FWRITELN

In a text formatting program there is a requirement for a buffer big enough to take a whole line of characters at a time (i.e. a string) and of procedures to move the line to and from a textfile in one operation. Accordingly input/output procedures have been developed to access textfiles in lines. These appear in Figure 8.1. The call FREADLN (INFILE, BUFFER) will read the next line of text from the textfile INFILE into the STRING called BUFFER. In line 6, the line separator from the previous line is

disposed of. The buffer is then filled, a character at a
time, until the line separator is detected (EOLN (INFILE)
is TRUE, lines 8 to 11). At this point a check (line 12)
is made that the line was not a blank line. If it was, it
is ignored and the next line is read; if not, the remainder
of BUFFER is filled with spaces (line 13). This is
important since the spaces will overwrite any characters
left over in BUFFER from a (longer) previously read line.
FWRITELN (lines 15 to 20) merely outputs the printable
characters in the buffer onto the indicated OUTFILE and
appends a line separator.

The Text Formatter

     The idea of a text formatting program is to exploit
the text handling capabilities of the computer (together
with its capacity to control the line printer) to produce
correctly formatted textual output. First the required text
is entered into a file using the system editor and without
much attention being paid to the layout of the text. If
this file were to be offered as input to a text formatting
program, the program would accept one line at a time and
"pack" an output buffer, producing an output file each line
of which is constructed according to some standard format;
for example, each output line would be filled with the
maximum number of whole words possible.

     Invariably, however, a simple line-width specification
will not be adequate for most text formatting tasks and the
user will want to impose other conditions on the text
output. The lines of text may perhaps be divided into
pages, which may or may not be numbered, each consisting
of a fixed number of lines, which may be single, double or
triple spaced. Furthermore, the text may need to be
subdivided into paragraphs, and each line could be

right-<u>justified</u> -- spaced out evenly between the left and
right margins. Sometimes the formatting scheme may need to
be temporarily suspended in order to deal with a title or
heading or a table of specially "hand-formatted" material.

   All this information has to be passed to the
formatting program and this can most easily be done by
embedding <u>formatting</u> <u>commands</u> in the input text. While the
program is processing the input text, it can trap each
formatting command and dynamically alter the formatting
specification to meet the requirements dictated by the new
information. Figure 8.2 tabulates some of the functions
which could be implemented under such a scheme. Note
particularly the syntax of the formatting commands. Each
command will appear on a line of its own, and begins with
a "." which is a very unlikely character for a line of text
to start with! In this way the program can recognize which
lines of the input file are formatting commands and which
are just plain text.

   Most of the formatting commands relate to the text
which follows the command, although some commands (e.g.
Break) relate to the text immediately before the command.
For this reason a great deal of care must be taken, during
programming, to keep the input and ouput file buffers
independent, and to "look ahead" at the incoming line of
text before writing out the latest line of output text.
It is also important to distinguish between those commands
which are effective for one line only (like .B for Break)
and those which alter the output format for all the ensuing
text until new commands are issued (like .M for Margin).

   The problem specification for PROGRAM PROFF is as
follows:

Write a program that allows a user to produce
formatted textfiles from named unformatted
textfiles in which are embedded the set of commands
listed in Figure 8.2.

FORMATTING FUNCTION	OVERRIDING COMMAND	RESULT OF COMMAND	DEFAULT
PAGE CONTROLS:			
+LENGTH-Number of lines to the page.	.Ln	SETS NUMBER OF LINES PER PAGE TO "n".	n=58
+NUMBER-Successively number each new page.	.Nn	STARTS NUMBERING AT "n".	TRUE n=2
	.O	SUPPRESSES PAGE NUMBERING.	FALSE
+SPACING-Intersperse blank lines between text lines.	.Sn	INTERSPERSES "n-1" BLANK LINES BETWEEN TEXT LINES.	FALSE n=1
LINE CONTROLS:			
+MARGINS-Inserts spaces to left and right of text on each line.	.Mlr	FIRST CHARACTER OF TEXT AT POSITION "l" AND LAST AT "r".	l=0 r=60
+FILL-Pack as many whole words as possible into each line.	.F .U(UNFILL)	INVOKES FILLING SUPPRESSES FILLING	TRUE FALSE
+JUSTIFY-Rearrange words in line so last word ends on last character position.	.J .R(RAGGED)	INVOKES JUSTIFICATION SUPPRESS JUSTIFICATION	TRUE FALSE
ONE-OFF COMMANDS: (Apply only to immediate text after which previous formatting resumed.)			
+INDENT-Insert spaces at beginning of next line.	.In	INDENTS "n" SPACES	
+BREAK-Terminate latest line without justifying or filling.	.Bn	TERMINATES LINE AND INSERTS "n". BLANK LINES.	
+PARAGRAPH-Terminate current line and indents following line.	.Pin	EQUIVALENT TO .Bn FOLLOWED BY .Ii	i=5 n=1
+CENTRE-Position next line of text in centre of output line. (for headings)	.C		FALSE

Fig. 8.2. Textformatting Commands

Assuming the string handling procedures described in
Chapter 7 and the file accessing procedures from Figure
8.1, the first step is to consider the main data structures
needed for the problem (see Figure 8.3). Both the input and
output files are textfiles and can be referenced by the file
identifiers INFILE and OUTFILE provided these are declared
as such (line 21). Likewise INFILENAME and OUTFILENAME are

```
  1: PROGRAM PROFF ;
  2:
  3: CONST MAXLINE = 80 ;
  4:
  5: TYPE FORMAT = RECORD
  6:                    NUMBER : BOOLEAN ;
  7:          -         FILL : BOOLEAN ;
  8:                    JUSTIFY : BOOLEAN ;
  9:                    PAGENUMBER : INTEGER ;
 10:                    INDENT : 0 .. MAXLINE ;
 11:                    LEFTMARGIN : 0 .. MAXLINE ;
 12:                    RIGHTMARGIN : 0 .. MAXLINE ;
 13:                    LINES : INTEGER ;
 14:                    SPACING : 1 .. 10
 15:                END ;
 16:
 17:      STRING = ARRAY[1..MAXLINE] OF CHAR ;
 18:
 19:
 20: VAR INFILENAME, OUTFILENAME : STRING ;
 21:     INFILE, OUTFILE : TEXT ;
 22:
121: PROCEDURE TEXTFORMAT ;
122: (* READS FROM INFILE, FORMATS AND WRITES FORMATTED TEXT TO OUTFILE *)
123:
499: BEGIN (* MAIN PROGRAM *)
500:     REPEAT
501:         WRITE ('FILENAME OR E TO EXIT --> ') ;
502:         READLN (INFILENAME) ;
503:         IF INFILENAME () 'E'
504:         THEN
505:         BEGIN
506:             RESET (INFILE, INFILENAME) ;
507:             WRITE ('NEW FILE NAME --> ') ;
508:             READLN (OUTFILENAME) ;
509:             REWRITE (OUTFILE, OUTFILENAME) ;
510:             TEXTFORMAT ;
511:             CLOSE (INFILE, LOCK) ;      (* UCSD ONLY *)
512:             CLOSE (OUTFILE, LOCK)       (* UCSD ONLY *)
513:         END
514:     UNTIL INFILENAME = 'E'
515: END.
```

Fig. 8.3. PROFF

strings which will contain the external file names, as
specified by the user. Finally, a look at Figure 8.2 will
show what a complex formatting "environment" the program
must maintain, utilize and occasionally amend. Clearly,
the record structure lends itself to the easy association
of data types suggested by the fields of FORMAT lines 5 to
15. While manipulating the text, the program will format
according to the specifications held in a FORMAT record,
and when obeying a formatting command, the program will
alter a field in a FORMAT record.

Having chosen the data structures, the next step is to
design and test the main program (Figure 8.3, lines 499 to

515). In order to enable a series of files to be formatted
successively, the main program consists of a loop (lines
500 to 514). Within this the user is asked for the input
file name (and can exit with "E") and an output file name.
The files are initialized for reading and writing
respectively, and the text is formatted (line 510). This is
the major ploy of top down design -- once the current
details (like filenames) have been dealt with, the "buck"
is passed to a procedure down the line -- in this case
TEXTFORMAT. Finally, the files are closed -- using the
UCSD instruction to close an external file (lines 511 and
512).

At this point it is necessary to test the code
currently written. No matter how trivial this may seem, it
is especially important at the initial stages of the design
since a logical error at this level of program could have
devastating results on the outcomes at lower levels. To
perform a test, a dummy procedure or _stub_ must be written
for TEXTFORMAT.

```
    e.g. PROCEDURE TEXTFORMAT;
         BEGIN
             FREADLN (INFILE, BUFFER);
             FWRITE (OUTFILE, BUFFER)
         END;
```

Thus when the main program calls TEXTFORMAT some sort
of action occurs, enough to test the continuity of the main
program. For procedures which return values, the stub has
to be more sophisticated and actually fake the return
values to enable testing of the logic of the module under
scrutiny. In this way the program can be built up as a
collection of tested procedures and stubs which combine to
form a _test harness_ for the procedure currently under
consideration.

```
121: PROCEDURE TEXTFORMAT ;
122: (* READS FROM INFILE, FORMATS AND WRITES FORMATTED TEXT TO OUTFILE *)
123:
124: VAR USERFORMAT : FORMAT ;
125:     INBUFFER, OUTBUFFER : STRING ;
126:     EMPTYINBUFFER, EMPTYOUTBUFFER : BOOLEAN ;
127:     CURRENTLINE : INTEGER ;
128:
129: PROCEDURE STANFORMAT ( VAR FORM : FORMAT ) ;
144:
145: PROCEDURE FLUSH (VAR BUFFER : STRING) ;
146: (* OUTPUTS SPACING BLANK LINES, FLUSHES BUFFER AND FILLS WITH SPACES *)
170:
171: FUNCTION COMMAND : BOOLEAN ;
172: (* TRUE IF IN BUFFER IS A COMMAND AND FALSE OTHERWISE *)
176:
177: PROCEDURE OBEY ( VAR FORM : FORMAT ) ;
178: (* CARRIES OUT FORMATTING COMMANDS *)
303:
304: PROCEDURE FILLOUT ;
305: (* TRANSFERS WORDS FROM INBUFFER TO OUTBUFFER UNTIL OUTBUFFER IS FULL *)
361:
362: FUNCTION READYOUTBUFFER : BOOLEAN ;
367:
368: FUNCTION SHOULDJUSTIFY : BOOLEAN ;
373: PROCEDURE ADJUST (VAR BUFFER : STRING) ;
374:
436:
437: PROCEDURE CLEAR (VAR OUTFILE : TEXT ; VAR OUTBUFFER : STRING ) ;
473:
474: BEGIN (* TEXTFORMAT *)
475:
476:     STANFORMAT(USERFORMAT ) ;
477:     CURRENTLINE := 1 ;
478:     EMPTYOUTBUFFER := TRUE ;
479:     WHILE NOT EOF (INFILE) DO
480:     BEGIN
481:         FREADLN (INFILE, INBUFFER) ;
482:         EMPTYINBUFFER := LENGTH(INBUFFER)=0 ; '
483:         IF COMMAND
484:         THEN OBEY(USERFORMAT) ;
485:         WHILE NOT EMPTYINBUFFER DO
486:         BEGIN
487:             IF USERFORMAT.FILL OR EMPTYOUTBUFFER THEN FILLOUT ;
488:             IF READYOUTBUFFER
489:             THEN
490:             BEGIN
491:                 IF SHOULDJUSTIFY THEN ADJUST (OUTBUFFER) ;
492:                 CLEAR (OUTFILE, OUTBUFFER)
493:             END
494:         END
495:     END ;
496:     WRITELN ('FORMATTING COMPLETED')
497: END ; (* TEXTFORMAT *)
```

Fig. 8.4. TEXTFORMAT

The next step is to implement TEXTFORMAT (Figure 8.4). TEXTFORMAT should begin by calling STANFORMAT to initialise the record with the predefined default values (see Figure 8.2). This technique minimizes the number of commands used

since only requirements at variance with the defaults need
to be explicitly mentioned. Local data structures include:
   (i) USERFORMAT -- the current formatting
   environment record -- since TEXTFORMAT has to
   process an entire file,
   (ii) the two strings INBUFFER and OUTBUFFER
   which act as windows on the files INFILE and
   OUTFILE,
   (iii) the BOOLEAN flags EMPTYINBUFFER and
   EMPTYOUTBUFFER to keep an eye on the status of the
   INBUFFER and OUTBUFFER.

   The processing algorithm will depend on the state of
the two flags, EMPTYINBUFFER and EMPTYOUTBUFFER. Only when
EMPTYINBUFFER is TRUE can another line of input text be read
in, while a TRUE EMPTYOUTBUFFER signals that OUTFILE has
already been written to. The while loop (lines 479 to 495)
will ensure that the entire input file is processed,
reading one line at a time into INBUFFER (line 481). The
contents of INBUFFER must either be a command (which must be
OBEYed -- line 484) or text. The text must be transferred
to OUTBUFFER, with reference to the conditions imposed by
the formatting record USERFORMAT. An initial stab at this
algorithm could be:

```
      WHILE NOT EMPTYINBUFFER DO
      BEGIN
            FILLOUT; (* transfer max. number of whole words
                           to OUTBUFFER observing MARGINS *)
         IF READYOUTBUFFER
         THEN
         BEGIN
               IF JUSTIFY THEN ADJUST; (* Right justify
                                             the line *)
               CLEAR(OUTBUFFER) (* write it to OUTFILE *)
         END
      END
```

Unfortunately, some of the formatting commands make the
solution more complicated than this. In particular, those
that apply to foregoing text (i.e. that which is in
OUTBUFFER before the command is encountered) require that
the text be retained in OUTBUFFER while the next input line
is checked to see if it affects the format ("lookahead").
Also there is no reason to suppose that just because
INBUFFER is empty OUTBUFFER is completely filled. The
differences between FILL and UNFILL, together with the
conditions imposed by BREAK, PARAGRAPH and EOF(INFILE) will
all have an effect on the state of READYOUTBUFFER. The
conditional (line 483) reflects the complexities of the
conditions on which READYOUTBUFFER would depend. Testing at
this level requires stubs for OBEY, FILLOUT, ADJUST and
CLEAR. OBEY should display the command passed (to test
whether the interface between the procedures is correct),
FILLOUT could simply transfer INBUFFER to OUTBUFFER and
CLEAR could write this to a disc file. If all is well at
this stage, OUTFILE should contain the text of INFILE
without the embedded formatting commands. The logical
paths dictated by both states of FILL should be tested in
turn (i.e. change the default value to false in STANFORMAT).

OBEY is clearly a straightforward application of the
CASE statement and as such does not warrant particular
scrutiny here. FILLOUT, on the other hand (line 304 to
359, Figure 8.5) offers more interesting possibilities,
since for the first time the details of handling a line of
text must be considered. Does one deal with words or
characters, for instance? In program PROFF a character
subdivision has been chosen. The available space in
OUTBUFFER is calculated by taking into account the margin
and indent format specifications and any possible OUTBUFFER
contents from a previous INBUFFER (PROCEDURE STARTINGPOINT,
Figure 8.5, lines 309 to 323). There follows a search from
the right hand side of INBUFFER until a space is found

```
177: PROCEDURE OBEY ( VAR FORM : FORMAT ) ;
178: (* CARRIES OUT FORMATTING COMMANDS *)
179:
180: VAR LEGAL : SET OF CHAR ;
181:     I : INTEGER ;
182:
183: FUNCTION PARAMETERS (BUFFER : STRING ) : BOOLEAN ;
188: FUNCTION NEXTPARAMETER (START : INTEGER) : INTEGER ;
202: PROCEDURE BLANK (VAR EMPTYOUTBUFFER : BOOLEAN ) ;
215: PROCEDURE CENTERED (VAR EMPTYOUTBUFFER : BOOLEAN ) ;
230: PROCEDURE NUM ;
236: PROCEDURE MARGIN ;
247: PROCEDURE PARAGRAPH (VAR EMPTYOUTBUFFER : BOOLEAN ) ;
265: PROCEDURE JUST ;
270: PROCEDURE UNFILL ;
276: BEGIN    (* OBEY *)
277:     LEGAL := ['B','C','F','I','J','L','M','N','O','P','R','S','U'] ;
278:     IF INBUFFER[2] IN LEGAL
279:     THEN
280:         WITH USERFORMAT DO
281:             CASE INBUFFER[2] OF
282:                 'B' : BLANK(EMPTYOUTBUFFER) ;
283:                 'C' : CENTERED(EMPTYOUTBUFFER) ;
284:                 'F' : FILL := TRUE ;
285:                 'I' : INDENT := NEXTPARAMETER(3) ;
286:                 'J' : JUST ;
287:                 'L' : LINES := NEXTPARAMETER(3) ;
288:                 'M' : MARGIN ;
289:                 'N' : NUM ;
290:                 'O' : NUMBER := FALSE ;
291:                 'P' : PARAGRAPH (EMPTYOUTBUFFER) ;
292:                 'R' : JUSTIFY := FALSE ;
293:                 'S' : SPACING := NEXTPARAMETER(3) ;
294:                 'U' : UNFILL
295:             END (* CASE *)
296:     ELSE
297:     BEGIN
298:     STWRITE(INBUFFER) ; WRITELN(' NOT RECOGNIZED')
299:     END ;
300:     FOR I := 1 TO MAXLINE DO INBUFFER[I] := ' ' ;
301:     EMPTYINBUFFER := TRUE
302: END ; (* OBEY *)
303:
304: PROCEDURE FILLOUT ;
305: (* TRANSFERS WORDS FROM INBUFFER TO OUTBUFFER UNTIL OUTBUFFER IS FULL *)
306: VAR POINTER : INTEGER ;
307:     START : 0..MAXLINE ;
308:
309: PROCEDURE STARTINGPOINT ;
310: VAR I : 1..MAXLINE ;
311: BEGIN
312:     IF EMPTYOUTBUFFER
313:     THEN
314:     BEGIN
315:         WITH USERFORMAT DO
316:         BEGIN
317:             FOR I := 1 TO MAXLINE DO OUTBUFFER[I] := ' ' ;
318:             START := LEFTMARGIN + INDENT + 1 ;
319:             INDENT := 0
320:         END (* WITH *)
321:     END
322:     ELSE START := LENGTH(OUTBUFFER) + 2
323: END ; (* STARTINGPOINT *)
324:
325: PROCEDURE FINDSTRING ;
326: VAR FREELENGTH : 1..MAXLINE ;
327:     SHORTENOUGH , ENDOFLINE, WHOLEWORD : BOOLEAN ;
328: BEGIN
329:     FREELENGTH := USERFORMAT.RIGHTMARGIN - START + 1 ;
330:     POINTER := LENGTH(INBUFFER) ;
```

```
331:
332:     REPEAT
333:         POINTER := POINTER - 1 ;
334:         SHORTENOUGH := POINTER < FREELENGTH ;
335:         ENDOFLINE := LENGTH(INBUFFER) = POINTER + 1 ;
336:         WHOLEWORD := INBUFFER[POINTER +1] = ' '
337:     UNTIL (SHORTENOUGH AND (ENDOFLINE OR WHOLEWORD)) OR (POINTER =0)
338: END ; (* FINDSTRING *)
339:
340: PROCEDURE MOVESTRING ;
341: VAR TEMPBUFFER : STRING ;
342: BEGIN
343:     COPY(INBUFFER, TEMPBUFFER, 1, POINTER + 1) ;
344:     DELETE (INBUFFER, 1, POINTER + 1) ;
345:     INSERT(TEMPBUFFER, OUTBUFFER, START)
346: END ; (* MOVESTRING *)
347: PROCEDURE SETFLAGS ;
348: BEGIN
349:     EMPTYINBUFFER:=(LENGTH(INBUFFER)=0)
350:                     OR (EOF(INFILE)AND(LENGTH(INBUFFER)=1)) ;
351:     EMPTYOUTBUFFER := LENGTH(OUTBUFFER)=0
352: END ; (* SETFLAGS *)
353:
354: BEGIN (* FILLOUT *)
355:     STARTINGPOINT ;
356:     FINDSTRING ;
357:     IF POINTER > 0 THEN MOVESTRING ;
358:     SETFLAGS
359: END ; (* FILLOUT *)
```

Fig. 8.5. OBEY

(i.e. there are a whole number of words to the left) such
that the lefthand substring would fit into OUTBUFFER (c.f.
FINDSTRING lines 325 to 338). The actual transfer is
handled by PROCEDURE MOVESTRING (lines 340 to 346).

PROCEDURE ADJUST (Figure 8.6, lines 373 to 435)
distributes the spare spaces, left over at the end of the
text line, between the words on the line. This is known as
"right justification". The technique is to advance down the
textfile from right to left searching for spaces. When a
space is found, another space from the pool of surplus
spaces (GAP) is added in. Care must be taken that two
adjacent spaces are not doubly added to, and also that,
when the left margin is reached, the process can be "turned
around" and used in the opposite direction.

```
373: PROCEDURE ADJUST (VAR BUFFER : STRING) ;
374:
375: VAR POINTER, NEWPOINTER, GAP, START : 0 .. MAXLINE ;
376:     DIRECTION : -1 .. 1 ;
377: FUNCTION INRANGE : BOOLEAN ;
378: BEGIN
379:     INRANGE := (POINTER)START)AND(POINTER(USERFORMAT.RIGHTMARGIN) AND
380:         (NEWPOINTER)=START)AND(NEWPOINTER(=USERFORMAT.RIGHTMARGIN)
381: END ; (* INRANGE *)
382: PROCEDURE SETUP ;
383: VAR ONEWORD : BOOLEAN ;
384:     I : 0 .. MAXLINE ;
385: BEGIN
386:     GAP := USERFORMAT.RIGHTMARGIN - LENGTH(BUFFER) ;
387:     POINTER := LENGTH(BUFFER) ;
388:     DIRECTION := 1 ;
389:     NEWPOINTER := POINTER + DIRECTION*GAP ;
390:     START := 0 ;
391:     REPEAT
392:         START := START + 1
393:     UNTIL BUFFER[START] <>' ' ;
394:     ONEWORD := TRUE ;
395:     FOR I := START TO LENGTH(BUFFER) DO
396:         IF BUFFER[I] = ' '
397:         THEN ONEWORD := FALSE ;
398:     IF ONEWORD THEN GAP := 0
399: END ; (* SETUP *)
400: PROCEDURE MOVECHARACTER ;
401: BEGIN
402:     BUFFER[NEWPOINTER] := BUFFER[POINTER] ;
403:     BUFFER[POINTER] := ' '
404: END ; (* MOVECHARACTER *)
405: PROCEDURE PADIFSPACE ;
406: BEGIN
407:     IF INRANGE AND (BUFFER[NEWPOINTER] = ' ')
408:     THEN IF BUFFER[NEWPOINTER+DIRECTION] <> ' '
409:         THEN
410:         BEGIN
411:             BUFFER[NEWPOINTER-DIRECTION] := ' ' ;
412:             GAP := GAP - 1
413:         END
414: END ; (* PADIFSPACE *)
415: PROCEDURE MOVEPOINTERS ;
416: BEGIN
417:     IF INRANGE
418:     THEN POINTER := POINTER - DIRECTION
419:     ELSE
420:     BEGIN
421:         POINTER := NEWPOINTER ;
422:         DIRECTION := -1*DIRECTION
423:     END ;
424:     NEWPOINTER := POINTER + DIRECTION*GAP
425: END ; (* MOVEPOINTERS *)
426:
427: BEGIN (* ADJUST *)
428:     SETUP ;
429:     WHILE GAP)0 DO
430:     BEGIN
431:         MOVECHARACTER ;
432:         PADIFSPACE ;
433:         MOVEPOINTERS
434:     END
435: END ; (* ADJUST *)
436:
437: PROCEDURE CLEAR (VAR OUTFILE : TEXT ; VAR OUTBUFFER : STRING ) ;
438: VAR I, LINESLEFT : INTEGER ;
439: PROCEDURE NEWPAGE (VAR CURRENTLINE : INTEGER) ;
440: VAR I : 1..MAXLINE ;
441: BEGIN
442:     WITH USERFORMAT DO
```

```
443:      BEGIN
444:         FOR I := 1 TO 3 DO
445:             WRITELN (OUTFILE) ;
446:         IF NUMBER
447:         THEN
448:         BEGIN
449:            FOR I := 1 TO RIGHTMARGIN - 7 DO
450:                WRITE (OUTFILE, ' ' ) ;
451:            WRITELN (OUTFILE, 'PAGE ', PAGENUMBER) ;
452:            PAGENUMBER :=  PAGENUMBER + 1
453:         END
454:         ELSE WRITELN (OUTFILE) ;
455:         WRITELN (OUTFILE) ; WRITELN (OUTFILE) ;
456:         CURRENTLINE := 3
457:      END (* WITH *)
458: END ; (* NEWPAGE *)
459: BEGIN (* CLEAR *)
460:      WITH USERFORMAT DO
461:      BEGIN
462:         IF (CURRENTLINE + SPACING) )= (LINES - 2)
463:         THEN
464:         BEGIN
465:            LINESLEFT := LINES - CURRENTLINE ;
466:            FOR I := 1 TO LINESLEFT DO WRITELN (OUTFILE) ;
467:            NEWPAGE (CURRENTLINE)
468:
469:         END ;
470:         FLUSH (OUTBUFFER)
471:      END (* WITH *)
472: END ; (* CLEAR *)
```

Fig. 8.6. ADJUST

Conclusion

The lower level procedures are fairly easy to understand and do not contribute to the overall strategy of the solution. There are a variety of other commands which could have been implemented and obviously there are different tactics for tackling problems like ADJUST and FILLOUT. Nevertheless, it is hoped that this program may serve as an illustration of the close parallel between an algorithm, as it is thought out, and its expression in Pascal code. A complete listing of PROFF appears in Appendix B.

Exercises : Implement the following enhancements to the text formatting program.

1) .T -- skip to the top of a new page.

2) .Z -- return to predefined standard format
(i.e. "Zero").

3) .N n p -- where 'p' is a flag which directs the
page number to the left hand, centre or right
hand side of the page

4) .H -- check if there is enough space below the
heading for the first line of text, and if not,
skip to a new page.

Chapter 9. Advanced Programming Techniques

As programmers become more experienced the pressures imposed on them while engaged in program writing begin to resolve themselves. Some of these pressures emerge from the run-time environment where particular restrictions as to memory usage or execution time may require the overall programming strategy to be considerably modified. These pressures are often alleviated by hardware enhancements -- like adding more memory or by the availability of such software tools as optimising compilers which reduce the effort required by the programmer to meet the run-time specificatins of the program.

Other, more numerous pressures exist at what might be described as "write-time". These may be imposed by the nature of the problem itself, by the algorithm which enables its solution, or by the syntax of the language in which the program is being written. A top-down design approach can help the programmer to make a complex problem more manageable. Likewise, the constructs of structured programming can help the programmer to express the solution (i.e. the program) simply and effectively.

Hardware improvements, software tools, sophisticated design techniques and a sympathetic language all contribute towards easing the programmer's load. But programming is still a tricky business that requires planning, concentration and skill and, inevitably, experienced programmers will learn to develop ploys to cut down coding,

speed up some forms of manipulation or generally take
further action to reduce both the write-time and run-time
pressures. In this chapter a small but popular sample of
these constructs and structures -- recursion, dynamic data
structures and variable field records -- are discussed,
together with their implementations in Pascal. The chief
problem, however, is not so much how the language realizes
the required constructs, as how the underlying logic can be
formulated to take advantage of the elegance or efficiency
offered by the indicated technique.

Recursive Programming

To some, <u>recursion</u>, or recursive programming,
represents the peak of "intellectual" programming while to
others it seems like a logical trick or an ineffectual
waste of time and space. The truth must lie between these
points of view since, while some desirable or even
necessary outcomes are only possible by means of recursive
methods, for most applications the result could often have
been achieved with less effort and with greater machine
efficiency by means of an iterative method. At the same
time, however, a language which incorporates the facility to
perform recursive algorithms offers an opportunity to
produce elegant and concise code which is usually more
readable than the iterative alternative.

Consider the problem of searching a character string
(called SENTENCE, say) for the first occurrence of a space.
 This can be written as a function which returns an
integer value equal to the position of the first space in
the string, if one exists, and equal to zero if no space
exists in the string. The call
        I := FIRSTSPACE(SENTENCE)
will initiate the <u>iterative</u> version of the function (Figure
9.1, lines 1 to 11). Tactically the function must search

the character positions one-by-one, keeping count of the
number of characters inspected and keeping a lookout for
the end of the string. The REPEAT-UNTIL construct controls
the search, moving from character to character until
something happens (i.e. until one of the UNTIL conditions
in line 7 is met).

```
 1: FUNCTION FIRSTSPACE (SENTENCE : STRING) : INTEGER ;
 2: VAR J : INTEGER ;
 3: BEGIN
 4:     J := 0 ;
 5:     REPEAT
 6:         J := J + 1
 7:     UNTIL (SENTENCE[J] = ' ') OR (J = LENGTH(SENTENCE)) ;
 8:     IF J = LENGTH(SENTENCE)
 9:     THEN FIRSTSPACE := 0
10:     ELSE FIRSTSPACE := J
11: END ; (FIRSTSPACE)
12:     ...
13: FUNCTION FINDSPACE(SENTENCE : STRING ; HERE : INTEGER) : INTEGER ;
14: BEGIN
15:     IF HERE < LENGTH(SENTENCE)
16:     THEN
17:     BEGIN
18:         IF SENTENCE[HERE] <> ' '
19:         THEN FINDSPACE := FINDSPACE(SENTENCE, HERE+1)
20:         ELSE FINDSPACE := HERE
21:     END
22:     ELSE FINDSPACE := 0
23: END ; (FINDSPACE)
```

Fig. 9.1. FIRSTSPACE and FINDSPACE

In the second example, (the recursive case, lines 13
to 23) control of the search is handled in a subtly
different way. The call
    I := FINDSPACE(SENTENCE,1)
initiates this version, the constant '1' indicating that the
search is to start at the first character position. First
note that lines 15 and 18 are testing for the same
conditions stipulated in line 7 and that the resulting
assignments correspond (i.e. line 9 and 22, line 10 and 20).
The search, however, is controlled by means of the
recursive function call in line 19 which has the effect of
restarting FINDSPACE but with a modified starting character
position HERE + 1 (=2 in the first case).

In an elementary example such as this the similarities between the iterative and recursive techniques are much more evident than the differences. Nevertheless, it should be possible to discern the major features of the recursive approach. Firstly, a recursive procedure "calls itself" -- (line 19). Secondly, however, a recursive procedure always contains an escape clause -- otherwise an infinite sequence of nested procedure calls will ensue. In FINDSPACE the escape clause consists of the different paths indicated by the conditionals on lines 15 and 18. Since these are of exactly the same nature as the loop-terminating conditions in FIRSTSPACE (line 7), the recursion is no more likely to "go infinite" than the loop (although careless programming can always bring this about).

Thirdly, compared with iteration, recursion tends not to produce code which executes particulary efficiently. Every procedure call implies another stack frame and set of local variables loaded onto the stack. This tends to eat up memory and also to slow down the program execution somewhat. On the other hand, recursion can be highly effective at write-time, producing concise, readable code which expresses the underlying algorithm clearly and elegantly. Proponents of recursion claim that recursive algorithms are more "natural" than their alternatives and certainly many mathematical relations may implicitly be expressed in recursive terms. Finally, once a programmer becomes accustomed to thinking along these lines, a recursive procedure is probably more "top-down" than its iterative equivalent in the sense that it usually requires less detailed analysis to realize a precise solution.

At run-time, the recursive mechanism depends heavily on the stack-oriented procedure call, as described in Chapter 7, to control the different levels of recurrence

and to ensure the proper returns. Of course the depth of
nesting possible depends on how much memory is available for
the stack to grow into. Some innocent-looking mathematical
recursive algorithms can nest to a fantastic depth very
rapidly so that any program containing procedure calls to
them runs out of memory and crashes.

Program ANAGRAM in Figure 9.2 is an example of a
slightly more complex recursive task which would be very
messy if tackled with iterative techniques. The idea is to
print out every permutation of the letters of a particular
input word (up to 10 characters). In the main program
(lines 30 - 40) the word is read in and its length

```
 1: PROGRAM ANAGRAM ;
 2: VAR I, LENGTH : INTEGER ;
 3:     LETTER, NEWWORD : ARRAY [1..10] OF CHAR ;
 4:     USED : ARRAY [1..10] OF BOOLEAN ;
 5: PROCEDURE PERMUTE (COUNTDOWN : INTEGER) ;
 6: VAR J : INTEGER ;
 7: BEGIN
 8:     IF COUNTDOWN = 0
 9:     THEN
10:     BEGIN
11:         WRITELN ;
12:         FOR I := LENGTH DOWNTO 1 DO
13:             WRITE (NEWWORD[I] )
14:     END
15:     ELSE
16:     BEGIN
17:         FOR J := 1 TO LENGTH DO
18:             BEGIN
19:                 IF NOT USED[J]
20:                 THEN
21:                 BEGIN
22:                     USED[J] := TRUE ;
23:                     NEWWORD[COUNTDOWN] := LETTER[J] ;
24:                     PERMUTE (COUNTDOWN - 1) ;
25:                     USED[J] := FALSE
26:                 END
27:             END
28:     END
29: END ; (* PERMUTE *)
30: BEGIN (* MAIN PROGRAM *)
31:     WRITE ('PLEASE TYPE IN YOUR WORD --) ') ;
32:     I := 0 ;
33:     REPEAT
34:         I := I + 1 ;
35:         USED[I] := FALSE ;
36:         READ (LETTER[I])
37:     UNTIL (I = 10) OR EOLN ;
38:     LENGTH := I -1 ;
39:     PERMUTE (LENGTH)
40: END .
```

Fig. 9.2. ANAGRAM

calculated. In line 40 the recursive procedure PERMUTE is
called. This procedure produces all the permutations
before it exits.

The algorithm hinges on the BOOLEAN array USED which
keeps track of which letters have already been used in the
current permutation -- the letters being held in LETTER in
their original order. The array NEWWORD is used to
accumulate the re-ordered letters one-by-one and the
re-ordering is achieved by recursively calling PERMUTE
(line 24) until every letter has been used (COUNTDOWN = 0)
at which point the escape clause (lines 9-14) is invoked,
printing out the current word and exiting. Control then
shifts back one level and one element of USED is
deallocated (line 25) and so on until a new permutation can
be formed. How far back control must go will depend on the
combined states of USED, J and COUNTDOWN but when all the
letters have been shuffled around to the original word,
control returns to the main program.

Program ANAGRAM has one recursive procedure. More
complicated is the situation where a procedure is required
to call a second procedure which in turn calls the first
procedure. Since a procedure can only be called if it is
on at most the same level or nested in the calling
procedure, the problem here arises as to which procedure to
declare first. The remedy lies in the Pascal facility to
make a "dummy" procedure declaration called a forward
reference. The format of a forward reference is as shown in
Figure 9.3.

This ploy provides the compiler with enough
information (i.e. the parameter list) to set up that part
of the stack frame which deals with communicating beyond
the scope of the procedure whilst FORWARD tells the
compiler to pick up the rest of the procedure when it is

```
1: PROCEDURE TRYAGAIN (PARAMETER LIST) ; FORWARD ;
2:
3: (* NO "BODY" FOLLOWS AS THIS IS THE FORWARD REFERENCE *)
4: PROCEDURE TRY (PARAMETER LIST) ;
5: BEGIN
6:     IF NOSUCCESS
7:     THEN TRYAGAIN (PARAMETERS)
8: END ;
9:
10: PROCEDURE TRYAGAIN ; (* NO PARAMETER LIST! *)
11: BEGIN (* BODY OF TRYAGAIN *)
12:     -
13:     - (* SOME CODE DEALING WITH NOSUCCESS *)
14:     -
15:     TRY (PARAMETERS)
16: END ;
17:
18: BEGIN (* MAIN PROGRAM *)
19:     TRY (PARAMETERS)
20: END .
```

Fig. 9.3. TRY and TRYAGAIN

next declared. Although the example is somewhat artificial, the necessity of the forward reference can be seen by considering the reaction of the compiler if the forward reference were omitted.

Dynamic Data Structures

At any point in a program the data which is being processed is normally held, either internally or externally, in one of the predefined data structures. Internally, the record is used to associate complex and varied data items together while an array offers the ability to contain a number of similar data items simultaneously and manipulate them at random. In a typical data processing application, therefore, the most flexible arrangement is probably an array of records since the bulk of the processing is likely to be concerned with manipulating matching fields within a group of records.

This is not as flexible as it might be, however. One problem is that the precise number of records needed in

memory at run-time is not necessarily known when the
program is written and will in any case vary from one run to
the next. The programmer must therefore declare the array
as large as the maximum number of records likely to be
required even though at least some of this space will be
wasted on most runs. For this reason, the array is known as
a static structure. Pascal is often criticized for not
providing for dynamic (i.e. run-time) allocation of array
space. In fact Pascal does provide a dynamic data type via
the pointer type. Instead of some particular variable (say a
record) being embedded in the stack, as with other
declarations, the pointer type declaration enables a
pointer variable to be placed in the stack, associating
(or binding) that pointer to the required data type (i.e. the
record). When the record is created (dynamically) the
memory locations will be allocated in a region of memory
known as the heap, and the starting address of the record
will be placed in the pointer variable on the stack. The
heap is usually located at the bottom of available memory
while the stack is located at the top. As the program
proceeds, the stack and heap grow towards one another, the
former as a result of successive procedure calls and
secondary processing; the latter as a result of the dynamic
 creation of new records -- see Figure 9.4. If the stack
and the heap touch, the program has run out of memory. The
pointer type is declared a follows:

    TYPE MARKERS =^DATATYPE
where MARKERS is the name of the pointer type and DATATYPE
is the name of the data type -- which need not be a record
-- to be dynamically allocated. The declaration

    VAR POINTER1, POINTER2, DUMMY : MARKERS ;
then binds the variable names POINTER1 etc. to the data type
DATATYPE. To initialise a pointer variable on the stack, a
value NIL is assigned. This is a reserved word indicating
that no address in the heap is being pointed to.

A variable of type DATATYPE may then be created by executing the statement

    NEW(POINTER1)

at which time the memory locations in the heap will be allocated and their starting address will be placed in POINTER1. Note that the variable has no name of its own and can only be referred to by means of POINTER1 as follows:

    POINTER1^.REFNUMBER := 301

MEMORY MAP

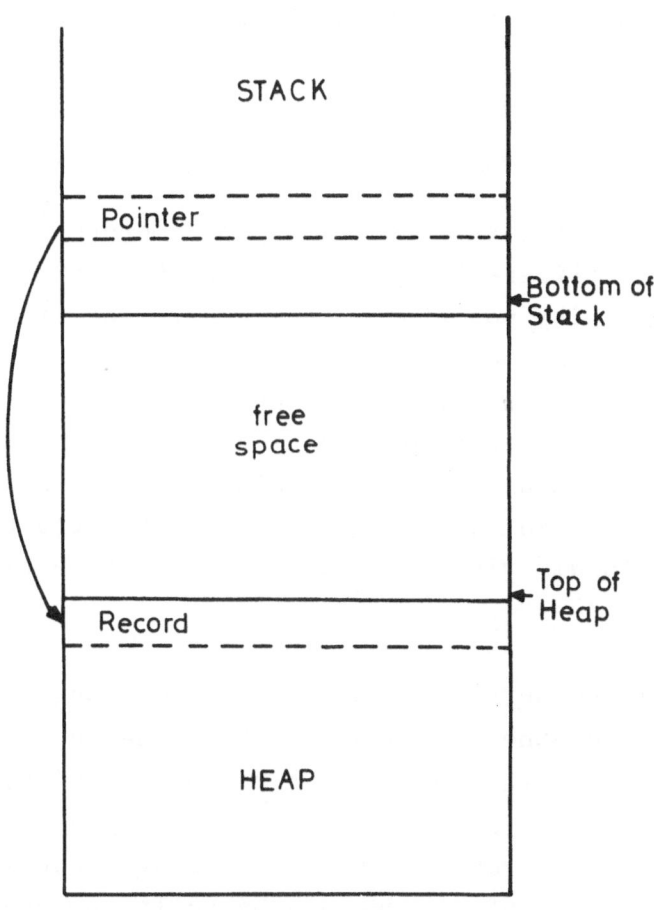

Fig. 9.4. Memory Map

assuming that DATATYPE is a record type and that an integer
field REFNUMBER has been declared.

In this way, a series of records may be built up in
the heap, each of which has its own pointer on the stack
through which it may be referenced. If extra pointers have
been declared (e.g. DUMMY) then one such record may have
more than one pointer pointing to it. So
    DUMMY := POINTER1
implies that DUMMY^ and POINTER1^ refer to the same record
on the heap. A record can be deallocated by
    POINTER2 := NIL
which means that the record will become inaccessible even
though the space on the heap will stay occupied. The
business of clearing up the deallocated regions of the heap
is known as "garbage collection" and is system dependent.

The advantage of using a heap is that different
records of the same type can easily be amended, enhanced or
sorted into a different order. In a static array a record
is accessed by its position in the array and if the elements
must be re-ordered, or one element eliminated say, a
considerable amount of manipulation is required. A dynamic
"array", on the other hand, can be created by defining an
array of pointers and re-ordered simply by redirecting the
pointers. Likewise, one record could be deleted by setting
its pointer to NIL without disturbing the other elements at
all.

A really powerful application can be brought about by
declaring one of the fields within the dynamic record as a
pointer type. By this means, one record in the heap can be
set up to reference another record simply by assigning its
pointer to the relevant field in the first record. In this
way, a linked list of records can be built up, consisting

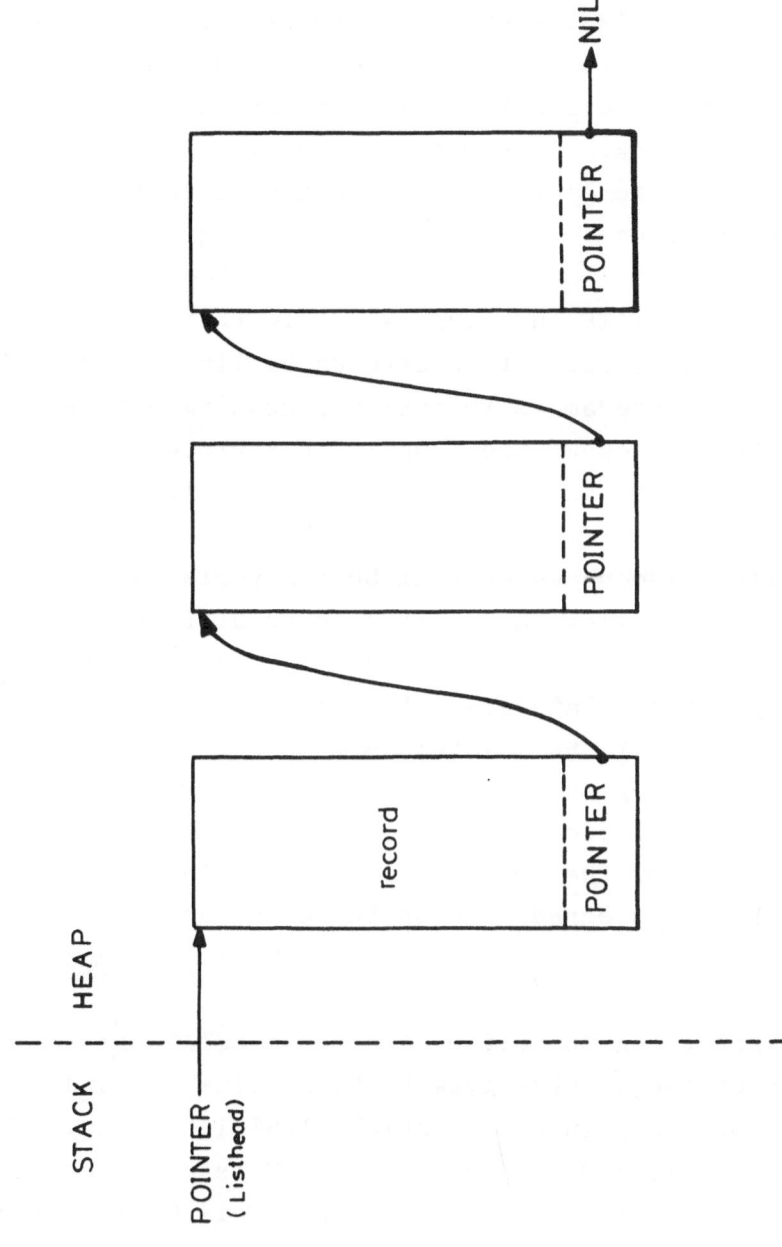

Fig. 9.5. Linked List

of a set of records whose structure (i.e. order) is defined
implicitly by the sequence of pointer fields rather than
explicitly by some static format arbitrarily declared at
compile-time. The last element of the linked list must
always have its pointer field set to NIL and the first
element (and only the first) will be referenced by a
pointer in the stack. Thus one pointer in the stack,
sometimes called the listhead, grants access to the entire
structure of records in the heap   -- see Figure 9.5.

Program ESTATE in Figure 9.6 illustrates some of
the data handling capabilities offered by linked lists. The
purpose of this program is to assist a housing estate
manager to keep track of the tenants in a block of flats.
Initially, the flats are created as a linked list of
records, called FLAT, in the heap. (FLAT is an example of
a variant field record which will be fully discussed in the
next section.) As flats are allocated to different people,
the relevant fields in FLAT are updated, and as families
move out the vacant flats are returned to the pool. Thus
two linked lists will be maintained -- one consisting of
the empty flats, beginning with the one that has been
vacant longest; the second containing the occupied flats in
alphabetic order of the tenants' surnames. Individual
flats will be transferred between these two as the occasion
arises.

The first thing to notice in program ESTATE is the
declaration of the pointer type POINTER (line 10) and the
declaration of the pointer variables FIRSTFILLED etc. as
type POINTER in line 22. The record FLAT is declared in
lines 14 to 21 and line 17 declares the field NEXT as a
field of type POINTER. It is this mechanism which allows
the linked list to be formed since the address of the next
flat will be stored in NEXT.

In order to make the program both interactive and
complete, the main program offers the user a MENU of
different options (lines 45-53) including:
  INITIALISE -- which "commissions" the block to
  start with;
  MOVEIN and MOVEOUT -- which manipulate the flats
  between the two linked lists;
  FREEFLATS and TENANTLIST -- which offer the user
  the opportunity of listing the vacant or occupied
  flats at any time.

Procedure INITIALISE (lines 64-84) constructs the
entire linked list once the number of flats is known (line
68). First, two listhead pointers are initialised (69 and
70) and a record of type FLAT is created in line 73. Then
the relevant data are assigned to the fields of the
variable LINK^ (74-82). Note the two pointer assignments
on lines 76 and 81. NEXT is the pointer field within the
record so that the first time through, NEXT is set to NIL and
this record will always be the last record in the list. In
line 84, the pointer to this record (LINK) is assigned to
FIRSTFREE so that when the next record is created, this
value can be placed into its NEXT field (line 79 again).
The second record is thus linked to the first.

Procedure MOVEIN is designed to allow a predefined
number of flats to be allocated to families. In order to
do this a second linked list is formed although no new FLAT
records will be created. Instead, some of the links in the
current vacant list will be broken and new ones forged to
build up a list of occupied flats. Procedure FINDFLAT
(90-99) tests for the first vacant flat and, if one is
there, passes its pointer address to the pointer NEXTFLAT
(line 97) so that when the next procedure, FILLFLAT
(100-143), needs the flat record it has merely to reference

```
 1: PROGRAM ESTATE ;
 2: TYPE DATE = RECORD
 3:       DAY : 1..31 ;
 4:       MONTH : 1..12 ;
 5:       YEAR : INTEGER
 6:       END ;
 7:  (* DATE *)
 8:       NAME = ARRAY [1..20] OF CHAR ;
 9:       OCCUPATION = (VACANT, FILLED) ;
10:       POINTER = ↑FLAT ;
11:       FAMILY = RECORD
12:           SURNAME : NAME ; SIZE : 1..20
13:           END ; (* FAMILY *)
14:       FLAT = RECORD
15:           NUMBER : INTEGER ;
16:           ROOMS : 1..10 ;
17:           NEXT : POINTER ;
18:           CASE STATUS : OCCUPATION OF
19:               VACANT : (LASTDATE : DATE) ;
20:               FILLED : (TENANTS : FAMILY)
21:           END ; (* FLAT *)
22: VAR FIRSTFILLED, FIRSTFREE, LINK : POINTER ;
23:       CHOICE : INTEGER ; NEWDATE : DATE ;
24: PROCEDURE STREADLN (VAR N : NAME) ;
25: VAR I, J : INTEGER ;
26: BEGIN
27:     READLN ;
28:     I := 0 ;
29:     REPEAT
30:         I := I + 1 ;
31:         READ(N[I])
32:     UNTIL EOLN OR (I=20) ;
33:     FOR J := I+1 TO 20 DO
34:         N[J] := ' '
35: END ; (* STREADLN *)
36: FUNCTION LENGTH(N : NAME) : INTEGER ;
37: VAR I : INTEGER ;
38: BEGIN
39:     I := 20 ;
40:     WHILE (I>0) AND (N[I] = ' ') DO
41:         I := I-1 ;
42:     LENGTH := I
43: END ; (* LENGTH *)
44:
45: PROCEDURE MENU ;
46: BEGIN
47:     WRITELN('0.   EXIT FROM THIS PROGRAM.') ;
48:     WRITELN('1.   SET UP A NEW ESTATE.') ;
49:     WRITELN('2.   MOVE NEW TENANTS IN.') ;
50:     WRITELN('3.   MOVE TENANTS OUT.') ;
51:     WRITELN('4.   SEE FREE FLATS.') ;
52:     WRITELN('5.   SEE LIST OF TENANTS.')
53: END ; (* MENU *)
54: PROCEDURE GETDATE ;
55: BEGIN
56:     WITH NEWDATE DO
57:     BEGIN
58:         WRITE('DAY ---> ') ; READ(DAY) ;
59:         WRITE('MONTH ---> ') ; READ(MONTH) ;
60:         WRITE('YEAR ---> ') ; READ(YEAR)
61:     END
62: END ; (* GETDATE *)
63:
64: PROCEDURE INITIALISE ;
65: VAR NUM, I : INTEGER ;
66: BEGIN
67:     GETDATE ;
68:     WRITE('NUMBER OF FLATS ---> ') ; READLN (NUM) ;
69:     FIRSTFILLED := NIL ;
70:     FIRSTFREE := NIL ;
```

```
71:     FOR I := 1 TO NUM DO
72:     BEGIN
73:         NEW(LINK) ;
74:         WITH LINK↑ DO
75:         BEGIN
76:             NEXT := FIRSTFREE ;
77:             WRITE('FLAT NUMBER---> ') ; READ (NUMBER) ;
78:             WRITE('NUMBER OF ROOMS---> ') ; READ(ROOMS) ;
79:             STATUS := VACANT ;
80:             LASTDATE := NEWDATE ;
81:             FIRSTFREE := LINK
82:         END
83:     END
84: END ; (* INITIALISE *)
85: PROCEDURE MOVEIN ;
86: VAR I, NUM : INTEGER ;
87:     FOUND : BOOLEAN ;
88:     NEXTFAMILY : FAMILY ;
89:     NEXTFLAT, PREVIOUSLINK : POINTER ;
90: PROCEDURE FINDFLAT ;
91: BEGIN
92:     IF FIRSTFREE = NIL
93:     THEN FOUND := FALSE
94:     ELSE
95:     BEGIN
96:         FOUND := TRUE ;
97:         NEXTFLAT := FIRSTFREE
98:     END
99: END ;
100: PROCEDURE FILLFLAT ;
101: PROCEDURE SETPOINTERS ;
102: VAR CONTINUE : BOOLEAN ;
103: FUNCTION BEFORE(N1, N2 : NAME ; P : INTEGER) : BOOLEAN ;
104: BEGIN
105:     IF P = LENGTH(N2)
106:     THEN BEFORE := FALSE
107:     ELSE IF P = LENGTH(N1)
108:         THEN BEFORE := TRUE
109:         ELSE IF ORD(N2[P]) < ORD(N1[P])
110:             THEN BEFORE := FALSE
111:             ELSE IF ORD(N1[P]) < ORD(N2[P])
112:                 THEN BEFORE := TRUE
113:                 ELSE BEFORE := BEFORE(N1, N2, P+1)
114: END ; (* BEFORE *)
115: BEGIN (* SETPOINTERS *)
116:     LINK := FIRSTFILLED ;
117:     PREVIOUSLINK := FIRSTFILLED ;
118:     CONTINUE := LINK <> NIL ;
119:     WHILE CONTINUE DO
120:     BEGIN
121:         IF BEFORE(NEXTFAMILY.SURNAME, LINK↑.TENANTS.SURNAME, 1)
122:         THEN CONTINUE := FALSE
123:         ELSE
124:         BEGIN
125:             CONTINUE := LINK <> NIL ;
126:             PREVIOUSLINK := LINK ;
127:             LINK := LINK↑.NEXT
128:         END
129:     END ;
130:     FIRSTFREE := NEXTFLAT↑.NEXT ; (* TAKE FLAT OFF FREE LIST *)
131:     NEXTFLAT↑.NEXT := LINK ; (* LINK NEW FLAT INTO OCCUPIED LIST *)
132:     IF (FIRSTFILLED = NIL) OR (PREVIOUSLINK=LINK)
133:     THEN FIRSTFILLED := NEXTFLAT
134:     ELSE PREVIOUSLINK↑.NEXT := NEXTFLAT
135: END ; (* SETPOINTERS *)
136: BEGIN (* FILLFLAT *)
137:     WITH NEXTFLAT↑ DO
138:     BEGIN
139:         STATUS := FILLED ;
140:         TENANTS := NEXTFAMILY ;
```

```
141:            SETPOINTERS
142:        END
143: END ; (* FILLFLAT *)
144: BEGIN (* MOVEIN *)
145:        WRITE ('HOW MANY NEW TENANTS---) ') ;
146:        READ (NUM) ;
147:        FOR I := 1 TO NUM DO
148:        BEGIN
149:            WITH NEXTFAMILY DO
150:                BEGIN
151:                    WRITE('SURNAME---) ') ; STREADLN(SURNAME) ;
152:                    WRITE('SIZE---) ') ; READ(SIZE) ;
153:                    FINDFLAT ;
154:                    IF FOUND
155:                    THEN FILLFLAT
156:                    ELSE WRITELN('CAN''T BE DONE.')
157:                END
158:        END
159: END ; (* MOVEIN *)
160: PROCEDURE MOVEOUT ;
161: VAR LASTNAME : NAME ;
162:     FOUND : BOOLEAN ;
163:     I, NUM : INTEGER ;
164:     EMPTYFLAT : POINTER ;
165: PROCEDURE EVICTIFTHERE ( VAR EMPTYFLAT, LINK : POINTER ) ;
166: BEGIN
167:     FOUND := TRUE ;
168:     IF LINK = NIL
169:     THEN FOUND := FALSE
170:     ELSE
171:     BEGIN
172:         IF LINK↑.TENANTS.SURNAME = LASTNAME
173:         THEN
174:         BEGIN
175:             EMPTYFLAT := LINK ;
176:             LINK := LINK↑.NEXT
177:         END
178:         ELSE EVICTIFTHERE (EMPTYFLAT, LINK↑.NEXT)
179:     END
180: END ; (* EVICTIFTHERE *)
181: PROCEDURE TIDYUP (VAR LINK : POINTER ; EMPTYFLAT : POINTER) ;
182: BEGIN
183:     IF LINK = NIL
184:     THEN
185:     BEGIN
186:         LINK := EMPTYFLAT ;
187:         LINK↑.NEXT := NIL ;
188:         LINK↑.STATUS := VACANT ;
189:         LINK↑. LASTDATE := NEWDATE
190:     END
191:     ELSE TIDYUP (LINK↑.NEXT, EMPTYFLAT)
192: END ; (* TIDYUP *)
193: BEGIN (* MOVEOUT *)
194:     GETDATE ;
195:     WRITE ('HOW MANY FAMILIES ARE LEAVING -->') ;
196:     READ (NUM) ;
197:     FOR I := 1 TO NUM DO
198:     BEGIN
199:         WRITE('WHAT IS THE SURNAME OF THE FAMILY THAT ARE LEAVING -->') ;
200:         STREADLN (LASTNAME) ;
201:         EVICTIFTHERE (EMPTYFLAT, FIRSTFILLED) ;
202:         IF FOUND
203:         THEN TIDYUP (FIRSTFREE, EMPTYFLAT)
204:         ELSE WRITELN (LASTNAME, ' DON''T LIVE HERE.')
205:     END
206: END ; (MOVEOUT)
207:
208: PROCEDURE FREEFLATS ;
209: BEGIN
210:     WRITELN ('FLAT NUMBER          ROOMS') ;
```

```
211:      LINK := FIRSTFREE ;
212:      WHILE LINK () NIL DO
213:      BEGIN
214:          WRITELN(LINK↑.NUMBER, '              ' , LINK↑.ROOMS) ;
215:          LINK := LINK↑.NEXT
216:      END
217: END ; (FREEFLATS)
218: PROCEDURE TENANTLIST ;
219: BEGIN
220:      WRITELN('NAME           FLAT NUMBER') ;
221:      LINK := FIRSTFILLED ;
222:      WHILE LINK () NIL DO
223:      BEGIN
224:          WRITELN (LINK↑.TENANTS.SURNAME, LINK↑.NUMBER) ;
225:          LINK := LINK↑.NEXT
226:      END
227: END ; (* TENANTLIST *)
228:
229: BEGIN (* MAIN PROGRAM *)
230:      REPEAT
231:      MENU ;
232:      WRITE ('YOUR CHOICE --) ') ; READ(CHOICE) ;
233:      WRITELN ; WRITELN ; WRITELN ;
234:      IF (CHOICE)5) OR (CHOICE(0) THEN CHOICE := 0 ;
235:      CASE CHOICE OF
236:          0 : WRITELN('GOOD BYE') ;
237:          1 : INITIALISE ;
238:          2 : MOVEIN ;
239:          3 : MOVEOUT ;
240:          4 : FREEFLATS ;
241:          5 : TENANTLIST
242:      END ; (* CASE *)
243:      WRITELN ; WRITELN ; WRITELN
244:      UNTIL CHOICE = 0
245: END .
```

Fig. 9.6. ESTATE

NEXTFLAT^ (line 137). FILLFLAT, however, also has the tricky
job of linking the new flat into the list of occupied flats
so that the tenants' names are in alphabetical order. This
is done in SETPOINTERS (102-135) with the help of the
BOOLEAN function BEFORE (105 and 107) which returns the value
TRUE provided that the first string passed to it (N1) comes
before the second (N2), taken alphabetically. BEFORE is a
recursive function (line 113) which calls itself as long as
there are stll uninspected characters left in the string
(tested for in lines 105 and 107) and as long as
corresponding characters in the two strings (referenced by
the INTEGER P) are identical (checked in lines 109 and
111). Note the use of the Pascal standard function ORD
which maps its argument (which must be a character) onto a
set of integers, one for each character in the character
set.

SETPOINTERS itself is an example of the ease with which a linked list can be used. Line 118 (and 125) ensures that the search loop will run until the end of the list is reached, if necessary. Line 127 drives the search through the list by redirecting the search pointer (LINK) to the record indicated by the current record's pointer field. Once the correct place in the list has been found, control moves to the final sequence of SETPOINTERS (130-134), where the new flat is detached from the list of vacant flats, its link pointer being assigned the address of the next record up the list while its address is passed to the pointer field of the last record down the list (or the listhead pointer if necessary). Procedure MOVEOUT (160-206) performs the opposite process, searching out specified occupied flats and removing them from the list (EVICTIFTHERE lines 165-180) and ensuring that the flat that has been vacant longest will be the first to be filled (TIDYUP lines 181-192). Further use is made of recursion in EVICTIFTHERE and TIDYUP, demonstrating how concisely a linked list may be traversed (lines 178 and 191). In comparison the procedures FREEFLATS and TENANTLIST access the same lists but iteratively. Note how EVICTIFTHERE deletes a record, pinpointing the flat to be cleared in line 175 and excluding it from the list by linking its immediate neighbours together in line 176.

Variant field records

It is a frequent occurrence that the data one wishes to associate together in one record will not fit conveniently into any fixed record format. For these occasions Pascal provides a means of building variants into the record declaration so that a portion of the record can contain alternative (and different) formats depending on the nature of the items in the fixed part of the record.

An example of this feature appears in the program in
Figure 9.6. The information required in the record of a
vacant flat (e.g. date last occupied) is quite different
from the information needed for an occupied flat (name of
tenants and size of family). Consequently, in the record
declaration of FLAT (lines 14 - 21) the first few fields
are common to both types of flat but at line 18 some sort
of split has to be made. This is done by means of a CASE
statement which must enumerate the different possibilities
open at this point. The format for such a variant field
declaration is as follows:

```
CASE tag field : type OF
     const1 : (fields of const1) ;
     const2 : (fields of const2) ;
     --
     --
```

Note that there is no "END" reserved word to close off the
case statement. The tag field is a variable (common to all
records) which acts as a selector, picking out the
appropriate variant format. In ESTATE the tag field is
STATUS (line 18) which can be either VACANT (implying a
variant field named LASTDATE) or FILLED (implying TENANTS).

When a record is assigned (e.g. lines 137-142), as
soon as STATUS is defined, the required variant field is
selected and can itself be subsequently assigned. If
STATUS is altered (lines 139 and 188) the new variant is
automatically switched in and overwrites the previous data.
Note that a record type may only contain one set of variant
fields (i.e. one CASE statement) although record types
(with their own variant fields) may be nested within the
variations. Figure 9.7 contains the syntax diagrams for
both pointer types and record field variants.

Conclusion

The use of recursion and linked lists may affect a
programmer's style as profoundly as the use of the control
and data structrures dealt with in earlier chapters. Any
technique which can contribute to the creation of concise
programs will repay the effort required to grasp it.

Exercise 1: Desk-run PERMUTE on your favourite four letter
word. Keep track of NEWWORD, USED, J and COUNTDOWN,
especially COUNTDOWN, which provides a measure of the depth
to which PERMUTE has been called.

Exercise 2: No one would use a program like ESTATE because
as soon as the machine is switched off, all the data would
be lost. Write procedures to dump both lists onto disc
files at the end of each day and to build up a new heap
from the same disc files when the system is booted up the
next morning.

Exercise 3: Modify FINDFLAT so that it finds the first
vacant flat in the list with sufficient rooms to provide at
least one room per person.

157

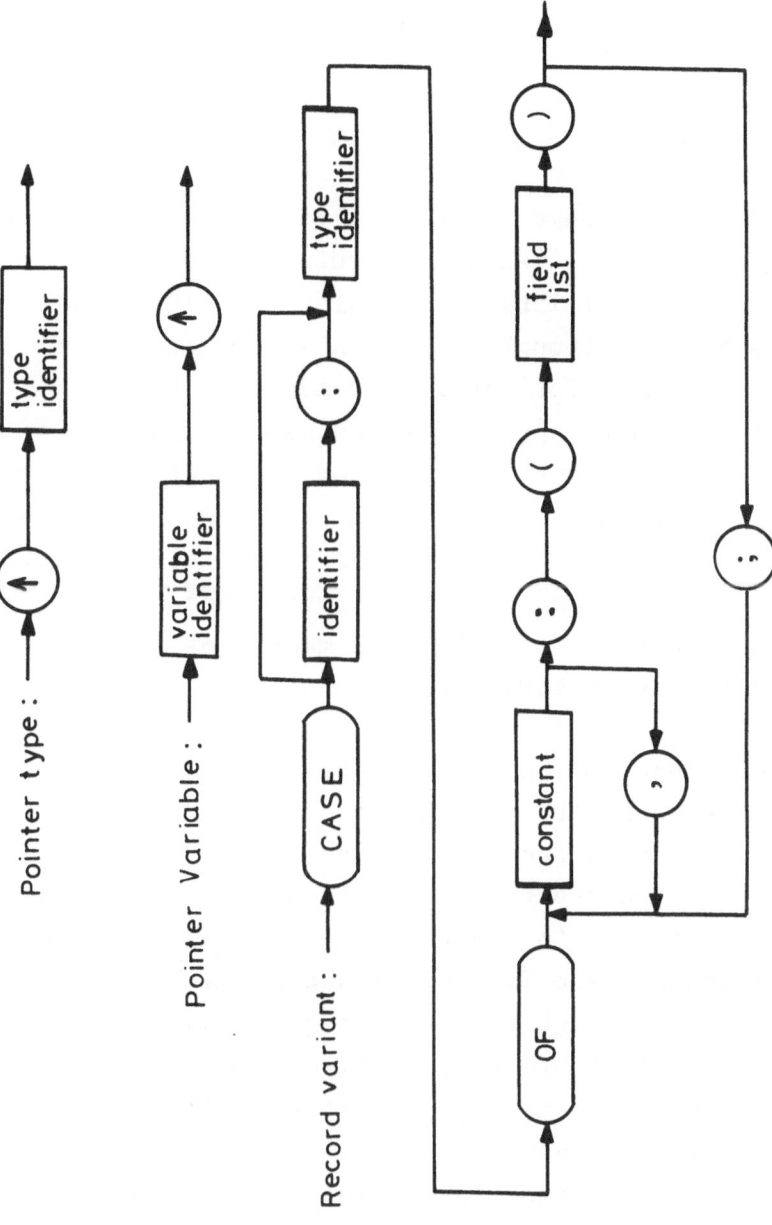

Fig. 9.7. Syntax Diagrams for POINTERS and RECORD VARIANTS

Chapter 10. The Finishing Touches

Programming languages should be viewed in evolutionary terms -- from low level languages (which are close to the machine) to high level languages (which are close to the programmer's mode of thought); from highly specialised languages constructed for particular machines or applications to general purpose languages designed to adapt to a variety of environments; and from languages offering easy access for the beginner to others that seem to promote the idea of a programmer as an esoteric specialist. In this context, Pascal was seen to be high level, general purpose and ideal for teaching -- it being a member of the "structured" family of languages.

From this description one would expect Pascal to be readable in the sense that variables can be given sensible names, that verbs give some indication of the actions they perform and that the program as a whole flows in a logical way; it should be easy to see what is going on at any given point. These aspects are implied by the words "high-level" and "structured" although they also require some effort and discipline on the part of the programmer who is trying for these ideals. At the same time, the term "general purpose" implies that the full range of programming features is available to the experienced programmer whilst the term "teaching" means not only that the language will encourage the beginner to adopt the structured programming strategies but also that simple working programs should be obtainable from a small subset of the language. In a language like

FORTRAN, mathematical statements can be written out almost "off the page" but the input/output instructions are so complex that the simplest program will often frustrate the beginner. BASIC, on the other hand, was designed for beginners.

Of course all this attention to making life easier for the programmer imposes great strains on the computer system and some high level structured languages are justifiably infamous for the "overhead" which they impose in terms of the amount of memory required, the execution times possible and the amount of secondary activity (e.g. compilation etc.) required to deliver the source code into executable form. Anyone used to these languages and thinking of switching to Pascal will probably regret the lack of some favourite feature. Among the features missing the definition of Standard Pascal are dynamic allocation of arrays (useful for general purpose matrix handling procedures), random access files, concurrent control structures (to allow two or more processes to be executed simultaneously), the capability to attach a set of operators tonewly defined data structures, restrictions on placement of declarations and the absence of a loop with the exit in the middle. Probably any scientific programmer would do without variant records in order to get dynamic arrays, while the commercial programmer is unlikely to think of Pascal as a serious alternative if it doesn't have random access files.

At the cost of these more unusual general-purpose features and with a certain spirit of compromise, Pascal succeeds in being reasonably frugal in terms of overheads when compared with other structured languages. To some mainframe programmers these concessions place Pascal in the lightweight category in the language stakes but it is just these features which make Pascal so suitable for

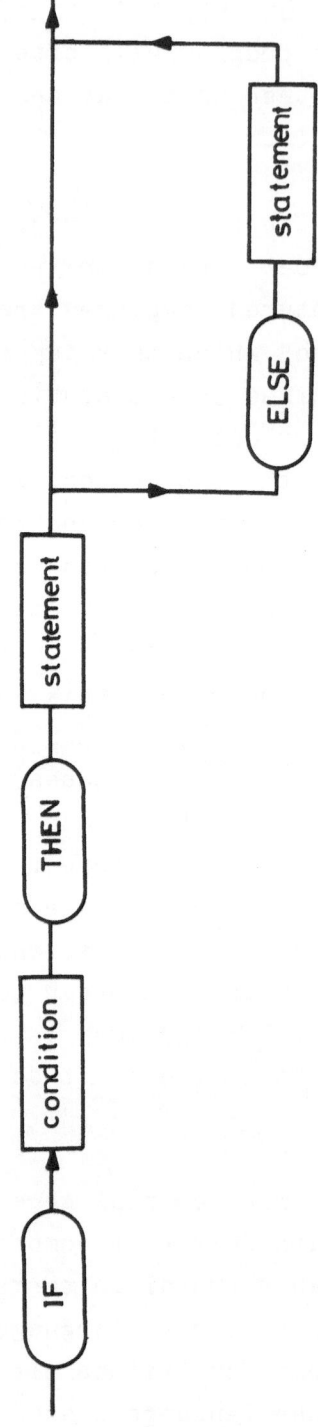

Fig. 10.1. Syntax Diagram for IF-THEN-ELSE

implementation on microcomputers and thus worthy of
consideration here.

The major method employed by the designers of Pascal to
achieve this machine efficiency has been through a very
tightly written compiler. Throughtout this book the aim has
been to help the reader develop an appreciation for (and
relationship with) this compiler. In order to help
implementers produce standard compilers rapidly, Wirth's
team wrote and made freely available three compilers
(written predominantly in Pascal) for Pascal. The first is
an officially recognized subset of Pascal called Pascal S,
the second is for standard Pascal while the third is for an
extended version of the language. The standard compiler
generates a pseudo machine code called P-code which can be
translated into machine code with much less effort than
Pascal.

Wirth's syntax diagrams are a visual representation of
the manner in which a compiler tackles source code, and can
thus be used as an aid to minimize syntactic error. The
syntax diagram in Figure 10.1 is a means of expressing what
the compiler expects to see and therefore reflects the way
code is actually laid out in the machine at compile time.
In contrast the flow diagram in Figure 10.2 is a way of
showing how program control will move (i.e. which code will
be executed) at run time. Pascal usually allows for the
production of sufficiently descriptive source code as to
make a visual representation of the program flow
unnecessary.

One device that Wirth adopts to reduce overheads is
the help that the compiler requires of the user. Thus the
declaration of all the variable names and and data types
before the action part of any procedure begins makes it much
easier for the compiler to allocate the working space for

162

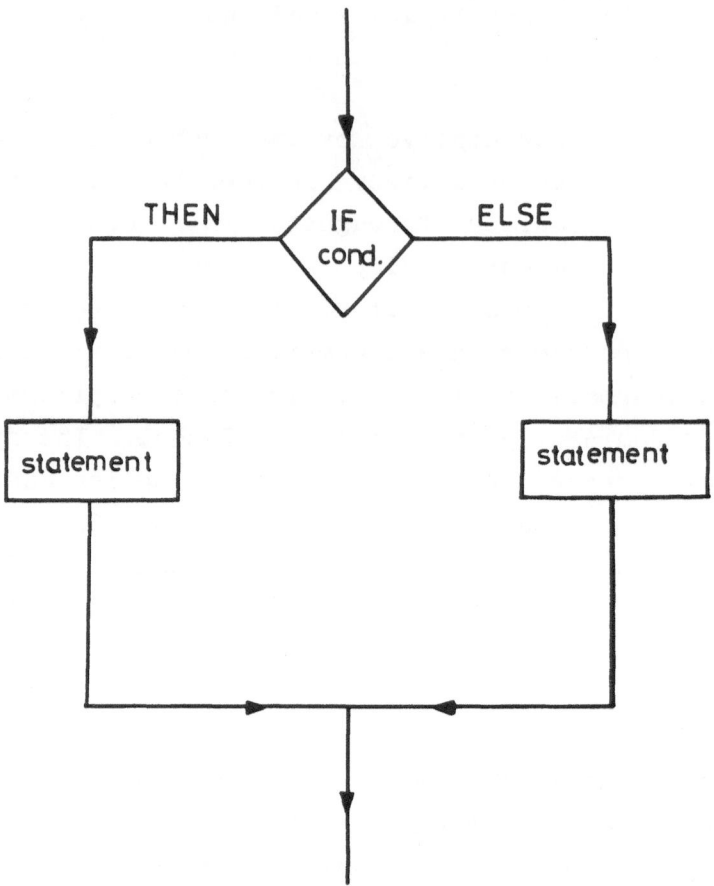

Fig. 10.2. Flow Diagram for IF-THEN-ELSE

that procedure and at the same time makes a clear
distinction between the data and the algorithmic portions
of the procedure. Similarly, the existence of reserved
words cuts the work of the compiler considerably at the
expense of a small degree of flexibility in the selection
of variable names.

The GOTO Statement

A GOTO statement is an instruction which transfers
controls from the current position to another specified

point in the program. This is a simple device which is
essential in many programming languages although it does tend
to break up the flow of control and make it more difficult
to follow. Since structured languages have been designed
to provide readable source code and since they are so
richly endowed with less abrupt methods of redirecting the
flow of control (using loops and branches), the use of the
GOTO statement is not generally necessary and is never
encouraged. Nevertheless, circumstances can occur,
particularly in dealing with error conditions, where the GOTO
statement is the most effective alternative and so it is
presented here for the sake of completeness.

In Pascal the GOTO reserved word is followed by an
unsigned integer called a label. On execution, control
will shift to the statement to which the same unsigned
integer refers (see Figure 10.3). Of course, each label
used must be declared in the declaration part of the
procedure so that the compiler can cope with the sudden
shifts in control. Each label can only be used once in the
block in which it is declared although it can be referenced
by any number of GOTO statments from anywhere within the
block. If one procedure is nested within another it is
incorrect to jump into the inside procedure, since it takes
a procedure call to set up the stack frame and pass
parameters etc. It is, however, possible to jump out of the
inside procedure although it is bad practice to leave a
procedure from two different points; the exiting GOTO
statement should be as close to the procedure END as
possible.

In fact UCSD does not allow any movement between
procedures via the GOTO statement at all, and there is even
a switch to disable the statement completely ... i.e. the
compiler will flag a GOTO as an error. This is done to
discourage student users from producing inadequately planned

GOTO Statement declaration

declaration

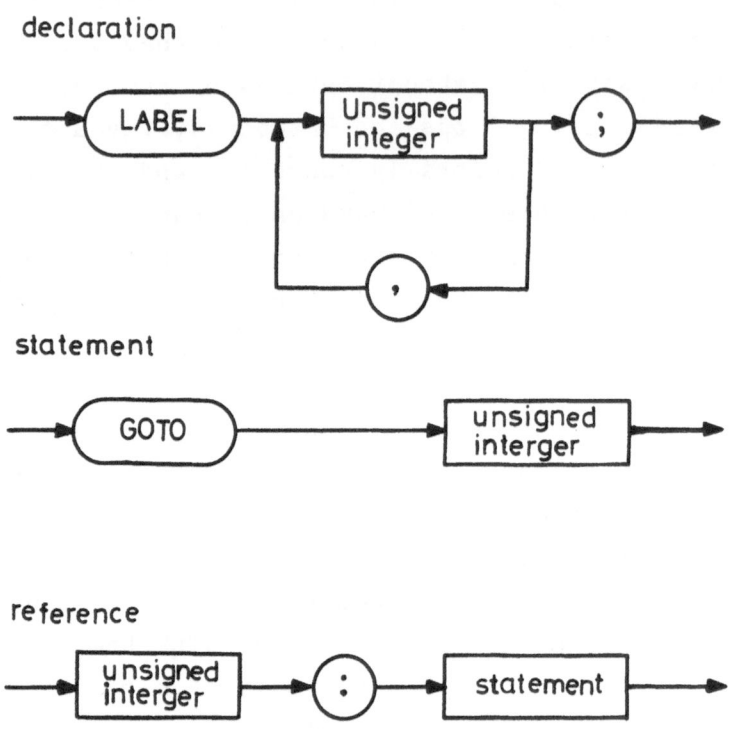

statement

reference

Fig. 10.3. Syntax Diagram for GOTO construct

programs where the GOTO is used to escape from the deadends
into which they program themselves.

Procedures as Parameters

    Pascal provides one facility which can be extremely
useful to programmers who may need to manipulate
mathematical functions. Instead of passing an array of
values to a procedure which is to perform some particular
operation on this data, Pascal allows the use of a function
identifier as a value parameter in the argument list. This

is clearly more efficient provided that the results of the
evaluation of the function in question are not required at
other points in the program.

    A simple illustration of this technique is a graph
plotting routine which plots out a set of y versus x
values. One method of achieving this is for one process to
pass an array of x and y values to the routine which then
simply plots them out. Consider however, the procedure call
    PROCEDURE PLOTGRAPH (FUNCTION FUNC : REAL ;
    XDOM, XMIN, XORIGIN : REAL; POINTS : INTEGER) ;
for plotting Y=FUNC(X) versus X over the domain XMIN to
XMIN+XDOM with the axes crossing at (XORIGIN, YORIGIN) and
with checks made for asymptotes etc. Then the calls
    PLOTGRAPH(SIN,1,0,0,0,100) and
    PLOTGRAPH(BESSELJ1,10,0,0,0,50)
will produce the corresponding graphs (provided the Bessel
function is defined).

Conclusion

    It is difficult to pinpoint what makes programming the
enjoyable activity it can be. Certainly, it has more to do
with doing than with reading and the authors hope that this
text will not have intruded into the reader's programming
time. Perhaps it has something to do with how easy the
language is to use with skill and versatility, in which
case, perhaps Pascal is a good candidate.

    Appendix A contains a brief language summary and a few
of the more useful syntax diagrams. It remains only to
wish the reader Happy Programming and may all your loops
terminate.

Appendix A. Language Summary

1. Standard Indentifiers

constants	FALSE	TRUE	
data types	BOOLEAN	CHAR	INTEGER
	REAL	(STRING)	TEXT
files	INPUT	OUTPUT	(INTERACTIVE)

2. Reserved Words

AND	ARRAY	BEGIN	CASE
CONST	DIV	DO	DOWNTO
ELSE	END	FILE	FOR
FORWARD	FUNCTION	GOTO	IF
IN	LABEL	MOD	NIL
NOT	OF	OR	PACKED
PROCEDURE	PROGRAM	RECORD	REPEAT
SET	THEN	TO	TYPE
UNTIL	VAR	WHILE	WITH

3. Standard Procedures (f=filename, x=identifier)

arithmetic procedures	ABS(x)	ARCTAN(x)
	COS(x)	EXP(x)
	LN(x)	SIN(x)
	SQR(x)	SQRT(x)
Boolean functions	EOF(f)	EOLN(f)
	ODD(x)	
data manipulation	CHR(x)	ORD(x)
	PRED(x)	ROUND(x)
	SUCC(x)	TRUNC(x)
file handling	GET(f)	PUT(f)

SYNTAX DIAGRAM FOR STATEMENT

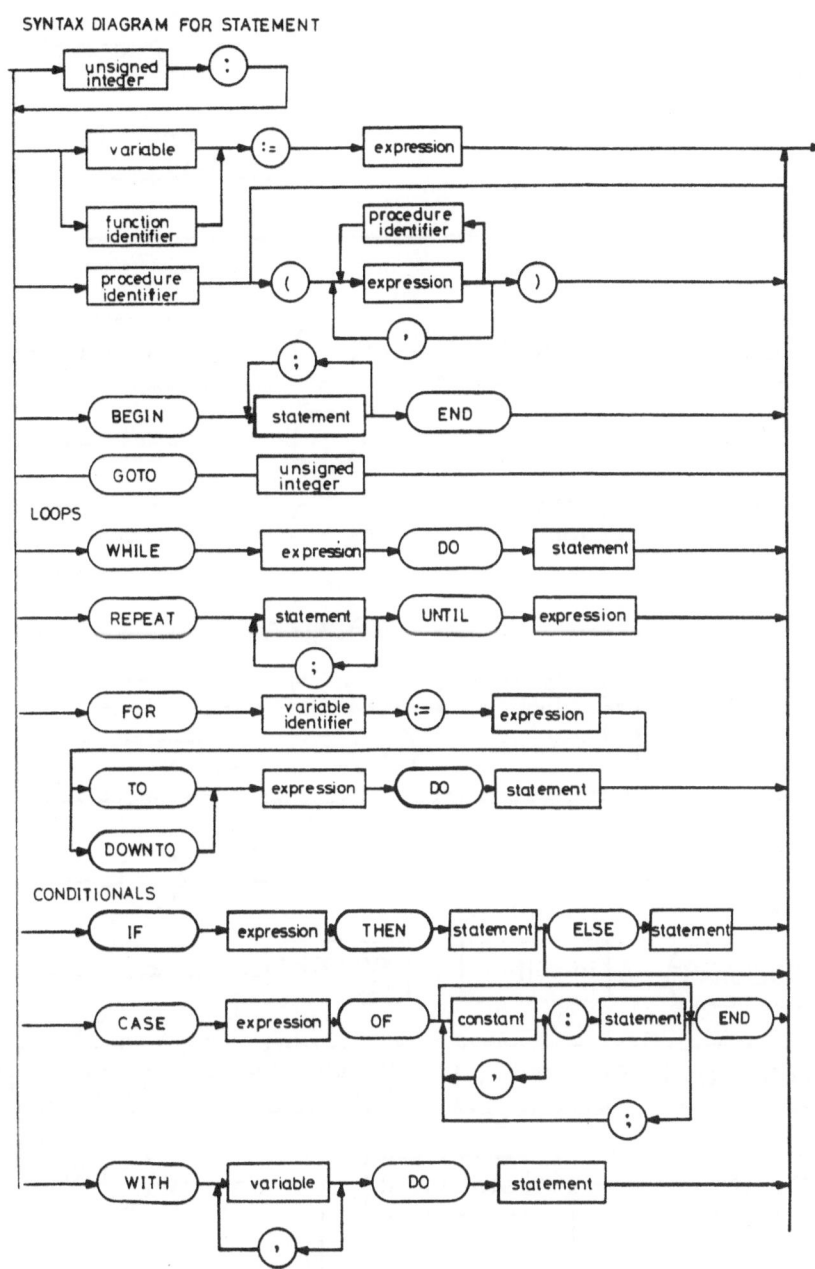

Fig. A.1. Complete Syntax Diagram for STATEMENT

BLOCK

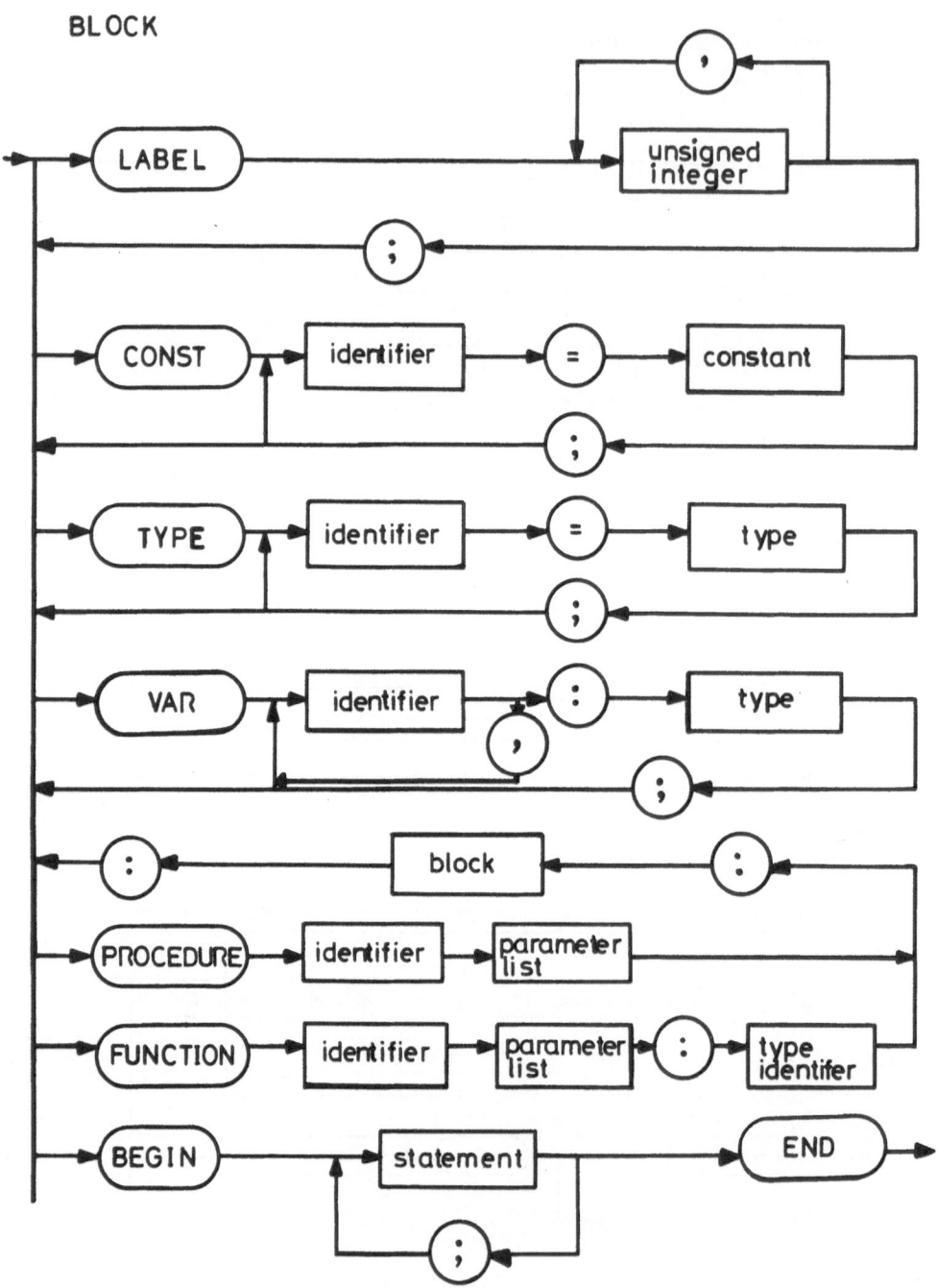

Fig. A.2. Complete Syntax Diagram for BLOCK

	RESET(f)	REWRITE(f)
	READ(f,x)	READLN(f,x)
others	WRITE(f,x)	WRITELN(f,x)
	DISPOSE(x)	NEW(x)
	PACK(x)	UNPACK(x)

Appendix B. Complete Program Listings

```
1: PROGRAM REPAYMENTS ;
2: VAR MIN, MAX, LOAN, REPAY, AMOUNTDUE, YEARS : INTEGER ;
3:     INTERESTRATE : REAL ;
4: PROCEDURE GETINPUTS;(*READ INTEREST RATE,NUM OF YEARS, MIN AND MAX LOANS*)
5: CONST IMIN = 2 ; IMAX =50 ;
6:       YMIN = 5 ; YMAX = 35 ;
7:       LMIN = 5 ; LMAX = 200 ;
8:
9: PROCEDURE GETINTEREST ; (* READS IN INTEREST RATE BETWEEN IMIN AND IMAX
10:                              AND CONVERTS IT TO A DECIMAL *)
11: BEGIN
12:     WRITELN('TYPE IN THE RATE OF INTEREST AS A PERCENTAGE.') ;
13:     REPEAT
14:         WRITE('A NUMBER BETWEEN ' , IMIN, ' AND ', IMAX, '--)' ) ;
15:         READLN(INTERESTRATE)
16:     UNTIL (INTERESTRATE)=IMIN) AND (INTERESTRATE(=IMAX) ;
17:     INTERESTRATE := INTERESTRATE/100 ; (* % --) DECIMAL *)
18: END ;
19:
20: PROCEDURE GETYEARS;(*READS DURATION OF LOAN BETWEEN YMIN AND YMAX YEARS*)
21: BEGIN
22:     WRITELN('TYPE IN THE NUMBER OF YEARS FOR WHICH MORTGAGE WILL RUN. ') ;
23:     REPEAT
24:         WRITE('A NUMBER BETWEEN ', YMIN, ' AND ', YMAX, '--)') ;
25:         READLN(YEARS)
26:     UNTIL (YEARS)=YMIN) AND (YEARS(=YMAX)
27: END ; (* GETYEARS *)
28:
29: PROCEDURE GETMIN ; (* READS, IN THOUSANDS, THE MINIMUM LOAN VALUE BETWEEN
30:                          LMIN AND LMAX AND CONVERTS IT TO POUNDS *)
31: VAR LOANMIN : INTEGER ;
32: BEGIN
33:     WRITELN('TYPE IN THE SMALLEST MORTGAGE YOU ARE INTERESTED IN,',
34:         'IN THOUSANDS.') ;
35:     REPEAT
36:         WRITE('A NUMBER BETWEEN ', LMIN, ' AND ', LMAX, '--)') ;
37:         READLN(LOANMIN)
38:     UNTIL (LOANMIN)=LMIN) AND (LOANMIN(=LMAX) ;
39:     MIN := LOANMIN*1000
40: END ; (* GETMIN *)
41:
42: PROCEDURE GETMAX ; (* LIKE GETMIN, BUT FOR THE MAXIMAL LOAN VALUE *)
43: VAR LOANMAX : INTEGER ;
44: BEGIN
45:     WRITELN ('TYPE IN THE LARGEST MORTGAGE YOU ARE INTERESTED IN, ' ,
46:         'IN THOUSANDS.') ;
47:     REPEAT
48:         WRITE('A NUMBER BETWEEN ', MIN DIV 1000, ' AND ', LMAX, '--)') ;
49:         READLN(LOANMAX)
50:     UNTIL (LOANMAX )MIN DIV 1000) AND (LOANMAX (=LMAX) ;
51:     MAX := LOANMAX*1000
52: END ; (* GETMAX *)
```

```
53: BEGIN (* GETINPUTS *)
54:     GETINTEREST ;
55:     GETYEARS ;
56:     GETMIN ;
57:     GETMAX
58: END ; (* GETINPUTS *)
59:
60: PROCEDURE PRINTHEADINGS ; (* PRINT OUT INTEREST RATE, NUMBER OF YEARS
61:                              AND TABLE HEADINGS *)
62: CONST SPACE = '                    ' ;
63: BEGIN
64:     WRITELN ; WRITELN ;
65:     WRITELN(SPACE, '**MONTHLY MORTGAGE REPAYMENTS**') ;
66:     WRITELN(SPACE, '--------- -------- -------------') ;
67:     WRITELN ;
68:     WRITELN('INTEREST RATE=',100*INTERESTRATE,'% OVER ', YEARS, ' YEARS');
69:     WRITELN('    LOAN      REPAYMENTS') ;
70:     WRITELN('    ----      ----------')
71: END ; (* PRINTHEADINGS *)
72:
73: PROCEDURE CALCULATEREPAY ; (* WORK OUT MONTHLY REPAYMENTS *)
74: VAR TOTALMONTHS : INTEGER ;
75:     MONTHLYINTERESTRATE, AMOUNTDUE : REAL ;
76: PROCEDURE TRYREPAY ; (* WORK OUT THE ACTUAL AMOUNT A GIVEN
77:     REPAYMENT WILL ACTUALLY PAY OFF *)
78: VAR MONTH : INTEGER ;
79: BEGIN (* CALCULATEREPAY *)
80:     FOR MONTH := 1 TO TOTALMONTHS DO
81:         AMOUNTDUE := (AMOUNTDUE - REPAY)*(1 + MONTHLYINTERESTRATE)
82: END ; (* TRYREPAY *)
83: BEGIN (* CALCULATEREPAY *)
84:     MONTHLYINTERESTRATE := INTERESTRATE/12 ;
85:     TOTALMONTHS := 12*YEARS ;
86:     REPAY := LOAN DIV TOTALMONTHS ;
87:     REPEAT
88:         AMOUNTDUE := LOAN ;
89:         REPAY := REPAY + 1 ;
90:         TRYREPAY
91:     UNTIL AMOUNTDUE(=0
92: END ; (* CALCULATEREPAY *)
93:
94: BEGIN (* MAIN PROGRAM *)
95:     GETINPUTS;
96:     PRINTHEADINGS ;
97:     LOAN := MIN ;
98:     WHILE LOAN (= MAX DO
99:     BEGIN
100:         CALCULATEREPAY ;
101:         WRITELN('    ', LOAN, '      ', REPAY) ;
102:         LOAN := LOAN + 1000
103:     END
104: END . (* REPAYMENTS *)
```

```
 1: PROGRAM OTHELLO ;
 2: CONST SCREENHEIGHT = 16 ;
 3: TYPE ROWNUM = '1'..'8' ;
 4:      COLCHAR = 'A'..'H' ;
 5:      DIR = (N, NE, E, SE, S, SW, W, NW) ;
 6:      MOVE = (FIRST, SECOND, EMPTY) ;
 7: VAR NOUGHT, CROSS : ARRAY[1..10] OF CHAR ;
 8:      BOARD : ARRAY[ROWNUM, COLCHAR] OF MOVE ;
 9:      MOVER, TARGET : MOVE ;
10:      COUNTER : 0..60 ;
11:      ROWNOW : ROWNUM ;
12:      COLNOW : COLCHAR ;
13:      ANSWER : CHAR ;
14:      LEGAL, GAMEOVER, NOMORE, PASS, FINISHED : BOOLEAN ;
15:      DIRECTION : DIR ;
16:      FLIPCOUNTER : ARRAY[DIR] OF 0..8 ;
17:
18: PROCEDURE WRITECROSS ;
19: VAR I : INTEGER ;
20: BEGIN
21:      FOR I := 1 TO 10 DO WRITE(CROSS[I])
22: END ; (* WRITECROSS *)
23:
24: PROCEDURE WRITENOUGHT ;
25: VAR I : INTEGER ;
26: BEGIN
27:      FOR I := 1 TO 10 DO WRITE(NOUGHT[I])
28: END ; (* WRITENOUGHT *)
29:
30: PROCEDURE INSTRUCTIONS ; (* PRINTS OUT RULES OF OTHELLO *)
31: PROCEDURE SCREEN1 ;
32: BEGIN
33:      WRITELN('OTHELLO IS A BOARD GAME PLAYED BETWEEN TWO PLAYERS. EACH ') ;
34:      WRITELN('PLAYER HAS A DIFFERENT COLOURED COUNTER. THE PLAYERS START') ;
35:      WRITELN('WITH TWO COUNTERS.EACH IN THE CENTRAL FOUR SQUARES OF THE') ;
36:      WRITELN('BOARD. THE FIRST PLAYER MUST PLACE A COUNTER IN AN EMPTY') ;
37:      WRITELN('SQUARE ADJACENT TO AN OCCUPIED SQUARE IN SUCH A WAY THAT ') ;
38:      WRITELN('AT LEAST ONE OF THE OPPENENT''S COUNTERS LIES BETWEEN THE ') ;
39:      WRITELN('CURRENT COUNTER AND ANOTHER OF HIS COUNTERS IN A STRAIGHT ') ;
40:      WRITELN('LINE DRAWN HORIZONTALLY, VERTICALLY, OR DIAGONALLY ACROSS') ;
41:      WRITELN('THE BOARD. ALL OF THE OPPONENTS COUNTERS SO ''SANDWICHED''') ;
42:      WRITELN('BECOME CAPTURED. THAT IS THEY CHANGE COLOUR.') ;
43:      WRITELN
44: END ; (* SCREEN1 *)
45: PROCEDURE SCREEN2 ;
46: BEGIN
47:      WRITELN('AS THE NUMBER OF COUNTERS BUILDS UP MORE AND MORE HAVE TO') ;
48:      WRITELN('BE SWAPPED IN EACH MOVE, SO OTHELLO IS CLEARLY A TEDIOUS') ;
49:      WRITELN('GAME TO PLAY BY HAND. THIS IMPLEMENTATION USES ''O'' AND ') ;
50:      WRITELN('''X'' TO REPRESENT THE DIFFERENT COLOURS AND EMPLOYS A') ;
51:      WRITELN('STANDARD A-H, 1-8 CHESSBOARD CONVENTION. THE PLAYER WITH') ;
52:      WRITELN('THE GREATER NUMBER OF COUNTERS AT THE END OF THE GAME') ;
53:      WRITELN('WINS. A PLAYER MAY BE FORCED TO PASS IF NO EMPTY SQUARE') ;
54:      WRITELN('EXISTS WHICH IS ADJACENT TO AN OPPONENT''S SQUARE') ;
55:      WRITELN('IN A LINE CONTAINING ONE OF HIS OWN.') ;
56:      WRITELN;
57: END ; (* SCREEN2 *)
58:
59: BEGIN (* INSTRUCTIONS *)
60:      SCREEN1 ;
61:      WRITE ('PLEASE PRESS RETURN TO SEE THE REST OF THE INSTRUCTIONS.') ;
62:      READLN ;
63:      SCREEN2 ;
64:      WRITE('PLEASE PRESS RETURN WHEN YOU ARE READY TO PLAY.') ;
65:      READLN
66: END ; (* INSTRUCTIONS *)
67:
68: PROCEDURE IDENTIFY ; (* ASKS FOR THE PLAYERS NAMES *)
69: VAR I : INTEGER ;
70: BEGIN
```

```
71:      FOR I := 1 TO 10 DO
72:      BEGIN
73:          CROSS[I] := ' ' ;
74:          NOUGHT[I] := ' '
75:      END ;
76:      WRITE('WHO''S GOING TO HAVE THE FIRST MOVE--)') ;
77:      I := 1 ;
78:      REPEAT
79:          READ(CROSS[I]) ;
80:          I := I + 1
81:      UNTIL EOLN OR (I)10) ;
82:      READLN ;
83:      WRITE('RIGHT ') ; WRITECROSS ; WRITELN( ' YOUR SYMBOL IS ''X''') ;
84:      WRITE('WHO''S NEXT--)') ;
85:      I := 1 ;
86:      REPEAT
87:          READ(NOUGHT[I]) ;
88:          I := I + 1
89:      UNTIL EOLN OR (I)10) ;
90:      WRITE('THANKS ') ; WRITENOUGHT ; WRITELN( 'MAY THE BEST PLAYER WIN!')
91: END ; (* IDENTIFY *)
92:
93: PROCEDURE STARTGAME ; (* INITIALIZES GAME BOARD *)
94: VAR ROW : ROWNUM ;
95:     COL : COLCHAR ;
96: BEGIN
97:      FOR ROW := '1' TO '8' DO
98:          FOR COL := 'A' TO 'H' DO
99:              BOARD[ROW, COL] := EMPTY ;
100:     BOARD['4', 'D'] := FIRST ;
101:     BOARD['4', 'E'] := SECOND ;
102:     BOARD['5', 'D'] := SECOND ;
103:     BOARD['5', 'E'] := FIRST ;
104:     COUNTER := 0 ;
105:     GAMEOVER := FALSE ;
106:     MOVER := FIRST
107: END ; (* STARTGAME *)
108:
109: PROCEDURE PRINTBOARD ; (* DISPLAYS CURRENT GAME BOARD *)
110: CONST TAB = '          ' ; (* 10 SPACES *)
111:       SPACE = '  ' ; (* 2 SPACES *)
112: VAR ROW : ROWNUM ;
113:     COL : COLCHAR ;
114:     I : INTEGER ;
115: BEGIN
116:     FOR I := 1 TO SCREENHEIGHT - 10 DO WRITELN ;
117:     WRITE(TAB, '   ') ;
118:     FOR COL := 'A' TO 'H' DO WRITE(SPACE, COL) ; (* COL. TITLES *)
119:     FOR ROW := '1' TO '8' DO
120:     BEGIN
121:         WRITELN  ;
122:         WRITE(TAB, ROW, SPACE) ; (* ROW TITLES *)
123:         FOR COL := 'A' TO 'H' DO
124:         BEGIN
125:             CASE BOARD[ROW, COL] OF
126:                 EMPTY : WRITE (SPACE, '.') ;
127:                 FIRST : WRITE (SPACE, 'X') ;
128:                 SECOND : WRITE (SPACE, 'O') ;
129:             END (* CASE *)
130:         END
131:     END
132: END ; (* PRINTBOARD *)
133:
134: PROCEDURE GETMOVE ; (* REQUESTS AND VALIDATES MOVE *)
135: VAR CORRECT : BOOLEAN ;
136:
137: PROCEDURE ASKFORMOVE ; (* REQUESTS APPROPRIATE MOVE *)
138: BEGIN
139:     WRITELN ;
140:     IF MOVER = FIRST
```

```
141:     THEN BEGIN WRITECROSS ; WRITE('''S MOVE --) ') END
142:     ELSE BEGIN WRITENOUGHT ; WRITE(' ''S MOVE --) ') END
143: END ; (* ASKFORMOVE *)
144:
145: PROCEDURE GETINPUT ;
146: VAR COLIN, ROWIN : BOOLEAN ;
147:     RANGE : SET OF CHAR ;
148:     RESPONSE : ARRAY[1..2] OF CHAR ;
149:     I : 1..2 ;
150:
151: PROCEDURE DETAILEDCHECK ; (* TESTS FOR AND ACCEPTS LEGAL MOVE *)
152: BEGIN
153:     FOR I := 1 TO 2 DO
154:         CASE RESPONSE[I] OF
155:             '1','2','3','4','5','6','7','8' : BEGIN
156:                                                 ROWNOW := RESPONSE|I| ;
157:                                                 ROWIN := TRUE
158:                                               END ;
159:             'A','B','C','D','E','F','G','H' : BEGIN
160:                                                 COLNOW := RESPONSE|I| ;
161:                                                 COLIN := TRUE
162:                                               END
163:         END ; (* CASE *)
164:         IF COLIN AND ROWIN
165:         THEN
166:         BEGIN
167:             IF BOARD[ROWNOW, COLNOW] = EMPTY
168:             THEN CORRECT := TRUE
169:             ELSE WRITELN('BAD MOVE - TRY AGAIN')
170:         END
171:         ELSE WRITELN( 'BAD MOVE - TRY AGAIN')
172: END ; (* DETAILED CHECK *)
173:
174: BEGIN (* GETINPUT *)
175:     COLIN := FALSE ;
176:     ROWIN := FALSE ;
177:     PASS := FALSE ;
178:     CORRECT := FALSE ;
179:     RANGE :=['1','2','3','4','5','6','7','8',
180:             'A','B','C','D','E','F','G','H','P'] ;
181:     READ(RESPONSE[1]) ; READ(RESPONSE[2]) ;
182:     IF RESPONSE[1]='P'
183:     THEN
184:     BEGIN
185:         CORRECT := TRUE ;
186:         PASS := TRUE
187:     END
188:     ELSE
189:         IF (RESPONSE[1] IN RANGE) AND (RESPONSE[2] IN RANGE)
190:         THEN DETAILEDCHECK
191:         ELSE WRITELN('IMPOSSIBLE MOVE - TRY AGAIN')
192: END ; (* GETINPUT *)
193:
194: BEGIN (* GETMOVE *)
195:     ASKFORMOVE ;
196:     REPEAT
197:         GETINPUT
198:     UNTIL CORRECT
199: END ; (* GETMOVE *)
200:
201:
202: PROCEDURE CHECKMOVE ;
203: VAR ROW : ROWNUM ;
204:     COL : COLCHAR ;
205:
206: PROCEDURE CHOOSESQUARE ; (* CHOOSE NEXT SQUARE FOR EXAMINATION *)
207: BEGIN
208:     CASE DIRECTION OF
209:         N : IF ROW='1' THEN FINISHED := TRUE ELSE ROW := PRED(ROW) ;
210:         NE : IF (ROW='1') OR (COL='H') THEN FINISHED := TRUE
```

```
211:                                              ELSE
212:                                              BEGIN
213:                                                   ROW := PRED(ROW) ;
214:                                                   COL := SUCC(COL)
215:                                              END ;
216:            E : IF COL = 'H' THEN FINISHED := TRUE
217:                        ELSE COL := SUCC(COL) ;
218:            SE : IF (ROW = '8') OR (COL = 'H') THEN FINISHED := TRUE
219:                    ELSE
220:                    BEGIN
221:                         ROW := SUCC(ROW) ;
222:                         COL := SUCC(COL)
223:                    END ;
224:            S : IF ROW = '8' THEN FINISHED := TRUE ELSE ROW := SUCC(ROW) ;
225:            SW : IF (ROW = '8') OR (COL = 'A') THEN FINISHED := TRUE
226:                                              ELSE
227:                                              BEGIN
228:                                                   ROW := SUCC(ROW) ;
229:                                                   COL := PRED(COL)
230:                                              END ;
231:            W : IF COL = 'A' THEN FINISHED := TRUE ELSE COL := PRED(COL) ;
232:            NW : IF (ROW = '1') OR (COL ='A') THEN FINISHED := TRUE
233:                                              ELSE
234:                                              BEGIN
235:                                                   ROW := PRED(ROW) ;
236:                                                   COL := PRED(COL)
237:                                              END
238:        END (* CASE *)
239: END ; (* CHOOSESQUARE *)
240:
241: PROCEDURE CHECKIT ; (* EXAMINE SQUARE *)
242: BEGIN
243:      IF BOARD[ROW, COL] = TARGET
244:      THEN FLIPCOUNTER[DIRECTION] := FLIPCOUNTER[DIRECTION] + 1
245:      ELSE
246:      BEGIN
247:          FINISHED := TRUE ;
248:          IF BOARD[ROW, COL] = MOVER
249:          THEN BEGIN IF FLIPCOUNTER[DIRECTION] > 0 THEN LEGAL := TRUE END
250:          ELSE FLIPCOUNTER[DIRECTION] := 0 (* EMPTY *)
251:      END
252: END ; (* CHECKIT *)
253: BEGIN (* CHECKMOVE *)
254:      LEGAL := FALSE ;
255:      IF MOVER = FIRST
256:      THEN TARGET := SECOND
257:      ELSE TARGET := FIRST ;
258:      FOR DIRECTION := N TO NW DO
259:      BEGIN
260:          FINISHED := FALSE ;
261:          FLIPCOUNTER[DIRECTION] := 0 ;
262:          ROW := ROWNOW ;
263:          COL := COLNOW ;
264:          REPEAT
265:             CHOOSESQUARE ;
266:             IF FINISHED (** EDGE REACHED **)
267:             THEN FLIPCOUNTER[DIRECTION] := 0
268:             ELSE CHECKIT
269:          UNTIL FINISHED
270:      END
271: END ; (* CHECKMOVE *)
272:
273: PROCEDURE FLIPS ;
274: VAR I : INTEGER ;
275:      ROW : ROWNUM ;
276:      COL : COLCHAR ;
277:
278: PROCEDURE NEXTSQUARE ; (* CHOOSE NEXT SQUARE FOR EXAMINATION *)
279: BEGIN
280:      CASE DIRECTION OF
```

```
281:          N : IF ROW='1' THEN FINISHED := TRUE ELSE ROW := PRED(ROW) ;
282:          NE : IF (ROW='1') OR (COL='H') THEN FINISHED := TRUE
283:                                          ELSE
284:                                          BEGIN
285:                                              ROW := PRED(ROW) ;
286:                                              COL := SUCC(COL)
287:                                          END ;
288:          E : IF COL = 'H' THEN FINISHED := TRUE
289:                           ELSE COL := SUCC(COL) ;
290:          SE : IF (ROW = '8') OR (COL = 'H') THEN FINISHED := TRUE
291:                    ELSE
292:                    BEGIN
293:                        ROW := SUCC(ROW) ;
294:                        COL := SUCC(COL)
295:                    END ;
296:          S : IF ROW = '8' THEN FINISHED := TRUE ELSE ROW := SUCC(ROW) ;
297:          SW : IF (ROW = '8') OR (COL = 'A') THEN FINISHED := TRUE
298:                                          ELSE
299:                                          BEGIN
300:                                              ROW := SUCC(ROW) ;
301:                                              COL := PRED(COL)
302:                                          END ;
303:          W : IF COL =·'A' THEN FINISHED := TRUE ELSE COL := PRED(COL) ;
304:          NW : IF (ROW = '1') OR (COL ='A') THEN FINISHED := TRUE
305:                                          ELSE
306:                                          BEGIN
307:                                              ROW := PRED(ROW) ;
308:                                              COL := PRED(COL)
309:                                          END
310:      END (* CASE *)
311: END ; (* NEXTSQUARE *)
312:
313: BEGIN
314:     BOARD[ROWNOW, COLNOW] := MOVER ;
315:     FOR DIRECTION := N TO NW DO
316:     BEGIN
317:         ROW := ROWNOW ;
318:         COL := COLNOW ;
319:         FOR I := 1 TO FLIPCOUNTER[DIRECTION] DO
320:         BEGIN
321:             NEXTSQUARE ;
322:             BOARD[ROW, COL] := MOVER
323:         END
324:     END
325: END ; (* FLIPS *)
326:
327: PROCEDURE GIVESCORE ;
328: VAR COL : COLCHAR ;
329:     ROW : ROWNUM ;
330:     FIRSTCOUNT, SECONDCOUNT : 0..60 ;
331: BEGIN
332:     PRINTBOARD ;
333:     FIRSTCOUNT := 0 ;
334:     SECONDCOUNT := 0 ;
335:     FOR ROW := '1' TO '8' DO
336:         FOR COL := 'A' TO 'H' DO
337:             IF BOARD[ROW, COL] = FIRST
338:             THEN FIRSTCOUNT := FIRSTCOUNT + 1
339:             ELSE SECONDCOUNT := SECONDCOUNT + 1 ;
340:     WRITELN ;
341:     WRITECROSS ; WRITELN( '            ', FIRSTCOUNT) ;
342:     WRITENOUGHT ; WRITELN( '            ', SECONDCOUNT) ;
343:     IF FIRSTCOUNT = SECONDCOUNT
344:     THEN WRITELN('IT''S A TIE')
345:     ELSE IF FIRSTCOUNT ) SECONDCOUNT
346:          THEN BEGIN WRITECROSS ; WRITELN(' WINS') END
347:          ELSE BEGIN WRITENOUGHT ; WRITELN(' WINS') END
348: END ; (* GIVESCORE *)
349:
350: PROCEDURE ANOTHERGO ;
```

```
351: VAR CONTINUE : CHAR ;
352: BEGIN
353:     WRITE('WOULD YOU LIKE ANOTHER GAME? TYPE Y OR N--) ') ;
354:     READLN(CONTINUE) ;
355:     IF CONTINUE = 'Y'
356:     THEN NOMORE := FALSE
357:     ELSE NOMORE := TRUE
358: END ; (* ANOTHERGO *)
359:
360: BEGIN (* MAIN PROGRAM *)
361:     WRITE('DO YOU WANT TO READ THE INSTRUCTIONS? TYPE Y OR N--)') ;
362:     READLN(ANSWER) ;
363:     IF ANSWER = 'Y' THEN  INSTRUCTIONS ;
364:     IDENTIFY ;
365:     REPEAT
366:     STARTGAME ;
367:         WHILE NOT GAMEOVER DO
368:         BEGIN
369:             REPEAT
370:                 PRINTBOARD ;
371:                 GETMOVE ;
372:                 IF PASS THEN LEGAL := TRUE ELSE CHECKMOVE
373:             UNTIL LEGAL ;
374:             IF NOT PASS
375:             THEN
376:             BEGIN
377:                 FLIPS ;
378:                 COUNTER := COUNTER + 1
379:             END ;
380:             IF MOVER = FIRST
381:             THEN MOVER := SECOND
382:             ELSE MOVER := FIRST ;
383:             IF COUNTER = 60
384:             THEN GAMEOVER := TRUE
385:         END ;
386:         GIVESCORE ;
387:         ANOTHERGO
388:     UNTIL NOMORE
389: END.
```

```
 1: PROGRAM PROFF ;
 2:
 3: CONST MAXLINE = 80 ;
 4:
 5: TYPE FORMAT = RECORD
 6:                    NUMBER : BOOLEAN ;
 7:                    FILL : BOOLEAN ;
 8:                    JUSTIFY : BOOLEAN ;
 9:                    PAGENUMBER : INTEGER ;
10:                    INDENT : 0 .. MAXLINE ;
11:                    LEFTMARGIN : 0 .. MAXLINE ;
12:                    RIGHTMARGIN : 0 ..  MAXLINE ;
13:                    LINES : INTEGER ;
14:                    SPACING : 1 .. 10
15:                  END ;
16:
17:     STRING = ARRAY[1..MAXLINE] OF CHAR ;
18:
19:
20: VAR INFILENAME, OUTFILENAME : STRING ;
21:     INFILE, OUTFILE : TEXT ;
22:
23: FUNCTION LENGTH (S:STRING) : INTEGER ;
24: VAR TEMP : 0..MAXLINE ;
25:     FOUND : BOOLEAN ;
26: BEGIN
27:     TEMP := MAXLINE ;
28:     FOUND := FALSE ;
29:     WHILE (TEMP>0) AND NOT FOUND DO
30:       IF S[TEMP] = ' '
31:       THEN TEMP := TEMP - 1
32:       ELSE FOUND := TRUE ;
33:     LENGTH := TEMP
34: END ; (* LENGTH *)
35:
36:
37: PROCEDURE STREADLN (VAR S : STRING ) ;
38: VAR I, J: 1..MAXLINE ;
39: BEGIN
40:     I := 1 ;
41:     READLN ;
42:     REPEAT
43:       READ(S[I]) ;
44:       I := I + 1
45:     UNTIL EOLN ;
46:     FOR J := 1 TO MAXLINE DO S[J] := ' '
47: END ; (* STREADLN *)
48:
49: PROCEDURE STWRITE (S:STRING) ;
50: VAR I, J : 1 .. MAXLINE ;
51: BEGIN
52:     IF LENGTH(S)>0
53:     THEN    FOR I := 1 TO LENGTH(S) DO
54:                   WRITE(S[I])
55: END ; (* STWRITE *)
56:
57: PROCEDURE COPY(SOURCE:STRING ;VAR DESTINATION:STRING; INDEX,SIZE:INTEGER);
58: VAR I, J : 1 .. MAXLINE ;
59: BEGIN
60:     FOR I := 1 TO SIZE DO
61:     BEGIN
62:         J := INDEX + I -1 ;
63:         DESTINATION[I] := SOURCE[J]
64:     END ;
65:     FOR I := SIZE + 1 TO MAXLINE DO
66:         DESTINATION[I] := ' '
67: END ; (* COPY *)
68:
69: PROCEDURE DELETE (VAR DESTINATION : STRING ; INDEX, SIZE : INTEGER) ;
70: VAR I : 0 .. MAXLINE ;
```

```
71: BEGIN
72:     FOR I := INDEX + SIZE TO MAXLINE DO
73:     BEGIN
74:         DESTINATION[I-SIZE] := DESTINATION[I] ;
75:         DESTINATION[I] := ' '
76:     END ;
77:     FOR I := 0 TO SIZE - 1 DO
78:         DESTINATION[MAXLINE - I] := ' '
79: END ; (* DELETE *)
80:
81:
82: PROCEDURE INSERT(SOURCE:STRING ; VAR DESTINATION:STRING ; INDEX:INTEGER) ;
83: VAR I, SIZE : 1..MAXLINE ;
84: BEGIN
85:     SIZE := LENGTH(SOURCE) ;
86:     IF SIZE + LENGTH(DESTINATION) > MAXLINE
87:     THEN WRITELN ('STRING OVERFLOW -- INSERTION NOT MADE')
88:     ELSE
89:     BEGIN
90:         IF LENGTH(DESTINATION) >= INDEX
91:         THEN FOR I := LENGTH(DESTINATION) DOWNTO INDEX DO
92:             DESTINATION [I+SIZE] := DESTINATION [I] ;
93:         FOR I := 1 TO SIZE DO
94:             DESTINATION[INDEX + (I-1)] := SOURCE[I]
95:     END
96: END ; (* INSERT *)
97:
98: PROCEDURE FREADLN (VAR INFILE : TEXT ; VAR BUFFER : STRING) ;
99: (* READLN INTO BUFFER FROM INFILE *)
100: VAR I, J : INTEGER ;
101: BEGIN
102:     REPEAT
103:         READLN(INFILE) ;
104:         I := 1 ;
105:         REPEAT
106:             READ(INFILE, BUFFER[I]) ;
107:             I := I + 1
108:         UNTIL EOLN(INFILE)
109:     UNTIL EOF(INFILE) OR (LENGTH(BUFFER) > 0) ;
110:     FOR J := I TO MAXLINE DO BUFFER[J] := ' '
111: END ; (* FREADLN *)
112:
113: PROCEDURE FWRITELN (VAR OUTFILE : TEXT ; BUFFER : STRING) ;
114: (* WRITELN BUFFER TO OUTFILE *)
115: VAR I, J : 1..MAXLINE ;
116: BEGIN
117:     FOR I := 1 TO LENGTH(BUFFER) DO WRITE (OUTFILE, BUFFER[I]) ;
118:     WRITELN (OUTFILE)
119: END ; (* FWRITELN *)
120:
121: PROCEDURE TEXTFORMAT ;
122: (* READS FROM INFILE, FORMATS AND WRITES FORMATTED TEXT TO OUTFILE *)
123:
124: VAR USERFORMAT : FORMAT ;
125:     INBUFFER, OUTBUFFER : STRING ;
126:     EMPTYINBUFFER, EMPTYOUTBUFFER : BOOLEAN ;
127:     CURRENTLINE : INTEGER ;
128:
129: PROCEDURE STANFORMAT ( VAR FORM : FORMAT ) ;
130: BEGIN
131:     WITH FORM DO
132:     BEGIN
133:         NUMBER := TRUE ;
134:         FILL := TRUE ;
135:         JUSTIFY := TRUE ;
136:         PAGENUMBER := 2 ;
137:         INDENT := 0 ;
138:         LEFTMARGIN := 0 ;
139:         RIGHTMARGIN := 60 ;
140:         LINES := 58 ;
```

```
141:        SPACING := 1
142:     END
143: END ;
144:
145: PROCEDURE FLUSH (VAR BUFFER : STRING) ;
146: (* OUTPUTS SPACING BLANK LINES, FLUSHES BUFFER AND FILLS WITH SPACES *)
147: VAR I : 1..MAXLINE ;
148: PROCEDURE LINESPACING ;
149: VAR I : 2 .. 10 ;
150: BEGIN
151:     IF USERFORMAT.SPACING)1
152:     THEN
153:         FOR I := 2 TO USERFORMAT.SPACING DO
154:         BEGIN
155:             WRITELN (OUTFILE) ;
156:             CURRENTLINE := CURRENTLINE + 1
157:         END
158: END ; (* LINESPACING *)
159: BEGIN (* FLUSH *)
160:     IF NOT EMPTYOUTBUFFER
161:     THEN
162:     BEGIN
163:         FWRITELN (OUTFILE, BUFFER) ;
164:         CURRENTLINE := CURRENTLINE + 1 ;
165:         LINESPACING
166:     END ;
167:     FOR I := 1 TO MAXLINE DO BUFFER [I] := ' ' ;
168:     EMPTYOUTBUFFER := TRUE
169: END ; (* FLUSH *)
170:
171: FUNCTION COMMAND : BOOLEAN ;
172: (* TRUE IF IN BUFFER IS A COMMAND AND FALSE OTHERWISE *)
173: BEGIN
174:     COMMAND := INBUFFER[1] = '.'
175: END ; (* COMMAND *)
176:
177: PROCEDURE OBEY ( VAR FORM : FORMAT ) ;
178: (* CARRIES OUT FORMATTING COMMANDS *)
179:
180: VAR LEGAL : SET OF CHAR ;
181:     I : INTEGER ;
182:
183: FUNCTION PARAMETERS (BUFFER : STRING ) : BOOLEAN ;
184: BEGIN
185:     PARAMETERS := LENGTH(BUFFER) ) 2
186: END ; (* PARAMETERS *)
187:
188: FUNCTION NEXTPARAMETER (START : INTEGER) : INTEGER ;
189: VAR I, NUM : INTEGER ;
190: BEGIN
191:     I := START ;
192:     WHILE INBUFFER[I] = ' ' DO I := I + 1 ;
193:     NUM := 0 ;
194:     WHILE INBUFFER[I] () ' ' DO
195:     BEGIN
196:         NUM := 10 * NUM + (ORD(INBUFFER[I]) - ORD('0')) ;
197:         I := I+1
198:     END ;
199:     NEXTPARAMETER := NUM
200: END ; (* NEXTPARAMETER *)
201:
202: PROCEDURE BLANK (VAR EMPTYOUTBUFFER : BOOLEAN ) ;
203: VAR I : 1..MAXLINE ;
204: BEGIN
205:     FLUSH (OUTBUFFER) ;
206:     IF PARAMETERS (INBUFFER)
207:     THEN
208:     FOR I := 1 TO NEXTPARAMETER(3) DO
209:     BEGIN
210:         WRITELN (OUTFILE) ;
```

```
211:            CURRENTLINE := CURRENTLINE + 1
212:        END
213: END ; (* BLANK *)
214:
215: PROCEDURE CENTERED (VAR EMPTYOUTBUFFER : BOOLEAN ) ;
216: VAR I, START, CENTRE : 0..MAXLINE ;
217: BEGIN
218:        FLUSH (OUTBUFFER) ;
219:        FREADLN (INFILE, INBUFFER) ;
220:        CENTRE := (USERFORMAT.RIGHTMARGIN - USERFORMAT.LEFTMARGIN) DIV 2 ;
221:        IF LENGTH(INBUFFER) )= CENTRE *2
222:        THEN START := USERFORMAT.LEFTMARGIN
223:        ELSE START := CENTRE - (LENGTH(INBUFFER) DIV 2) ;
224:        FOR I := 1 TO LENGTH(INBUFFER) DO
225:            OUTBUFFER[START + I]:= INBUFFER[I] ;
226:        EMPTYOUTBUFFER := FALSE ;
227:        FLUSH(OUTBUFFER)
228: END ; (* CENTERED *)
229:
230: PROCEDURE NUM ;
231: BEGIN
232:        USERFORMAT.NUMBER := TRUE ;
233:        IF PARAMETERS(INBUFFER)THEN USERFORMAT.PAGENUMBER := NEXTPARAMETER(3)
234: END ; (* NUM *)
235:
236: PROCEDURE MARGIN ;
237: BEGIN
238:        FLUSH (OUTBUFFER) ;
239:        WITH USERFORMAT DO
240:        BEGIN
241:            LEFTMARGIN := NEXTPARAMETER(3) ;
242:            RIGHTMARGIN := NEXTPARAMETER(6) ;
243:            IF LEFTMARGIN+20 )= RIGHTMARGIN THEN RIGHTMARGIN := LEFTMARGIN+20
244:        END
245: END ; (* MARGIN *)
246:
247: PROCEDURE PARAGRAPH (VAR EMPTYOUTBUFFER : BOOLEAN ) ;
248: VAR I, SKIPLINES : INTEGER ;
249: BEGIN
250:        FLUSH (OUTBUFFER) ;
251:        IF PARAMETERS(INBUFFER)
252:        THEN
253:        BEGIN
254:            USERFORMAT.INDENT:=NEXTPARAMETER(3) ; SKIPLINES :=NEXTPARAMETER(6);
255:            CURRENTLINE := CURRENTLINE + SKIPLINES ;
256:            FOR I := 1 TO SKIPLINES DO WRITELN (OUTFILE)
257:        END
258:        ELSE
259:        BEGIN
260:            USERFORMAT.INDENT := 5 ;
261:            WRITELN (OUTFILE) ; CURRENTLINE := CURRENTLINE + 1
262:        END
263: END ; (* PARAGRAPH *)
264:
265: PROCEDURE JUST ;
266: BEGIN
267:        USERFORMAT.JUSTIFY := TRUE ;
268:        USERFORMAT.FILL := TRUE
269: END ; (* JUST *)
270: PROCEDURE UNFILL ;
271: BEGIN
272:        USERFORMAT.FILL := FALSE ;
273:        USERFORMAT.JUSTIFY := FALSE ;
274: END ; (* UNFILL *)
275:
276: BEGIN     (* OBEY *)
277:        LEGAL := ['B','C','F','I','J','L','M','N','O','P','R','S','U'] ;
278:        IF INBUFFER[2] IN LEGAL
279:        THEN
280:            WITH USERFORMAT DO
```

```
281:                 CASE INBUFFER|2| OF
282:                     'B' : BLANK(EMPTYOUTBUFFER) ;
283:                     'C' : CENTERED(EMPTYOUTBUFFER) ;
284:                     'F' : FILL := TRUE ;
285:                     'I' : INDENT := NEXTPARAMETER(3) ;
286:                     'J' : JUST ;
287:                     'L' : LINES := NEXTPARAMETER(3) ;
288:                     'M' : MARGIN ;
289:                     'N' : NUM ;
290:                     'O' : NUMBER := FALSE ;
291:                     'P' : PARAGRAPH (EMPTYOUTBUFFER) ;
292:                     'R' : JUSTIFY := FALSE ;
293:                     'S' : SPACING := NEXTPARAMETER(3) ;
294:                     'U' : UNFILL
295:             END (* CASE *)
296:        ELSE
297:        BEGIN
298:        STWRITE(INBUFFER) ; WRITELN(' NOT RECOGNIZED')
299:        END ;
300:        FOR I := 1 TO MAXLINE DO INBUFFER|I| := ' ' ;
301:        EMPTYINBUFFER := TRUE
302: END ; (* OBEY *)
303:
304: PROCEDURE FILLOUT ;
305: (* TRANSFERS WORDS FROM INBUFFER TO OUTBUFFER UNTIL OUTBUFFER IS FULL *)
306: VAR POINTER : INTEGER ;
307:     START : 0..MAXLINE ;
308:
309: PROCEDURE STARTINGPOINT ;
310: VAR I : 1..MAXLINE ;
311: BEGIN
312:     IF EMPTYOUTBUFFER
313:     THEN
314:     BEGIN
315:         WITH USERFORMAT DO
316:         BEGIN
317:             FOR I := 1 TO MAXLINE DO OUTBUFFER[I] := ' ' ;
318:             START := LEFTMARGIN + INDENT + 1 ;
319:             INDENT := 0
320:         END (* WITH *)
321:     END
322:     ELSE START := LENGTH(OUTBUFFER) + 2
323: END ; (* STARTINGPOINT *)
324:
325: PROCEDURE FINDSTRING ;
326: VAR FREELENGTH : 1..MAXLINE ;
327:     SHORTENOUGH , ENDOFLINE, WHOLEWORD : BOOLEAN ;
328: BEGIN
329:     FREELENGTH := USERFORMAT.RIGHTMARGIN - START + 1 ;
330:     POINTER := LENGTH(INBUFFER) ;
331:
332:     REPEAT
333:         POINTER := POINTER - 1 ;
334:         SHORTENOUGH := POINTER < FREELENGTH ;
335:         ENDOFLINE := LENGTH(INBUFFER) = POINTER + 1 ;
336:         WHOLEWORD := INBUFFER[POINTER +1] = ' '
337:     UNTIL (SHORTENOUGH AND (ENDOFLINE OR WHOLEWORD)) OR (POINTER =0)
338: END ; (* FINDSTRING *)
339:
340: PROCEDURE MOVESTRING ;
341: VAR TEMPBUFFER : STRING ;
342: BEGIN
343:     COPY(INBUFFER, TEMPBUFFER, 1, POINTER + 1) ;
344:     DELETE (INBUFFER, 1, POINTER + 1) ;
345:     INSERT(TEMPBUFFER, OUTBUFFER, START)
346: END ; (* MOVESTRING *)
347: PROCEDURE SETFLAGS ;
348: BEGIN
349:     EMPTYINBUFFER:=(LENGTH(INBUFFER)=0)
350:                     OR (EOF(INFILE)AND(LENGTH(INBUFFER)=1)) ;
```

```
351:     EMPTYOUTBUFFER := LENGTH(OUTBUFFER)=0
352: END ; (* SETFLAGS *)
353:
354: BEGIN (* FILLOUT *)
355:     STARTINGPOINT ;
356:     FINDSTRING ;
357:     IF POINTER > 0 THEN MOVESTRING ;
358:     SETFLAGS
359: END ; (* FILLOUT *)
360:
361:
362: FUNCTION READYOUTBUFFER : BOOLEAN ;
363: BEGIN
364:     READYOUTBUFFER := NOT EMPTYOUTBUFFER AND ((NOT EMPTYINBUFFER) OR
365:                         EOF(INFILE) OR NOT USERFORMAT.FILL)
366: END ; (* READYOUTBUFFER *)
367:
368: FUNCTION SHOULDJUSTIFY : BOOLEAN ;
369: BEGIN
370:     SHOULDJUSTIFY := USERFORMAT.JUSTIFY AND NOT (EOF(INFILE) AND
371:                         EMPTYINBUFFER)
372: END ; (* SHOULDJUSTIFY *)
373: PROCEDURE ADJUST (VAR BUFFER : STRING) ;
374:
375: VAR POINTER, NEWPOINTER, GAP, START : 0 .. MAXLINE ;
376:     DIRECTION : -1 .. 1 ;
377: FUNCTION INRANGE : BOOLEAN ;
378: BEGIN
379:     INRANGE := (POINTER>START)AND(POINTER<USERFORMAT.RIGHTMARGIN) AND
380:         (NEWPOINTER>=START)AND(NEWPOINTER<=USERFORMAT.RIGHTMARGIN)
381: END ; (* INRANGE *)
382: PROCEDURE SETUP ;
383: VAR ONEWORD : BOOLEAN ;
384:     I : 0 .. MAXLINE ;
385: BEGIN
386:     GAP := USERFORMAT.RIGHTMARGIN - LENGTH(BUFFER) ;
387:     POINTER := LENGTH(BUFFER) ;
388:     DIRECTION := 1 ;
389:     NEWPOINTER := POINTER + DIRECTION*GAP ;
390:     START := 0 ;
391:     REPEAT
392:         START := START + 1
393:     UNTIL BUFFER[START] <>' ' ;
394:     ONEWORD := TRUE ;
395:     FOR I := START TO LENGTH(BUFFER) DO
396:         IF BUFFER[I] = ' '
397:         THEN ONEWORD := FALSE ;
398:     IF ONEWORD THEN GAP := 0
399: END ; (* SETUP *)
400: PROCEDURE MOVECHARACTER ;
401: BEGIN
402:     BUFFER[NEWPOINTER] := BUFFER[POINTER] ;
403:     BUFFER[POINTER] := ' '
404: END ; (* MOVECHARACTER *)
405: PROCEDURE PADIFSPACE ;
406: BEGIN
407:     IF INRANGE AND (BUFFER[NEWPOINTER] = ' ')
408:     THEN IF BUFFER[NEWPOINTER+DIRECTION] <> ' '
409:         THEN
410:             BEGIN
411:                 BUFFER[NEWPOINTER-DIRECTION] := ' ' ;
412:                 GAP := GAP - 1
413:             END
414: END ; (* PADIFSPACE *)
415: PROCEDURE MOVEPOINTERS ;
416: BEGIN
417:     IF INRANGE
418:     THEN POINTER := POINTER - DIRECTION
419:     ELSE
420:     BEGIN
```

```
421:            POINTER := NEWPOINTER ;
422:            DIRECTION := -1*DIRECTION
423:        END ;
424:        NEWPOINTER := POINTER + DIRECTION*GAP
425: END ; (* MOVEPOINTERS *)
426:
427: BEGIN (* ADJUST *)
428:        SETUP ;
429:        WHILE GAP)0 DO
430:        BEGIN
431:            MOVECHARACTER ;
432:            PADIFSPACE ;
433:            MOVEPOINTERS
434:        END
435: END ; (* ADJUST *)
436:
437: PROCEDURE CLEAR (VAR OUTFILE : TEXT ; VAR OUTBUFFER : STRING ) ;
438: VAR I, LINESLEFT : INTEGER ;
439: PROCEDURE NEWPAGE (VAR CURRENTLINE : INTEGER) ;
440: VAR I : 1..MAXLINE ;
441: BEGIN
442:        WITH USERFORMAT DO
443:        BEGIN
444:            FOR I := 1 TO 3 DO
445:                WRITELN (OUTFILE) ;
446:            IF NUMBER
447:            THEN
448:            BEGIN
449:                FOR I := 1 TO RIGHTMARGIN - 7 DO
450:                    WRITE (OUTFILE, ' ' ) ;
451:                WRITELN (OUTFILE, 'PAGE ', PAGENUMBER) ;
452:                PAGENUMBER :=  PAGENUMBER + 1
453:            END
454:            ELSE WRITELN (OUTFILE) ;
455:            WRITELN (OUTFILE) ; WRITELN (OUTFILE) ;
456:            CURRENTLINE := 3
457:        END (* WITH *)
458: END ; (* NEWPAGE *)
459: BEGIN (* CLEAR *)
460:        WITH USERFORMAT DO
461:        BEGIN
462:            IF (CURRENTLINE + SPACING) )= (LINES - 2)
463:            THEN
464:            BEGIN
465:                LINESLEFT := LINES - CURRENTLINE ;
466:                FOR I := 1 TO LINESLEFT DO WRITELN (OUTFILE) ;
467:                NEWPAGE (CURRENTLINE)
468:
469:            END ;
470:            FLUSH (OUTBUFFER)
471:        END (* WITH *)
472: END ; (* CLEAR *)
473:
474: BEGIN (* TEXTFORMAT *)
475:
476:        STANFORMAT(USERFORMAT ) ;
477:        CURRENTLINE := 1 ;
478:        EMPTYOUTBUFFER := TRUE ;
479:        WHILE NOT EOF (INFILE) DO
480:        BEGIN
481:            FREADLN (INFILE, INBUFFER) ;
482:            EMPTYINBUFFER := LENGTH(INBUFFER)=0 ;
483:            IF COMMAND
484:            THEN OBEY(USERFORMAT) ;
485:            WHILE NOT EMPTYINBUFFER DO
486:            BEGIN
487:                IF USERFORMAT.FILL OR EMPTYOUTBUFFER THEN FILLOUT ;
488:                IF READYOUTBUFFER
489:                THEN
490:                BEGIN
```

```
491:                    IF SHOULDJUSTIFY THEN ADJUST (OUTBUFFER) ;
492:                    CLEAR (OUTFILE, OUTBUFFER)
493:               END
494:          END
495:      END ;
496:      WRITELN ('FORMATTING COMPLETED')
497: END ; (* TEXTFORMAT *)
498:
499: BEGIN (* MAIN PROGRAM *)
500:      REPEAT
501:          WRITE ('FILENAME OR E TO EXIT --> ') ;
502:          READLN (INFILENAME) ;
503:          IF INFILENAME <> 'E'
504:          THEN
505:          BEGIN
506:              RESET (INFILE, INFILENAME) ;
507:              WRITE ('NEW FILE NAME --> ') ;
508:              READLN (OUTFILENAME) ;
509:              REWRITE (OUTFILE, OUTFILENAME) ;
510:              TEXTFORMAT ;
511:              CLOSE (INFILE, LOCK) ;      (* UCSD ONLY *)
512:              CLOSE (OUTFILE, LOCK)       (* UCSD ONLY *)
513:          END
514:      UNTIL INFILENAME = 'E'
515: END.
```

Appendix C. Glossary of Terms

Actual Parameter -- An actual parameter is a variable or
expression contained in a procedure or function call that
replaces the formal parameter which is a part of the
procedure or function declaration.

Address -- The address of a storage location in computer
memory is the number needed to access its contents.

Algorithm -- A statement that expresses a task in terms of
a series of unambiguous subtasks.

Array -- A data structure which contains elements all of
the same type. Each element in an array can be accessed by
means of a unique set of indices and hence directly.

ASCII -- The American Standard Code for Information
Interchange. Each of 96 displayable characters and 32
control characters has a unique numeric value. This gives
a total of 128 different characters which can be
represented in 7 bits.

Assembly Language, Assembler -- An assembly language is a
language similar to machine code with the operation codes
represented as mnemonics and the addresses represented as
identifiers. An assembler is a program that translates a
program written in assembly language into machine code.

Assignment Statement -- An assignment statement contains
the assignment operator ":=". On the left side of the

assignment operator is a variable whose value is replaced by the value of the expression on the right side of the assignment operator.

Batch Mode -- A program is executed in batch mode when it is submitted together with all required input data (on punch cards, paper tape, disc/tape file) to the operating system and when it has completed execution, the results output (either on line printer paper or disc/tape file).

Binary -- Two-valued number system. Compare with ten-valued "decimal" number system.

Bit -- A binary digit, that is a 0 or 1.

Bit Pattern -- A sequence of bits that can be interpreted in several ways such as as a number, character or as a machine code instruction.

Block -- A block consists of a set of declarations (labels, constants, types, variables and or procedures) followed by a compound statement. Any Pascal program consists of a program heading, a block and END., whereas any procedure consists of a procedure heading followed by a block.

Body of a loop -- The simple or compound statement that is executed each time the condition which controls the loop is met.

Boolean -- 1. Term used to describe anything relating to the two-valued (binary) logic system developed by 19th Century English mathematician George Boole.
    -- 2. A two-valued variable or expression, the "values" being TRUE or FALSE.

Branch -- A programming construct consisting of a condition

which can take two or more values and a list of
corresponding options. Depending on the value of the
condition one of these options is executed. Pascal has two
forms of branch constructs: IF..THEN..ELSE.. and CASE..OF.

Buffer Variable -- See File Window.

Bug -- An error in a program. Removing bugs is called
"debugging".

Byte -- The number of bits used to store a character within
the computer.

Call -- The initiation of a procedure or function.

Call-By-Reference -- When an actual parameter is
substituted for a formal parameter within a procedure or
function it is known as a call-by-reference-parameter, and
the parameter is said to be passed "by reference".

Call-By-Value -- When a parameter is passed "by value" in a
procedure call, a new local variable is created and
initialised to the value of the actual parameter.

Character -- Some symbol associated with text -- e.g.
letter of the alphabet, punctuation mark or decimal digit.
(See also ASCII, Control Character.)

Code -- 1. A set of rules for interpreting a series of bit
patterns -- so "machine code" is a set of bit patterns
which represent different instructions for a particular
computer, and ASCII code is a set of bit patterns which
represent different characters etc.
    -- 2. To code means to write an algorithm in a
computer language.

Comment -- A program statement ignored by the compiler, useful for giving information to human readers of the program.

Compiler -- A program that translates a program written in a high level language into its machine code equivalent.

Compile-time -- During compilation.

Compound Statement -- A group of Pascal statments that are surrounded by BEGIN..END.

Condition -- An expression which produces a value, generally TRUE or FALSE, (but which can take any scalar value), the state of which determines the branch to be executed in IF and CASE statements and how many times a WHILE or REPEAT loop is executed.

Conditional -- See Branch.

Constant -- A data element whose value is assigned during compilation and cannot be changed during execution of the program.

Construct -- See Control Structure.

Control Character -- Non-printing character used to format input or output on a VDU or printer, such as CR, rubout etc.

Control Structure -- A device for controlling the order in which the statements of a program are executed. Three control structures (the sequence (the default order of execution), the loop and the branch) are said to constitute Structured Programming if they are exclusively used in a program.

Control Variable -- A scalar variable which is initialised
and then incremented or decremented to control the number
of times a FOR..DO loop is executed.

Data -- Information supplied to and manipulated by a
program.

Data Structure -- A logical framework for related variables
which allows them to be dealt with as a single unit or
individually. Examples from Pascal include Arrays and
Records.

Data Types -- Data is stored in bit patterns and must be
interpreted by the program. In Pascal data can be stored
as one of several types i.e. INTEGER, REAL, BOOLEAN, CHAR
or scalar type.

Debug -- To correct a program that contains bugs or errors.

Declaration -- The specification of all identifiers to be
used in a program or procedure, together with their types,
in order to give the compiler information about what
storage space should be allocated.

Default Value -- A common or frequently held value assigned
to a variable to save the user from the effort of manually
inputting it. The program must give the user an opportunity
to override this value should other circumstances obtain.
In programs that require a large amount of user input,
defaults can save considerable time can be saved at the
keyboard.

Delimiter -- A delimiter is a symbol or a pair of symbols
used to mark the beginning and end of an entity. Pascal
uses single quotes as string delimiters and curly brackets
or (* and *) as comment delimiters.

Direct Access -- A method of obtaining individual records within a disc file in which the program provides a record number which is used to position the read/write head of the disc drive in the correct place so that the record can be accessed without having to access any other records. Standard Pascal does not support direct access (also called random access) files; however, most implementations of Pascal on microcomputers do.

Dynamic Data Structure -- A data structure which grows and shrinks during program execution. In Pascal dynamic data structures are accessed through a pointer type and held in the "heap".

Editor -- A program provided as part of an operating system that allows a user to input and alter a program.

Execution -- The performance, by the computer, of the tasks described in a program.

Expression -- A sequence of constants and identifiers separated by operators that has a value (numeric, character or Boolean), which is the result of some processing at run-time.

File -- A collection of data external to a program and held on disc, tape or cards.

File Window -- Given a typed file, the file window (also called the buffer variable) is a variable held in memory of the same type as the file elements. Every element (generally a record) read from the file into main memory or written from main memory to the file uses the file window.

Field -- One of the variables within a record.

Flag -- A variable, generally Boolean, which is set in a program to show that some event has occurred, and is tested later on to determine whether a course of action dependent on that event may proceed.

Formal Parameter -- An identifier declared in a procedure or function declaration and used throughout the procedure or function. When the procedure or function is called, the formal parameter is replaced by an actual parameter.

Forward reference -- Normally, procedures must be declared before they can be called, but if two procedures call each other then both cannot be declared before being called. Instead, the reserved word FORWARD is used to tell the compiler that a reference will be made to a procedure whose declaration will be supplied subsequently.

Function -- A procedure that returns a value. It is called by referencing its identifier (with appropriate parameters) wherever a variable of its type would be acceptable.

Garbage Collection -- A technique employed by the run-time system to recover unused heap space freed when a dynamic data structure contracts.

Global Variable -- A variable that is declared in the declaration part of the main program block and hence accessible to the main program and all procedures, except when a variable with the same identifier is declared within a procedure. In the latter case, the global variable goes temporarily out of scope.

Heading

    The first line of a program, procedure or function is called its heading.

Heap -- The area set aside in main memory at run-time to hold dynamic data structures. (Compare Stack.)

High Level Language -- Any language such as Pascal in which most single instructions will translate into several machine code instructions.

Identifier -- A name given to a data type, data item, data structure, procedure or function. Identifiers can be of any length but on most implementations only the first eight characters are significant.

Indentation -- Non-functional blank spaces inserted at the left of Pascal program code so that the structure of the program is visible.

Initialise -- To give a variable an initial value (usually zero) before using it in a program.

Integer -- Pre-declared Pascal type for (a limited range of) whole numbers.

Interpreter -- A program which takes as input a program written in either a high level language (e.g. BASIC, APL) or pseudo code (many Pascal systems) and translates and executes each statement one at a time.

Iterative -- Repetitive. Many mathematical functions are evaluated iteratively, that is, an initial solution is proposed, then tested and if not sufficiently accurate, the solution is improved upon and tested again. This process continues (using a loop construct) until the solution is deemed sufficiently accurate to stop.

Jump -- A control structure which directs control from one

point in the program to another out of the normal sequence.
(GOTO)

Linkage Loader -- A systems program that takes as input
relocatable object code that is produced when a source
program is compiled along with any standard functions from
the library called in the user program, and produces as
output a machine code program that is ready to be executed.

Linked List -- A dynamic data structure where each element
consists of a data item and a pointer to the next element.

Listhead -- A pointer to the first element in a linked list.

Local Variable -- A variable declared within the block
where it is used.

Loop -- A sequence of program steps that is repeated a
controlled number of times. Pascal provides three
constructs for coding loops (FOR-DO, WHILE-DO, REPEAT-UNTIL).

Machine Code or Language -- The instructions that a
computer's hardware actually executes.

Main Memory -- Immediate access storage locations. This is
where the stack, heap and code that is actually being
executed are located.

Master File -- In a data processing environment, the master
file is the main file on which all alterations are made.
(See update).

Module -- A functionally separate section of a program,
generally a procedure. A modular program is one where each
subtask is dealt with in its own distinct procedure.

Nesting -- When a logical construct has the same type of construct within itself, e.g. a loop within a loop, procedure inside a procedure.

Object Program -- A machine code program, the translation of some high-level language program as output by the compiler.

Operand -- A data item which is to be manipulated in the instruction within which it occurs.

Operator

A symbol such as +, := etc. which indicates that certain operations to take place.

Overlay -- In a computer system where memory is smaller than that required to hold the whole object program either the user or the system divides the program into sections such that only a few of these sections are in main memory at any one time and when a new section is needed it is written into main memory over an old section.

Packed, Packing -- The process of allocating the smallest amount of memory required for a structured type (record or array) is called packing. The structured type is called a PACKED type.

Parameter -- A variable passed between a calling and a called procedure or function.

Parameter List -- The list of variables in a procedure or function heading together with their corresponding types.

Peripheral -- A device added on to a computer (CPU plus

memory) usually used for either backing store (disc and
tape drives), or human communication (terminal and printer).

Pointer -- A variable, usually integer, containing
information about the location of some data (usually a
specific array or stack element). By changing the value
the pointer contains, different elements can be located.

Pop -- When an element is removed from a stack it is said
to be popped off the stack.

Predecessor -- In a list of scalar items the predecessor
of a given item is the adjacent item occuring earlier in
the list.

Procedure -- A procedure is a subprogram or subroutine,
similar in form to a program. It must be declared in the
declaration part of a program and is executed when its name
is called.

Program Stub -- When developing a program or a section of
a program instead of writing the code for each procedure
that is called a short piece of code called a program stub
is written, in order to test the logic of the code being
currently written.

Push -- When an element is placed on a stack it is said to
be pushed onto the stack.

Range -- The set of values that a given variable make
take.

Real -- A pre-declared Pascal type for decimal numbers.

Record -- A structured type consisting of several related

data items of different types, called fields. Records tend
to be grouped together in files.

Recursive -- A procedure or function is said to be
recursive if it contains a call to itself.

Reserved word -- A word that cannot be used as an
identifier because it is already a word within the
programming language.

Relational Operator -- An operator such as $\frac{1}{4}$, $\frac{1}{2}$ or =
which is used to compare two operands.

Return, Return Address -- After a procedure completes its
processing, program control transfers to the first program
statement following the one where the procedure was called.
 The address where program control is transferred to is
called the return address and flow of control is said to
return to the calling routine. Any result passed back to
the calling procedure will have been "returned".

Rogue Value -- A value put at the end of a data input
stream that is out of the normal range of input data and
whose purpose is to signal to the program that the input
stream is finished.

Run-time -- The period of time when a program is executing.

Scalar -- A variable or constant which can have any of an
ordered set of values which is listed in its declaration.

Scope -- A set of procedures within which a variable is ·
defined.

Set -- A reserved word for a BOOLEAN array. If an element

is TRUE   the corresponding item is said to be a member of the SET.

Sequential Access -- A method of reading or writing to a file where the next item (usually a record) which can be accessed is the one that immediately follows the last one accessed.

Side Effect -- The alteration of the value of a variable brought about by making an assignment to that variable in a procedure in which it is not declared and to which it is not passed.

Source program -- High-level language program which becomes the input for the compiler at compile-time.

Stack -- 1. In general, a list of elements such that the last element input is the first element that can be accessed.
         -- 2. Area of memory set aside to hold declared variables and procedure calls at run-time (hence Run-Time Stack).

Stack Frame -- Region of the stack containing all data relevant to a single procedure or function call. When the call is made, the whole frame is popped onto the stack.

Standard Function -- A function supplied with in a Pascal system. A standard function isn't declared within a program but can be used just by calling its name (e.g. x:=sin(y)).

Statement -- A single program instruction.

Statement Separator -- A symbol (;) which is used to separate two statements in the action part of a program.

Static Data Structure -- A data structure such as an ARRAY
or RECORD which has its space allocated at compile time,
via a declaration statement.

Stepwise Refinement -- A method of program development.
First the main program is written, but whenever a problem
is encountered it is given a name and passed over. When the
main program has been completed each of the subproblems is
tackled in the same way. This process of successively
decomposing a problem into subproblems is continued until the
problems that are left can be easily coded.

String -- A collection of characters between quotes
(literal string). Most versions of Pascal for
microcomputers have a predeclared STRING data type which is
equivalent to a PACKED ARRAY OF CHAR.

Structured Programming -- A technique of coding where all
control structures are sequences, loops or conditionals.
It is also known as "GOTOLESS" programming in contrast
with "spaghetti" programming where the jump construct is
also allowed.

Subrange -- A variable can be declared such that it is
only allowed to take on values in a subset of the full
range available (hence subrange).

Subroutine -- A word used for a procedure in many
programming languages.

Subscript -- An index used to access an element of an
array.

Successor -- In a list of scalar items the successor of a
given item is the adjacent item occuring later in the list.

Syntax, Syntax Diagram -- The set of rules describing what constitutes a grammatically correct program. A syntax diagram is a pictorial form designed by Wirth to state the rules clearly. A syntactically correct program will compile.

Tag Field -- In a record with a variant field the tag field is the variable in the CASE clause which picks out the currently valid variant.

Terminator -- A symbol used to show a given piece of code is finished. In the declaration part of a program the semicolon is the statement terminator whereas a full stop is the program terminator.

Test Harness -- A test harness is code written to "go around" a procedure to allow it to be tested without having to write the whole program in which the procedure is to appear.

Textfile -- A file whose component items are characters is referred to by the reserved word TEXTFILE.

Top Down Design -- See Stepwise Refinement.

Type -- A data type defines the set of values a variable may take.

Update -- A file is updated when the records within the file are changed to the latest values.

Validation -- The process of checking that the input values are within a reasonable range and hence probably not erroneous.

Value Parameter -- See Call-By-Value.

Variable -- A memory location or collection of locations where a data item is stored and altered and referred to by an identifier.

Variable Parameter -- See Call-By-Reference.

Variant Field -- One of a choice of several alternative fields which can optionally be defined as the last field of a record.

Workspace -- An area in memory that holds temporary values of variables during execution (in Pascal, the Stack and the Heap).

K. L. Bowles
Microcomputer
Problem Solving Using Pascal
Springer Study Edition
1977. 110 figures. IX, 563 pages
DM 24,80
ISBN 3-540-90286-4

"...The text is an integral part of revolutionary environment for computing education... By using PASCAL, Bowles is able to introduce algorithm development and problem solving as components of top-down, stepwise design. Procedures are introduced right from the start. Flow of control is presented in terms of modern programming principles (sequence, selection and iteration). Recursion is presented as an obvious extension of the procedure mechanism. Data structures are explained fully and clearly..."   *PASCAL News*

K. Jensen, N. E. Wirth
Pascal User Manual and Report
Springer Study Edition
2nd corrected reprint of the 2nd edition. 1978.
VIII, 167 pages
DM 19,80
ISBN 3-540-90144-2
(Originally published as Lecture Notes in Computer Science, Volume 18)

"The PASCAL language was created to provide a teaching language which would present programming as a systematic discipline and whose structure would instill a good programming style and habits in the student. The same aims of clarity and logical presentation have been embodied in this text which is addressed to the mature programmer who wishes to learn the language without formal instruction... The present volume is in two parts, a user manual for self-study, and a report designed for those who wish to implement the language... Examples abound, ranging from syntax to programs, and where possible specifications and examples are given graphically. Each of the two parts is well organized and logically complete, and each has its own separate index. The entire work is well organized and well presented and the joint authors are to be jointly commended upon the result."*CIPS-Computer Magazine*

Springer-Verlag
Berlin
Heidelberg
New York

S. Alagić, M. A. Arbib

The Design of Well-Structured and Correct Programs

1978. 68 figures. X, 292 pages
(Texts and Monographs in Computer
Science)
Cloth DM 29,50
ISBN 3-540-90299-6

Contents: Introducing Top-Down Design. –
Basic Compositions of Actions and Their
Proof Rules. – Data Types. – Developing
Programs With Proofs of Correctness. –
Procedures and Functions. – Recursion. –
Programming With and Without Gotos.

Springer-Verlag
Berlin
Heidelberg
New York

"…The authors have been largely sucessful
in achieving their stated aims. The book is
clearly written as well as being attractively
printed… It represents, among other things,
a thorough and worthwhile attempt to
inform a relatively wide readership about the
axiomatic approach to program semantics
and correctness. For that reason alone, many
computer scientists… should find it worth
reading…"

Computing Reviews